John Bunyan:
Reading Dissenting Writing

Religions and Discourse

Edited by James Francis

Volume 12

PETER LANG
Oxford · Bern · Berlin · Bruxelles · Frankfurt a.M. · New York · Wien

N. H. Keeble (ed.)

John Bunyan: Reading Dissenting Writing

PETER LANG
Oxford · Bern · Berlin · Bruxelles · Frankfurt a.M. · New York · Wien

Bibliographic information published by Die Deutsche Bibliothek
Die Deutsche Bibliothek lists this publication in the Deutsche National-
bibliografie; detailed bibliographic data is available on the Internet at
‹http://dnb.ddb.de›.

British Library and Library of Congress Cataloguing-in-Publication Data:
A catalogue record for this book is available from *The British Library*,
Great Britain, and from *The Library of Congress*, USA

ISSN 1422-8998
ISBN 3-906768-52-X
US-ISBN 0-8204-5864-3

© Peter Lang AG, European Academic Publishers, Bern 2002
Hochfeldstrasse 32, Postfach 746, CH-3000 Bern 9, Switzerland
info@peterlang.com, www.peterlang.com, www.peterlang.net

All rights reserved.
All parts of this publication are protected by copyright.
Any utilisation outside the strict limits of the copyright law, without
the permission of the publisher, is forbidden and liable to prosecution.
This applies in particular to reproductions, translations, microfilming,
and storage and processing in electronic retrieval systems.

Printed in Germany

Contents

Acknowledgements 7
List of Contributors 9
List of Abbreviations 13

Portrait of Bunyan 14
Introduction 15

1 THOMAS N. CORNS
　Bunyan, Milton and the Diversity of Radical
　Protestant Writing 21

2 WILLIAM LAMONT
　Bunyan and Baxter: Millennium and Magistrate 39

3 W. R. OWENS
　Reading the Bibliographical Codes:
　Bunyan's Publication in Folio 59

4 TAMSIN SPARGO
　Bunyans Abounding, or the Names of the Author 79

5 MICHAEL DAVIES
　'Stout & Valiant Champions for God': the Radical
　Reformation of Romance in *The Pilgrim's Progress* 103

6 VERA CAMDEN
　'That of *Esau*': the Place of Hebrews xii.16, 17 in
　Grace Abounding 133

7 NANCY ROSENFELD
　'So counterfeit holy would this Divel be': Debate and
　Disinformation as Satanic Strategies in Milton and Bunyan 165

8   ARLETTE ZINCK
    From Apocalypse to Prophecy: the Didactic Strategies of
    The Holy War 183

9   ROGER POOLEY
    The Life and Death of Mr. Badman and Seventeenth-Century
    Discourses of Atheism 199

10 DAVID HAWKES
    Master of His Ways? Determinism and the Market in
    The Life and Death of Mr. Badman 211

11 PETER MARBAIS
    The Tormented Body in *The Life and Death of Mr. Badman* .. 231

12 STUART SIM
    'Transworld Depravity' and 'Invariant Assertions':
    John Bunyan's Possible Worlds 245

Bibliography 263
Index 273

Acknowledgements

This volume was made possible, first, by the willingness of contributors to put forward their essays for inclusion and then to tolerate my various editorial interferences; secondly, by the care and attentiveness with which office staff in the Department of English Studies at the University of Stirling – Anne-Marie McCormack, Tracy Gardner and, in particular, Susan Dryburgh – prepared camera-ready copy for the publisher; and thirdly by the generosity of the International John Bunyan Society which made a grant towards the cost of publication. I am most truly grateful to them all.

NHK

List of Contributors

VERA CAMDEN is Associate Professor of English at Kent State University, Ohio, where, as President of the International John Bunyan Society, she organized and hosted the Third Triennial Conference of the Society in 2001. She is the editor of *The Narrative of the Persecutions of Agnes Beaumont* (1991) and guest editor of a special issue of *Bunyan Studies* on 'Dissenting Women' (1998). Professor Camden is also a practising psychoanalyst and chairs the Faculty Committee of the Cleveland Psychoanalytic Institute. A Member of the American Psychoanalytic Association, she chairs the Committee on Research and Special Training's (CORST) Essay Prize in Psychoanalysis and Culture. She is co-editor of *American Imago*, a journal of applied psychoanalysis.

THOMAS N. CORNS is Professor of English and Head of the School of Arts and Humanities at the University of Wales, Bangor. His principal publications include *The Development of Milton's Prose Style* (1982), *Milton's Language* (1990), *Uncloistered Virtue: English political literature 1640–1660* (1992), *Regaining 'Paradise Lost'* (1993) and the Twayne guide to Milton's prose (1998). He edited *The Cambridge Companion to English Poetry: Donne to Marvell* (1993) and *The Royal Image: representations of Charles I* (1999). With Ann Hughes and David Loewenstein he is editing the complete works of Gerrard Winstanley and he is the lead researcher of a group considering the provenance of Milton's *De Doctrina Christiana*.

MICHAEL DAVIES is Lecturer in English at the University of Leicester, England, where he completed his doctoral thesis on the theology and writings of John Bunyan in 1997. He has recently published essays on John Bunyan, on nonconformity in the Restoration, and on the 'Catholic Shakespeare', and he has also contributed a number of articles on seventeenth-century Baptists (including Henry Adis and John Child) to the *New Dictionary of National Biography*. His book

Graceful Reading: theology and narrative in the works of John Bunyan is forthcoming from Oxford University Press.

DAVID HAWKES is Associate Professor of English at Lehigh University, Pennsylvania. He is the author of *Ideology* (1996) and *Idols of the Market-Place: idolatry and commodity fetishism in English literature, 1580–1680* (2001). His essays have appeared in such journals as *Studies in English Literature*, *The Huntington Library Quarterly*, *Journal of the History of Ideas*, *Renaissance Studies* and *The Eighteenth Century: Theory and Interpretation*.

N. H. KEEBLE is Professor of English Studies and Deputy Principal at the University of Stirling, Scotland. He is the author of *Richard Baxter: Puritan Man of Letters* (1982) and *The Literary Culture of Nonconformity in later seventeenth-century England* (1987); and the editor of a collection of tercentenary essays, *John Bunyan: Conventicle and Parnassus* (1988), an anthology illustrating *The Cultural Identity of Seventeenth-Century Woman* (1994), *The Cambridge Companion to Writing of the English Revolution* (2001) and texts by Richard Baxter, John Bunyan and Lucy Hutchinson. With Geoffrey F. Nuttall he compiled a two-volume *Calendar of the Correspondence of Richard Baxter* (1991). He is currently editing a tract for the Yale edition of the *Prose Works of Andrew Marvell* and his study of the 1660s is forthcoming from Blackwell.

WILLIAM LAMONT retired as Professor of History in 1999 after thirty-three years teaching at the University of Sussex, England. He has published a trilogy of studies of *Puritanism and the English Revolution* (1991), which originally appeared separately as *Marginal Prynne* (1963), *Godly Rule: politics and religion 1603–60* (1969) and *Richard Baxter and the Millennium* (1979); an edition of Richard Baxter's *A Holy Commonwealth* (1994); and a discussion of the historiographical debate on Puritanism: *Puritanism and Historical Controversy* (1996). He is at present completing the first full-length study of a sect once thought to be extinct by the nineteenth century: *The Muggletonian History 1652–1979*.

List of Contributors 11

PETER MARBAIS primarily researches and writes upon Daniel Defoe as a doctoral candidate at Kent State University, Ohio. His dissertation concerns the female agents in *Moll Flanders* and *Roxana* and the issues of illegitimate children, midwives and infanticide in the narratives and in Defoe's England. His published works include reviews of science fiction criticism in *Extrapolation*. He currently teaches English literature at Bethany College, Lindsberg, Kansas.

W. R. OWENS is Senior Lecturer and Head of the Department of Literature at the Open University, England. His publications include an edition of Bunyan's *Grace Abounding* (1987), a co-edited volume of essays, *John Bunyan and His England 1628–1688* (1990), volumes XII and XIII of the *Miscellaneous Works of John Bunyan* (1994), and two co-edited books: *Shakespeare, Aphra Behn and the Canon* (1996) and *A Handbook to Literary Research* (1998). He has also published extensively on Daniel Defoe, in collaboration with P. N. Furbank. Their joint books include *The Canonisation of Daniel Defoe* (1988), *Defoe De-Attributions* (1994), and *A Critical Bibliography of Daniel Defoe* (1998). They are currently general editors of a 44-volume edition of *The Works of Daniel Defoe* being published by Pickering & Chatto.

ROGER POOLEY teaches in the School of English and Philosophy at Keele University, England. He has published *English Prose of the Seventeenth Century, 1590–1700* (1993) as well as a number of articles and chapters on Bunyan. He is the co-editor of *The Discerning Reader: Christian perspectives on literature and theory* (1995).

NANCY ROSENFELD teaches in the Department of English Language and Literature at the University of Haifa and in the Department of English at the Jezreel Valley College, Israel. She wrote her doctoral dissertation on the Satan character in the writings of Milton, Bunyan and John Wilmot, 2nd Earl of Rochester, and she is the author of several articles and conference papers on Milton, Bunyan and Keats.

STUART SIM is Professor of English Studies at the University of Sunderland, England. A founder and joint editor of *Bunyan Studies*, he has published widely on modern critical and cultural theory and on seventeenth- and eighteenth-century prose fiction (including the study *Negotiations with Paradox: narrative practice and narrative form in Bunyan and Defoe* (1990)). His most recent books are *Bunyan and Authority* (2000, with David Walker); *Post-Marxism: an intellectual history* (2000); and *Lyotard and the Inhuman* (2001).

TAMSIN SPARGO is Reader in Cultural History at Liverpool John Moores University, England. She is the author of *The Writing of John Bunyan* (1997), *Foucault and Queer Theory* (1999) and *Reading the Past: literature and history* (2000). She is currently writing a volume on John Bunyan for the British Council's 'Writers and their Work' series and researching the life of a forgotten American criminal.

ARLETTE ZINCK is Assistant Professor of English at The King's University College, Edmonton, Alberta. She was one of the organisers of the International John Bunyan Society's first triennial conference in 1995 and one of the editors of a volume of selected papers from that conference, *Awakening Words: John Bunyan and the language of community* (2000).

List of Abbreviations

GA   John Bunyan, *Grace Abounding to the Chief of Sinners*, ed. Roger Sharrock (Oxford: Clarendon Press, 1962)

HW   John Bunyan, *The Holy War*, ed. Roger Sharrock and James Forrest (Oxford: Clarendon Press, 1980)

MB   John Bunyan, *The Life and Death of Mr. Badman,* ed. James F. Forrest and Roger Sharrock (Oxford: Clarendon Press, 1988)

MW   John Bunyan, *Miscellaneous Works*, gen. ed. Roger Sharrock, 13 vols. (Oxford: Clarendon Press, 1976–94)

PP   John Bunyan, *The Pilgrim's Progress*, ed. James Blanton Wharey, 2nd edn. ed. Roger Sharrock (Oxford: Clarendon Press, 1960)

Engraved frontispiece portrait by John Sturt to the 1692 edition of John Bunyan's *Works*, edited by Charles Doe and published by William Marshall (see further p. 70 below). (By permission of the British Library (shelfmark 697.m.17).)

Introduction

During the last ten or fifteen years there has been, if not an explosion, then certainly a very marked increase in scholarly, critical and theoretical interest in the work of John Bunyan. The publication in 1994 of the final volume of the Oxford English Texts edition of Bunyan's *Miscellaneous Works* concluded the project of publishing his complete works which had begun in 1960 with the appearance of Roger Sharrock's edition of *The Pilgrim's Progress*. Six years earlier, the tercentenary of Bunyan's death in 1988 had been marked by international conferences and by the publication of four volumes of original essays.[1] That year also saw the publication of Christopher Hill's biography of Bunyan, *A Turbulent, Seditious and Factious People: John Bunyan and his church*, setting Bunyan in that tradition of radical Puritanism which during the previous twenty years Hill's own work had established as a focus of historiographical interest.[2] This contextualization has been developed especially by the historian Richard L. Greaves, whose research in public and church records has led to a number of studies, culminating in his collected essays, which have established with a new clarity and precision Bunyan's position within the complex politics of the nonconformist response to Restoration persecution.[3] Since the mid 1980s, literary scholars have similarly sought to define more subtly Bunyan's place within the culture of Puritanism. Kathleen Swaim's study of the relationship of *The Pilgrim's Progress* to the homiletic, allegorical and narrative discourses of Puritanism is an example, as is Isabel Rivers' study of the

---

1   Edited by Robert G. Collmer (Kent OH, 1989), N. H. Keeble (Oxford, 1988), Ann Laurence, W. R. Owens and Stuart Sim (London and Ronceverte WV, 1990) and M v. Os and G. J. Schutte (Amsterdam, 1990).
2   Oxford, 1988; published in the United States as *A Tinker and a Poor Man: John Bunyan and his church, 1628–1688* (New York, 1989).
3   Richard L. Greaves, *John Bunyan and Nonconformity* (London and Rio Grande OH, 1992). Professor Greaves's own biography of Bunyan is in preparation.

literature of later Puritanism and its rival ecclesiastical traditions;[4] so, too, though in a very different way, is John Stachniewski's claim in his *The Persecutory Imagination: English Puritanism and the Literature of Religious Despair*[5] that readings of Puritanism have been altogether too 'up-beat', giving 'the brighter side of protestantism [...] disproportionate attention'. We have still not fully assimilated his analysis of the 'rebarbitiveness of Christianity' in the seventeenth century, nor accommodated his forceful representation of Calvinist discourse as a pernicious agent of menace, disorientating and disheartening.[6] These various approaches may, in a general way be described as 'historicist'. Nearly thirty years ago *The Pilgrim's Progress* was the subject of essays in Stanley Fish's *Self-Consuming Artifacts* and in Wolfgang Iser's *The Implied Reader*,[7] but Bunyan did not attract sustained theoretical attention until the 1990s. Three critically radical and challenging studies then appeared in quick succession: Stuart Sim's *Negotiating with Paradox: narrative practice and narrative form in Bunyan and Defoe*, Thomas Luxon's *Literal Figures: Puritan allegory and the Reformation crisis in representation* and Tamsin Spargo's *The Writing of John Bunyan*.[8]

This increasing scholarly interest in Bunyan both inspired, and was inspired by, the journal *Bunyan Studies*, founded in 1988 by W. R. Owens, Stuart Sim and David Gay, and by the establishment of the International John Bunyan Society, with Richard L. Greaves as its first president. The Society held its first triennial conference at the University of Alberta, Edmonton, Canada, in 1995. Selected pro-

---

4   Kathleen Swaim, *Pilgrim's Progress, Puritan Progress: discourses and contexts* (Urbana and Chicago, 1993); Isabel Rivers, *Reason, Grace and Sentiment: a study of the language of religion and ethics in England, 1660–1780*, vol. I: *Whichcote to Wesley* (Cambridge, 1991). See also: N. H. Keeble, *The Literary Culture of Non-conformity in Later Seventeenth-Century England* (Leicester, 1987).
5   Oxford, 1991.
6   Stachiewski, *Persecutory Imagination*, pp. 2, 3, 4.
7   Respectively Berkeley, Los Angeles, and London, 1972; London, 1974.
8   Respectively Hemel Hempstead, 1990; Chicago and London, 1995; Aldershot and Brookfield VT, 1997.

ceedings from that conference appeared last year.[9] The present collection derives from the Society's second conference, held at the University of Stirling, Scotland, in 1998.

The collection's subtitle may be read both as a summary of the business of all the essays ('reading dissenting writing'), and also as a menu of their related concerns. In this latter sense ('reading, dissenting, writing'), it points to the collection's adoption of a variety of reader responses and of approaches to Bunyan's work; to its intention to push beyond received critical orthodoxies; and to its engagement with the nature of Bunyan's publications and with the cultural circumstances which shaped them. These approaches begin with two essays which explore the political and religious context of Bunyan's work by placing him beside Milton and Baxter, his two most eminent Puritan and nonconformist contemporaries. These pairings have been made before, but previously Milton has been likened to Bunyan, not contrasted with him as he is by Thomas N. Corns, and Baxter has been supposed a figure less disturbing to the body politic than Bunyan, whereas William Lamont argues the contrary case (drawing upon unpublished manuscript materials to do so). Each of these essays raises searching questions about our characterizations of the later Puritan tradition and discountenances easy generalizations about Bunyan's position within nonconformist culture.

The two succeeding essays turn to the material evidence. W. R. Owens examines the planning, editing and production of the first collected edition of Bunyan, Charles Doe's 1692 folio. He presents new evidence of its publishing history and discusses the 'meanings' conveyed by its 'bibliographic codes'. Reflection on the diversity of the forms of naming and of representations of the author on title-pages produced throughout Bunyan's publishing career leads Tamsin Spargo to discuss the kinds of authority claimed by 'John Bunyan' and to consider the various readings and responses these representations appear to demand. She finds that the answers to the questions 'who do we mean by "John Bunyan"?' and 'what is it that we do when we read "John Bunyan"?' are by no means as straightforward as might be

---

9   David Gay, James G. Randall and Arlette Zinck (ed.), *Awakening Words: John Bunyan and the language of community* (Newark DE and London, 2000).

supposed. Like Owens, she finds that the words on the page are by no means the only medium of the text's communication with the reader.

The symposium then moves to essays focused on particular texts. That *The Pilgrim's Progress* is in one sense a species of romance has long been recognised: the point is, as Michael Davies acknowledges in his essay, 'a mouldy issue'. However, he brings a new precision to our understanding of both this generic affiliation and the generic radicalism of *The Pilgrim's Progress*, arguing that it 'should not be considered as romance at all (Puritan or otherwise) but a rewriting of romance which deconstructs the genre's features' to serve Bunyan's theology. The next two essays deal with *Grace Abounding*. Focusing on Bunyan's preoccupation with a single Biblical passage, Vera Camden draws on the insights of present-day psychology to interpret Bunyan's reliance upon insistent linguistic refrains and his obsession with the story of Esau's loss of his birthright. Her essay illuminates the ways in which Bunyan's agonised turning and returning to what for him became talismanic Biblical verses 'delivered the key to his imaginative flourishing and his genius as both writer and preacher'. Nancy Rosenfeld's essay explores Bunyan's dramatization of temptation through a comparison of his Devil with Milton's Satan, finding, despite their very different generic obligations, unexpected points of contact in the two writers' presentation of temptation. *The Holy War* has often been reproved for the incompetencies of its repetitive plotting and for its inconclusiveness. Arlette Zinck answers these charges by demonstrating that the work is to be read not as a straightforward linear narrative but as a form of apocalyptic prophecy addressed to the immediate (and so inconclusive) experience of its readers. In contrast to some of his contemporaries' headier prophetic discourses, Bunyan, with pastoral caution, avoids the specious assurance of confident predictions of victory in his representation of the experience of the saints.

Roger Pooley's essay is the first of three on *Mr. Badman*. This proportion reflects the increasing interest in this as 'a pivotal work' (in David Hawkes's phrase) and as a text which is peculiarly susceptible to the kinds of attention contemporary criticism brings to bear. Like Corns and Lamont, Pooley addresses an aspect of context, in his case a context provided by intellectual history. He examines the elusiveness and varieties of atheism and its meanings in the early modern period persuasively to demonstrate that they provide 'an important and neglected context' for *Mr. Badman*. Noting, as have other commentators, the tensions between allegorical and realistic methods in *Mr. Badman*, David Hawkes goes on to show that allegorically Badman is 'an embodiment of the market economy' and that this is a key both to Bunyan's realistic specificity and to the text's denunciation of him as evil. This essay again enriches our sense of relevant contexts for Bunyan by calling, like Pooley, upon Hobbes, and also upon seventeenth-century writings on economics and upon Mandeville. In the third essay on *Mr. Badman*, Peter Marbais takes up a currently topical line (though not one previously applied to Bunyan) in an examination of Bunyan's problematic representation of the body, and especially of the relationship between spiritual and physical well-being (or ill-health).

The collection concludes with Stuart Sim's philosophically informed theoretical essay which applies to Bunyan 'possible worlds theory' in order to elucidate his fictionalising of predestinarianism. Sim is interested particularly in the question, 'is it the case that soteriological necessity dictates certain narrative moves to the exclusion of others?' Having explored some of the paradoxes and puzzles of Calvinism, Sim's conclusion is that a 'soteriological necessity drives narrative necessity in Bunyan', constraining even God himself.

1

THOMAS N. CORNS
Bunyan, Milton and the Diversity of Radical Protestant Writing

'Milton and Bunyan' seemed and still seems an obvious enough theme for a soi-disant Miltonist like me to take for a collection such as this. The connections run deep in the critical tradition. Christopher Hill has written only two literary biographies – on Milton and on Bunyan. His extraordinary and magisterial study, *The English Bible and the Seventeenth-Century Revolution*, culminates in an account of Milton and Bunyan, though with a more surprising coda on Marvell.[1] Again, N. H. Keeble has published on 'Restoration Images in Milton and Bunyan', and his deeply influential book, *The Literary Culture of Nonconformity in Later Seventeenth-Century England*, persistently and ingeniously holds Milton and Bunyan together, in a curious trinity that has Richard Baxter as its third entity.[2] I want to return to consider the interpretations of Hill and Keeble and others a little later in this account.

---

1 Christopher Hill, *The English Bible and the Seventeenth-Century Revolution* (London, 1993).
2 N. H. Keeble, *The Literary Culture of Nonconformity in Later Seventeenth-Century England* (Leicester, 1987), *passim*, and '"Till one greater man / Restore us": Restoration Images in Milton and Bunyan', *Bunyan Studies*, 6 (1995/6), 6–33, reprinted in David Gay, James G. Randall and Arlette Zinck (ed.), *Awakening Words: John Bunyan and the language of community* (Newark DE and London, 2000), pp. 27–50. Pertinently, that number of *Bunyan Studies* also contains P. J. H. Titlesla, 'The "pretty young man Civility": Bunyan, Milton and Blake and Patterns of Puritan Thought' (pp. 34–43), and Arlette M. Zinck, '"Doctrine by Ensample": Sanctification through Literature in Milton and Bunyan' (pp. 44–55).

My larger thesis is, put broadly, an inversion of Tolstoy's dictum, 'All happy families are alike but an unhappy family is unhappy after its own fashion': 'All unhappy dissenting groups are alike but a happy dissenting group is happy after its own fashion.' Or less whimsically, we may more usefully and much more easily generalize about common elements in the dissenting tradition before 1640 and after the Restoration than in the period in between. Milton and Bunyan will constitute my case study, but others could have served.

Milton and Bunyan appear almost as the default options, and the reasons for their unique status as Puritan exemplars within the literary tradition are multiple and complex. In part, the explanations are literary. Their most widely read works are narrative, though they lived and wrote in ages in which other modes, preeminently the discursive but also the lyric and the dramatic, predominated. The narrative mode, however, predominates in the eighteenth and subsequent centuries: *Paradise Lost* and *The Pilgrim's Progess*, fortuitiously, anticipate the power of the narrative line that overwhelms the literary tradition on the rise of the novel. In Milton's case, understanding the story emerges as an informing critical concern, manifest in the addition of the prefatory abstracts to each book of the second edition. Indeed, while these are termed 'arguments', they address overwhelmingly the clarification of the narrative line: what happens, not why, is their subject. Similarly, Bunyan's allegory retains still a status as proto-novel. Paula R. Backscheider, no naive reader, lines him up with Swift and Defoe in her *A Being More Intense*.[3] Similar connections are of course commonplace in earlier accounts of the novel tradition.

Again, subtler mechanisms of cultural ideology allowed the passage of Bunyan and Milton while their radical confrères were marginalised, suppressed or ignored. *Paradise Lost* functions as a sort of manifesto for literary neoclassicism in the Augustan age, though in the process its vital distinctions from the cultural assumptions of Dryden and Pope were largely ignored; and its claimed transcendence over classical epic led to a perception of the poem as the definitive vernacular emulation of Homer and Virgil. Bunyan serves a similar role in low culture to that served by Milton in high culture. A plain

---

[3] Paula R. Backscheider, *A Being More Intense* (New York, 1984).

style, an obvious accessibility in his most recurrently reprinted works match eighteenth-century and later concerns with meeting the widened market afforded by advances in literacy and the growth of the reading public. In an odd sort of way, perhaps Milton and Bunyan were more deserving of that happy afterlife in the English tradition denied to Gerrard Winstanley and Jacob Bauthumley. They wrote more and they kept writing, not letting setbacks like imprisonment and personal ruin arrest their output; Winstanley and the Ranters simply stopped. Moreover, more people had read them or had heard of them. Nothing by Winstanley went into a third edition. *Grace Abounding* probably had six life-time editions; *The Pilgrim's Progress*, Part I, about a dozen. Milton had a continental readership for his Latin prose, which may have included the Queen of Sweden. Charles II probably knew who both of them were.

So it is not remarkable that Milton and Bunyan survive into the early eighteenth century as others do not. And their fate is curiously similar thereafter, as their texts become appropriated by a subtly transformed cultural establishment. Milton, of course, is Addisonised. The oeuvre is reduced to a narrow subset; the political prose remains available to Whig theorists and is rediscovered by English Jacobins, but it is the great narrative of *Paradise Lost* by which he is represented. A burgeoning editorial tradition – Patrick Hume, Thomas Newton, Thomas Warton and others – repeatedly ties his text to Virgil's and to Homer's while eschewing its political or – in any detailed sense – its theological components. James Patterson's title, *A Complete Commentary, with Etymological, Explanatory, Critical and Classical Notes on Paradise Lost* (1744), defines well the priorities. Addison's eighteen essays in *The Spectator*[4] secure the transformation of Milton from 'that late Villain'[5] whose posthumous publications the state hunted down to definitive laureate of English Protestantism. The essays further narrow the range of the poem, offering in its selection a

---

4 Joseph Addison and Sir Richard Steele, *The Spectator*, Saturday issues from 5 January to 3 May 1712.
5 The phrase belongs to Sir Joseph Williamson, the civil servant whose task it was to hunt down Milton's literary *Nachlass*, Public Record Office, PRO SP 104/66/120.

text that is politically and theologically negligible and of no abiding intellectual interest. On Addison's account, not even what Satan has to say is upsetting or subversive.

Bunyan is similarly assimilated into the English cultural establishment. Controversial Bunyan disappears. Even *Grace Abounding*, with its throbbing anxieties and documented persecution, is much less frequently reprinted. Meanwhile *The Pilgrim's Progress*, rendered particularly ecumenical by its second part, gets translated for the benefit of supposedly benighted peoples everywhere. Hence the translations of the high Victorian period into Tamil, Dakota, Fanti, Ibo, Luo, Maori, Rarotonga, Eskimo, Ganda, Tahiti, etc. The characteristic sequence of imperialism runs: trader – missionary – translator of Bunyan. Interestingly, the process is initiated by translation into Welsh.[6] Adjacently, Bunyan is transposed into friendlier forms for immature readers, as in Mrs. Edward Ashley's precisely titled *The Pilgrim's Progress for the Little Ones, in words of one syllable* (1907), and many similar publications of the Victorian and Edwardian period.

Both Bunyan and Milton experienced a kind of appropriation in some ways more repressive than oblivion and censorship. A tradition of distortive critical reception bequeaths them to us as urgent cases for recontextualisation in the fabric of Civil War radicalism. As we do so, however, the connections evaporate, particularly for their writings before the early 1660s. Theologically, politically, culturally, aesthetically, socially, stylistically, rhetorically, in terms of their sources and influences, and in numerous aspects of self-representation, almost nothing connects them.

Let us take a simple example: going to jail. Charles II returned to England on 25 May 1660. It was wholly predictable and in a sense wholly proper that Milton, as best known apologist for the killing of his father, should be arrested and prosecuted. Indeed, in the propaganda skirmishes which preceded the Restoration, the 'speu of every drunkard, every ribald',[7] Milton's arrest and punishment were occa-

---

6 Translated as *Taith neu siwrnai y pererin* (1688).
7 Don M. Wolfe (ed.), *The Complete Prose Works of John Milton*, 8 vols. (New Haven and London, 1953–83), 7 (rev. edn.): 452.

sionally anticipated. One royalist adversary – perceptively, perhaps – suggests that when Milton's turn comes to be carried to Tyburn, his eccentricities will prompt him to ask to be taken in a wheelbarrow.[8] Milton's response to such gathering dangers accords with his resumed republican writing of early 1660; he does the best he can, though probably with little expectation of success. In the case of imprisonment, the best he can do is to secure as much personal equity as possible and to hide. Early in May we find him transferring a government bond to Cyriack Skinner. The document is doubly significant in that it confirms that Jeremy Picard was acting as secretary or amanuensis to him in 1660, which is an important detail connecting Milton with the scribe of the document now known as the manuscript of *De Doctrina Christiana*. And then Milton hides, with a still unidentified friend, until on 29 August the Act of Oblivion, which guarantees he will not be executed, receives the royal assent. (Perhaps I could remark in passing that Bunyan actually did something rather similar with his own property when he anticipated arrest in 1685.) Milton emerges from hiding, though later in the year a short period of imprisonment, in the Tower of London, occurs in rather uncertain circumstances. He is, an early biographer tells us, 'quickly set a liberty', though on one contemporary Dutch account it would seem he had given certain guarantees for future conduct: he 'was freed through good promises.' A question was later asked in the House of Commons by Marvell about the excessive fees he had been charged for incarceration.[9] Certainly, some contemporaries were surprised at the leniency of his treatment. Gilbert Burnet, for example, thought it 'an odd strain of clemency'.[10] Nor did Milton engage in any action that would leave him open to further persecution, living untroubled by the state for another fourteen years.

8   Anon., *The Character of the Rump* (1660), pp. 2–3.
9   Gordon Campbell, *A Milton Chronology* (Basingstoke, 1997), pp. 190–4.
10   Osmund Airy (ed.), *Burnet's History of My Own Time*, 2 vols. (Oxford, 1897–1900), 1: 283, quoted in P. J. Kitson, 'The Seventeenth–Century Influence on the Early Religious and Political Thought of S. T. Coleridge', Hull Ph.D. thesis (1984), p. 248.

At a purely pragmatic level all of that is unremarkable. A blind man in his early fifties with enough friends and connections and enough money to navigate a way out of prison and with other imperatives, in the form of at least two ongoing writing projects, chose not to die or degenerate in prison as in the fates of Colonel John Hutchinson or James Harrington. His action also matches the rhetoric and the perspective he previously brought to bear on the witness of faith through martyrdom. His concerns in the two editions of *The Readie and Easie Way to Establish a Free Commonwealth* (1660) are with the godly remnant, who risk persecution but who do not seek it. Again, the exigencies of debate had previously required a separation of suffering and morality. In *Of Reformation* (1641), he had been constrained to distinguish the bravery of episcopalian Marian martyrs from the dishonesty of their conduct in office: the fact that they could die well did not mean that they were right in their advocacy of prelatical church government.[11] In his greatest polemical challenge, responding to the presentation in *Eikon Basilike* of Charles I's evident courage and his claim to the status of martyr, Milton must argue that empty heroism is not ethically significant and cannot devalue the process of Providence that brought him to execution. Indeed, though Milton does indeed write a text about prison, *Samson Agonistes*, incarceration in that text is less a testament of faith than evidence of failure: it is what happens to armed saints when they let themselves down. Within the play the theme of Manoa's negotiations for Samson's release remains unresolved by the time that his regeneration and death render it irrelevant; Milton himself had left 'the mill' as expeditiously as he could.

At the time of the Restoration, Bunyan lived altogether more obscurely than Milton, though well enough known to the restored political elite of his locality, as Hill has demonstrated.[12] By May 1660, he had probably committed no offences under currently enforced legislation that would have merited incarceration, though his preaching had already attracted the attention of local magistrates. Indeed, his

---

11   Wolfe (ed.), *Prose Works of Milton*, 1: 603–04.
12   Christopher Hill, *A Turbulent, Seditious, and Factious People: John Bunyan and his church* (Oxford, 1988), pp. 105–10.

published oeuvre, far from being seditious, showed an admirable orthodoxy in its refutations of Quakerism; no one was ever punished in the seventeenth century for being unkind to Quakers.

Bunyan's arrest in November 1660 must have been within days of Milton's; far from being 'quickly set at liberty', however, he spent the next twelve years in jail.[13] Remarkably Bunyan represents his incarceration both as elective and as a component in his spiritual regeneration. Far from avoiding capture, he attended a meeting in the knowledge that a warrant had been issued. Far from seeking speedy delivery, he declined to give undertakings to discontinue preaching. Keeble hints at what seems altogether likely: that Bunyan commits himself to a process of competitive suffering, demonstrating that Baptists can match the constancy of witness shown by Quakers.[14] Indeed, the account in *A Relation* presents each early stage of the judicial process as a kind of invitation to betray the testimony he must bear: as 'Mr. *Foster* of Bedford' put it, 'if you will promise to call the people no more together, you shall have your liberty to go home: for my brother is very loath to send you to prison, if you will be but ruled'.[15]

The issues are symbolic as well as biographical: the prison is incorporated into his rhetorical and theological systems too. As Keeble puts it, 'to attend the meeting and so allow himself to be silenced was Bunyan's most eloquent testimony to the world, but primarily his most moving sermon to his people', albeit a 'sermon which could be preached only once'.[16] As Bunyan writes, however, the prison context, frequently felt, affirms his validity as witness to his faith. Part I of *The Pilgrim's Progress* begins in the prisonhouse, which functions as the necessary context for holy meditation: 'As I walk'd through the wilderness of this world, I lighted on a certain place, where was a Denn; And I laid me down in that place to sleep:

---

13 My information rests here primarily on his accounts in *Grace Abounding* and *A Relation of the Imprisonment of Mr. John Bunyan*, and Hill's interpretation of these.
14 Keeble, *Literary Culture*, p. 50.
15 *A Relation*, in *GA*, p. 109.
16 Keeble, *Literary Culture*, p. 78.

And as I slept I dreamed a Dream' (*PP*, p. 8). A marginal note from the third edition onwards glosses 'Denn' as 'The Gaol'; the phrasing suggestions his abode there is an elective, a place he lights on and adopts.

In *Grace Abounding* incarceration and prosecution supply much of the narrative. It is in prison that the critical phase in his spiritual salvation occurs, through which he feels confirmed in his faith and commitment. Of course, the narrative is reconstructed some while after the event, but its vividness lends plausibility, as, contemplating execution, he connects that literal leap from the ladder with a leap of faith:

> I thought with myself, if I should make a scrabling shift to clamber up the Ladder, yet I should either with quaking or other symptoms of faintings, give occasion to the enemy to reproach the way of God and his People, for their timerousness: this therefore lay with great trouble upon me, for methought I was ashamed to die with a pale face, and tottering knees, for a Cause as this (*GA*, §334).

The account seems shaped by recollection – he writes after the event about a time before it – of the execution of Hugh Peter, whose 'scrabling shift' and reported reluctance to jump off the ladder provided royalist narratives of the execution of regicides with a solitary useful detail.[17] As Bunyan continues to meditate on last things, resignation to God's will suddenly brings comfort:

> I thought also, that God might chuse whether he would give me comfort now, or at the hour of death; but I might not therefore chuse whether I would hold my profession or no: I was bound, but he was free: yea, it was my dutie to stand to his Word, whether he would ever look upon me or no, or save me at the last: Wherefore, thought I, the point being thus, I am for going on, and venturing my eternal state with Christ, whether I have comfort here or no; if God doth not come in, thought I, I will leap off the Ladder even blindfold into Eternitie, sink or swim, come heaven, come hell; Lord Jesus, if thou wilt catch me, do; if not, I will venture for thy Name (GA, §337).

---

17 See Raymond Phineas Stearns, *The Strenuous Puritan: Hugh Peter 1598–1660* (Urbana, 1954), p. 418, for an account of conflicting reports.

At that point, 'the word dropped upon me, *Doth Job serve God for nought?*' (*GA*, §338).

Milton often writes about himself, in the Latin defences, in his response to *A Modest Confutation*,[18] in invocations in *Paradise Lost*, and in that long and curious digression in *The Reason of Church-Government* (1642), but he never describes an analogous spiritual experience. Milton on Milton's account is always godly; his young manhood a model of chaste conduct; his salvation is never in doubt. When the young poet anticipates the millennium in the Nativity Ode, it is with an eagerness to see the devastation wrought by the infant Jesus more widely extended. When he repeats the process at the end of *Of Reformation* he once more anticipates the joy of the godly, perhaps rendered more joyous still by the contemplation of the sufferings of the damned, especially bishops. The Lady in *Comus* (1637) chooses the godly way, and various apparatuses of divine intervention swing into action to secure her liberation and salvation. The fallen Adam and Eve do have a somewhat disturbed night, but once they recognise the proper nature of repentance, they progress speedily on a soterial fast-track.

Of course, what we are seeing is a theory of salvation that differs hugely from Bunyan's. Milton's Arminianism is as discernible in his earliest poetry as it is in his last. Salvation stands open to all who, in godly fashion, align themselves with the divine will. As the Father puts it, 'Man shall not quite be lost, but saved who will,/ Yet not of will in him, but grace in mee/ Freely voutsaf't'.[19] Thereafter, salvation follows smoothly for those who listen to conscience: 'Light after light well used they shall attain,/ And to the end persisting, safe arrive'.[20] The godly retain responsibility for their conduct, but it is a responsibility they are capable of sustaining. As the Arminian Independent John Goodwin, whose position seems close to Milton's, put it, the covenant of grace between the Father and the Son, which is dramatised by Milton in Book 3, is 'to give Assurance unto [...] Men, that upon *their*

---

18 *An Apology against a Pamphlet Call'd A Modest Confutation of the Animadversions upon the Remonstrant against Smectymnuus* (1642).
19 *Paradise Lost*, 3: 173–5.
20 *Paradise Lost*, 3: 196–7.

Faith and Repentance, and *their* Perseverance in both unto the end, they shall have Salvation and Eternal Life conferred upon them'.[21]

The Arminian position, Goodwin's and Milton's, offers a calm reassurance to its subscribers. Bunyan's version of covenant theology, even in its most theoretical exposition, in *The Doctrine of the Law and Grace Unfolded*, emerges as a singularly terrifying soteriology. Salvation is dreadful, an active process in which the godhead acts on chosen individuals, squeezing them to destruction:

> when a man is soundly killed to all his sins, to all his righteousness, to all his comforts whatsoever, and sees that there is no way but the devil must have him, but he must be damned in hell, if he be not clothed with Jesus Christ; Oh! then (saith he) give me Christ on any terms whatsoever he cost: though he cost me friends, though he cost me comforts, though he cost me all that ever I have; yet like the wise merchant in the Gospel they will sell all to get that pearl. I tell you when a soul is brought to see its want of Christ aright, it will not be kept back, Father, Mother, Husband, Wife, Lands, Livings, nay, life and all shall go, rather then the soul will miss of Christ (*MW*, 2:144).

Here Bunyan discusses the chosen ones, whom God elects to kill spiritually that they may be reborn. At the heart of his theory of salvation abides a central mystery, in his phrase 'the pinch of the whole discourse', namely, '*Who* they are that are actually brought into this free and unchangeable grace' (*MW*, 2: 136). The process requires a spiritual agony, the kind he exemplifies dramatically in the account in *Grace Abounding* of his own moment of recognition in the Gethsemane of the Bedford jail. Salvation is terrible, worked through terror, and the terror comes in no small measure through an awareness of its proximity to damnation. An awesome algorithm of anxiety recurs in Bunyan's writing: to presume salvation is to court damnation through presumption; to doubt salvation is to court damnation through faithlessness and despair. Indeed, published first as a broadside in 1663 or 1664, Bunyan's *Mapp Shewing the Order and Causes of Salvation and Damnation* is precisely an algorithm, a flow chart – if this, then that – defining a process leading to heaven or hell, which

---

21 · Quoted by R. L. Greaves in *MW*, 2: xxvii.

seem terribly close to each other (*MW*, 12: 416–23). *The Doctrine of the Law and Grace Unfolded* ends:

> I might lay thee down severall considerations to stir thee up to mend thy pace towards heaven; but I shall not: there is enough written already to leave thy soul without excuse, and to bring thee down with a vengeance into hell fire, devouring fire, the lake of fire, eternall, everlasting fire; Oh! to make thee swim and roul up and down in the flames of the furnace of fire (MW, 2: 226).

Milton in *Paradise Lost* can vividly depict the landscape of hell – even the architecture of hell, as in *Of Reformation* he can, gleefully and wittily, imagine the torments of the damned, relieved only by the thought that the prelates are in a lower condition than they. But in Milton hell is for other people; in Bunyan, it stands open for people like him, like his readers, like everyone.

As the climactic moment passes, Bunyan in *Grace Abounding* has a Bible text come to mind, 'the word dropped upon me, *Doth Job serve God for nought*?'. Milton and he in their theological systems both give a primacy to the Bible, but their modes of use and interpretation differ radically. Certainly, in a tract like *The Doctrine of the Law and Grace Unfolded*, Bunyan assembled a cluttered marginalia of Biblical reference, but his dialectic is unmethodical. The key texts work on him, vitally suggesting themselves to him in moments of need, as in the Bedford jail – or as the Book works on the protagonist of Part I of *The Pilgrim's Progress*. He opens it, he reads the right bit and it does its work. Or Evangelist appears with a '*Parchment-Roll*', and again, just the right text, '*Fly from the wrath to come*', identified in the margin as Mathew iii. 3.7 (*PP*, pp. 9–10). An exterior agency mystically presents the text. In stark contrast, at least as early as *Tetrachordon* (1645) Milton is fascinated by the possibilities of formal exegesis, of developing reading strategies to reduce to order a seeming chaos of conflicting texts through postulating non-literal modes of interpretation. The provenance of *Christian Doctrine* has recently received thorough review.[22] I subscribe to the view that Milton was engaged, probably in the very late 1650s, in a process of

---

22 See Gordon Campbell *et al.*, 'The Provenance of *De Doctrina Christiana*', *Milton Quarterly*, 17 (1997), 67–121.

assembling, from one or more sources and from his own research, an exhaustive account of Christian doctrine, tallying, juxtaposing and reconciling the evidence of the sacred text. As a process and a methodology it stands at a far remove from the de-intellectualised but potent primitivism of Bunyan's approach.

Centring the Bible is essential to Bunyan's self-definition. Significantly, it allows him to represent his separateness from Quakers. Milton and Bunyan contrast interestingly in their perception and representation of Quakerism in the late 1650s. Milton never uses the word 'Quaker'. However, latterly several critics have remarked on Quakerish elements in his last verse. Certainly after the Restoration, Milton counted some prominent Quakers, such as Thomas Ellwood, among his unusually wide circle of friends. (I continue to be amazed that Miltonists habitually dismiss this important, courageous, trusted and intelligent writer and Quaker activist; the reductive perspective survives into Shawcross's recent biography, where he appears as 'honest and naive'.)[23] We know, too, that when Milton fled plague-stricken London in 1665, he went to Chalfont St Giles, a centre of Quaker activity, and that the cottage was rented on his behalf by Ellwood. However, the clearest flirtation with Quaker values and ideals, it seems to me, comes in the tracts of 1659, *Considerations Touching the Likeliest Means to Remove Hirelings out of the Church* and *A Treatize of f Civil Power*. There Milton praises the ministry of modestly educated amateurs. Christ's first ministers were 'unlearned men', as were the earliest true Protestants.[24] He writes warmly and at some length in praise of itinerant preachers, going out, in the footsteps of the apostles, to spread the gospel where it has least penetrated, and he writes, too, in praise of the informality of such missions:

> For notwithstanding the gaudy superstition of som devoted still ignorantly to temples, we may be well assur'd that he who disdaind not to be laid in a manger, disdains not to be preachd in a barn; and that by such meetings as these, being, indeed, most apostolical and primitive, they will in a short time advance more in Christian knowledge and reformation of life, then by the many

---

23 John T. Shawcross, *John Milton: the self and the world* (Lexington, 1993), p. 149.
24 Wolfe (ed.), *Prose Works of Milton*, 7: 302.

years preaching of such an incumbent [...] as will be meanly hir'd to abide long in those places.[25]

Of course, by the late 1650s the group most associated with itinerant preaching and informality of meeting place and an unlearned and unbeneficed ministry was most certainly the Quakers. For Milton, a revolutionary from a securely propertied background, an air of radical chic surrounds Quakerism. Moreover, in some of the more speculative elements in early Quakerism, especially in notions of the Christ within, of the pre-eminence of an interiorised spirit validating the actions of the godly, Milton probably encountered a radical and challenging version of the godhead that approximated to the more heterodox elements of his personal theology.

That interiority is sometimes adduced as a defining component of radical Protestantism. However, if we look at Bunyan's anti-Quaker writing, and particularly at *Some Gospel-Truths Opened* (1656) and *A Vindication of Some Gospel-Truths Opened* (1657), such interiority is hotly disputed. Quakers, in a more spiritual version of an idea recurrent in Winstanley, speak frequently of the individual resurrection of Christ within each believer, at the same time down-valuing the significance of a historical Christ, 'the man Jesus', and redefining the millennium as a current process not a future event. Bunyan's two tracts celebrate the incarnate Christ in explicitly and doggedly literal terms, what he calls 'the simplicity that is in Christ' (*MW*, 1: 100.). His Christ is an historical figure, who physically ascended, body and spirit, who lives in body and spirit above the clouds, who is external from the godly but influences from that position of exteriority, and who will physically return, body and spirit, to effect a physical resurrection of the godly in a single, real-time event, in conflict with the Quaker fantasy:

> *The new and false Christ, is a Christ crucified within, dead within, rizen againe within, and ascended within in opposition of the Son of Mary, who was crucified without, dead without, and ascended in a cloud away from his Disciples in heaven* [...] *without them* (*MW*, 1: 19–20).

25 Wolfe (ed.), *Prose Works of Milton*, 7: 304–5.

(It is pertinent here to recall Milton's own enthusiastic celebration of the 'paradise within' available to the godly.)[26] Bunyan's exteriorising doctrine allows him to make an early flourish of a recurrent anti-Quaker tactic, associating them with Ranters:

> let us a little compare the principles of a *Ranter* and a *Quaker* together, and it will clearly appear, that in many of their Principles (at least) they agree, or jump in one: As first, the *Ranters* will owne Christ no other waies, then only within: and, this is also the principle of the *Quakers*, they will not owne Christ without them. 2. the *Ranters*, they crie down all teaching, but the teaching within; and so do the Quakers (*MW*, 1: 138).

I think here of Tiny Rowland's famous advice that one cannot have too many enemies. The dictum certainly holds true among mid-century radicals. Explicit formulations of belief or policy are very rare, though of course there are exceptions such as Leveller manifestoes or Winstanley's *The Law of Freedom in a Platform* (1651). Groups habitually define themselves through their difference from rival groups. The Quakers' speculative and elusive theology serves Bunyan well in establishing the sober literalism of his own doctrinal position, while making a sort of plea for an orthodoxy, indeed a respectability, which differentiates his Baptists from groups perhaps, in his view, even worthy of suppression.

Milton's enemies are quite different. Chief among them are the Presbyterians, vehemently flayed in poems of the mid-1640s, in the tracts of 1649, and in *The Readie and Easie Way*, sometimes with an exuberance that threatened the polemical coherence of what he was doing. In terms of the enemies by whom they define themselves, Milton and Bunyan do not remotely approach each other. Milton, incidentally, never attacks Baptists. In his early prose, he notes that the term is sometimes used as a generalized reproach, but it is not one he repeats; a possibly negative aspect of his reference to them in the first edition of *The Doctrine and Discipline of Divorce* (1643) is clarified in an addition to the second edition.[27] The chapter on baptism in *Christian Doctrine*, while showing signs of inconsistency, as it

---

26 *Paradise Lost*, 12: 587.
27 Wolfe (ed.), *Prose Works of Milton*, 2: 278.

stands is sympathetic to Baptists' views of the sacrament, and he praises at least one leading Baptist – the 'virtuous father' in the sonnet 'Lawrence of virtuous father virtuous son' was Henry Lawrence, a significant figure in Baptist theology.[28]

Examples and aspects separating Milton and Bunyan could be multiplied. Bunyan's self-representation makes him appear a little poorer than he probably was – 'my fathers house being of that rank that is meanest, and most despised of all the families of the land' (*GA*, §2) – not really; they were more prosperous than agricultural day-labourers, for example. Milton makes himself appear perhaps a little richer, playing up the gentlemanly grand tour and his indifference to mere wage-labour. Bunyan condemns his father's malign influence; Milton, constructing an ancestry for himself, does the opposite (though the late Jeremy Maule disclosed significant information about the probably rather unpuritanical nature of his father's religious predilections).[29] Bunyan emphasises the rights of the poor and uneducated to know and speak of religion; Milton occasionally agrees, though in *Colasterion* (1645) a rather different class perspective emerges.

Much could be made of their characteristic modes of expression, of the genres they chose, of the audiences they address, in their pre-1660 publications. The whole hortatory, evangelical dimension is missing in Milton, who never addresses the salvation of his readers. Again, England slips from a relatively permissive republic to a very repressive monarchy without Bunyan seemingly noticing – or at least engaging with the issue in print. They talk about a wholly different sphere of human experience, to different people, and for different purposes. Milton, in *The Readie and Easie Way*, for example, in part addresses a readership he profoundly despises, to scare them into a course of action that would serve to do the right thing for the wrong reason. Bunyan's address to his readers functions within a radically different perspective – to tell the perceived truth; his holy terror has no Machiavellian justification.

28 Richard L. Greaves and Robert Zaller, *Biographical Dictionary of British Radicals in the Seventeenth Century*, 3 vols. (Brighton, 1983), 2: 175–6.
29 In an unpublished paper to the British Milton Seminar, March 1997.

As I began by claiming, a happy dissenting group is happy after its own fashion – though Milton, I suspect, is really a group of one, and 'happiness' does not immediately suggest itself as a term for Bunyan's religious sensibility. In the 1650s, largely unconstrained by the civil magistrate, an extraordinary diversity of belief, opinion and practice emerges admitting a variety as great as that which, by the late 1650s, separated rentier-class, politically connected, metropolitan, speculative, Arminian and spiritually content Milton from relatively indigent, politically inert, provincial, literalist, Calvinist and spiritually tortured Bunyan. Indeed, the most influential accounts of the intellectual and literary history of 1640–60 engage this diversity. Thus Hill's *The World Turned Upside Down*[30] celebrates the complexities, the variety and vigour, of radical thought in the period, like a botanist admiring a thousand flowers blooming. The study itself reflects something of the headiness of the late 1960s and early seventies, as the direct-action radicalism of the former mutated into the cultural diversities of the latter. Nigel Smith's two major studies of the period, in rather different ways, address and define diversities. *Perfection Proclaimed*[31] is like a generative syntax of the radical *langue* by which the infinite *paroles* of individual belief and expression were generated. Again, his *Literature and Revolution*[32] has a sort of evolutionary metaphor informing it, as though changes in objective conditions suddenly permitted the infinite sporting of literary kinds.

At 1660, however, or shortly thereafter, that impulse changes radically into a kind of convergent evolution in which all species of radical dissent adopt analogous survival strategies, or else they perish. The seminal text is probably Hill's *The Experience of Defeat: Milton and some contemporaries*. Published in 1984, it is replete with the dismay and alienation of the British Left in the period immediately after the Falklands War and the ensuing Thatcher landslide. It is an

---

30 Christopher Hill, *The World Turned Upside Down: radical ideas during the English revolution* (London, 1972).
31 Nigel Smith, *Perfection Proclaimed: language and literature in English radical religion 1640–1660* (Oxford, 1989).
32 Nigel Smith, *Literature and Revolution in England, 1640–1660* (New Haven, 1994).

extended essay on unhappy radicals being unhappy in very similar ways, and rings as true of radicals of the 1980s as of the 1660s. Indeed, Hill ends, almost in a spirit of lamentation: 'In 1644 Milton saw England as "a nation of prophets". Where are they now?'[33]

The simple answer was: surviving as best they could, and despite the horrors of the early 1980s or the 1660s, survive they did. Most pertinent for this argument is Keeble's *Literary Culture of Nonconformity*, published in 1987, which demonstrates that such survival assumes an active, ingenious and courageous aspect shared across a very wide range of dissent, and expressed in shared value systems, in redefined attitudes among dissenting groups, and in changes and developments in characteristic modes of expression. As Keeble generalizes, literary dissent 'was [...] creative, positive and salutary in its demotic realism, its subjective authenticity and its sensitivity to the numinous'.[34]

In a sense, however, to generalize about post-1660 dissent is made easier by the actions of the restored establishment, which also implacably generalized. On the eve of the Restoration, Milton challenged the newly kingified Presbyterians with what was likely to happen to them once kingship returned: did they really think Charles II would forgive them their treatment of his father? To a Presbyterian, a Congregationalist was altogether a different kind of Puritan; Baptists knew their own divisions intimately; and they most certainly understood precisely what separated them from Quakers. But by 1662 they are all roughly equated as obnoxious dissenters by those whose political will mattered. The effect reverses the transitions around 1640. In the late 1630s Lilburne hazarded extreme penalties to circulate the work of writers who, by the early 1640s, seemed to him sell-outs and apostates.

A complex and fissured tradition becomes simplified, then, under external pressure. Finally, that connection of Bunyan and Milton, chimerically constructed by an eighteenth- and nineteenth-century critical practice – Bunton and Milyan – and unsustainable in the con-

---

33 Christopher Hill, *The Experience of Defeat: Milton and some contemporaries* (London, 1984), p. 328.
34 Keeble, *Literary Culture*, p. 283.

text of the 1650s, starts to make sense. It works at the level of detail as well as at the level of larger abstraction. For example, naively but necessarily, I have interpreted *Grace Abounding* as a document relating to the late 1650s and very early in the 1660s; but it is a text Bunyan refreshes throughout his life, and the additions and changes can be plotted against the changing experience of dissent in the 1660s and into the 1670s, as grim endurance is replaced by a recognition of new possibilities, a renewed impulse to mobilise the faithful to his particular agenda, and indeed by Bunyan's need to protect his own position within the movement.[35] Similarly, the post-1660 Milton oeuvre reflects initially a grim endurance, a short-term pessimism with optimism endlessly postponed; but in the 1670s, in *Paradise Regained* and in *Samson Agonistes*, it shows a more active role for the godly. Again, in the 1670s, both Milton and Bunyan recognise advantages in a new ecumenicalism, redefining Protestantism in a broader way. Thus, in *Of True Religion, Heresy and Schism* (1673), Milton's only post-1660 pamphlet, a certain opportunism informs his attempts to define toleration in purely anti-Catholic terms. Similarly, although Part I of *The Pilgrim's Progress* remains replete with many of Bunyan's characteristic values and anxieties, both its success and the facility with which it secured a broad Protestant readership indicate how far he had journeyed from the sectaries' turf-wars of the 1650s.

---

35 See Thomas N. Corns, 'Bunyan's *Grace Abouding* and the Dynamics of Restoration Nonconformity', in Neil Rhodes (ed.), *English Renaissance Prose: history, language, and politics* (Tempe, 1997), pp. 259–70.

2

WILLIAM LAMONT
Bunyan and Baxter: Millennium and Magistrate

Near the end of their lives both John Bunyan and Richard Baxter committed themselves to manuscript observations on the millennium. What better time to think on last things? D. H. Lawrence, dying of tuberculosis in 1929, likewise composed his own remarkable *Apocalypse* as his last work. Millenarian reflections are not necessarily subversive in their implications, although Norman Cohn's seminal study, *The Pursuit of the Millennium*, has made that linkage seem compelling.[1] In the case of Bunyan and Baxter, moreover, there is a piquant extra ingredient: both men would not submit their manuscript thoughts to a public audience. Proof positive, therefore, of sinister designs?

One historian would have leapt to such a conclusion, we may be sure. Michael Walzer's *The Revolution of the Saints* is a book with a thesis: Puritan ideology, in his view, is as much the motor of the seventeenth-century English Revolution as Marxism was of 'modernising' twentieth-century movements.[2] Bunyan – the proletarian tinker/hero of Christopher Hill's study[3] – can be made to fit into this pattern rather better, it is true, than the moderate, respectable nonconformist Richard Baxter. It is, however, damning evidence that both should wish *to keep secret* their thoughts on the millennium: how wise then of the authorities of the day to lock up both men!

1   Norman Cohn, *The Pursuit of the Millennium* (London, 1957). And for a different view, see: William Lamont, *Godly Rule: politics and religion, 1603–60* (London, 1969).
2   Michael Walzer, *The Revolution of the Saints* (London, 1966) and 'Puritanism as a revolutionary ideology', *History and Theory*, 3 (1963–4), 59–90.
3   Christopher Hill, *A Turbulent Seditious and Factious People: John Bunyan and his church* (Oxford, 1988).

To this there are two objections to be made. The first is that neither was sent to prison for his millenarian beliefs (which were as opaque to governments as to most of their peers). Baxter pointed out, with dry wit, that it was the other way round. His millenarian studies were a consequence, not a cause, of his imprisonment. At last he had been provided with a decent sabbatical to work out what he really thought about Revelation.[4] The second is that it assumes a revolutionary intent held by most English Puritans. Walzer is not an oddball in holding such a view. Nevertheless it runs counter to a contrary historiographical tendency, which emphasises the deferential, magistrate-revering side of Puritanism: the greatest exponent of that view is Patrick Collinson.[5] No comparative analysis of Bunyan's and Baxter's millenarian manuscripts has been undertaken up until now, and yet the fruit of such a study might be an enhanced understanding of the nature of Puritanism. Both men *professed* loyalism in their printed writings. Do those private papers (unpublished while they were alive) throw a different light on their public face? Let me begin this brief essay by declaring my hand. Both men, I will argue, are as loyalist in private as they were in public; the differences between two sorts of Puritanism – the 'world turned upside down' perspective of a Bunyan and the deferential respectability of a Baxter – seem to me to have been overblown; the authorities had, in fact, more to fear from Baxter than from Bunyan, and this, it will be argued, not because Baxter's commitment to the authority of the magistrate was less than Bunyan's (some Walzerian subscription in secret to a revolutionary ideology), but because, we shall find paradoxically, it was *more*. It was the genuineness of Baxter's commitment to magistracy – for him and for many of his fellow Puritans – which would make it in the end such a *destabilising* concept.

Though Bunyan and Baxter come from different traditions within Puritanism, there has been a tendency to obscure what they have in common. To start with what Bunyan himself called a 'dreadful Story' about the life and death of one Dorothy Mateley:

---

4   Doctor Williams's Library, London, *Baxter Treatises*, vol. vii, fol. 295.
5   Among his many writings, see especially: Patrick Collinson, *The Religion of Protestants* (Oxford, 1982), pp. 141–88.

Now upon the 23. of *March*, 1660. this *Dorothy* was washing of Ore upon the top of a steep Hill, about a quarter of a mile from *Ashover*, and was there taxed by a Lad for taking of two single Pence out of his Pocket, (for he had laid his Breeches by, and was at work in his Drawers;) but she violently denyed it, wishing, *That the ground might swallow her up if she had them:* She also used the same wicked words on several other occasions that day.

Now one *George Hodgkinson* of *Ashover*, a man of good report there, came accidentally by where this *Dorothy* was, and stood still a while to talk with her, as she was washing her Ore; there stood also a little Child by her *Tub-side*, and another a distance from her, calling aloud to her to come away; wherefore the said *George* took the Girle by the hand to lead her away to her that called her: But behold, they had not gone above ten yards from *Dorothy*, but they heard her crying out for help; so looking back, he saw the *Woman*, and her *Tub*, and *Sive*, twirling round, and sinking into the ground. Then said the man, *Pray to God to pardon thy sin, for thou art never like to be seen alive any longer.* So she and her Tub twirled round and round, till they sunk about three yards into the Earth, and then for a while staid. Then she called for help again, thinking, as she said, that she should stay there. Now the man, though greatly amazed, did begin to think which way to help her; but immediately a great stone which appeared in the Earth, fell upon her head, and brake her Skull, and then the Earth fell in upon her, and covered her. She was afterwards digged up, and found about four yards within ground, with the Boys two single Pence in her pocket, but her *Tub* and *Sive* could not be found (*MB*, p. 33).

So much for what we might call 'the tale of the tub'. Now for another equally 'dreadful' story, but this time from a different source. There once was a conformist parishioner, Mr Martin of Walsall. He did not appreciate his good fortune in having as a minister the redoubtable Anthony Lapthorne, known as a 'rustic thunderer' in the Latimer mould. When the pulpit thunder proved too much for Martin, he would up and leave. He did this once too often. What happened? 'The ground opened and swallowed him for good. 'Ever after that, Lapthorne had a ready moral at hand for his congregation: 'when any one would goe out of Church at a blustering passage, Mr. Lapthorne would call to him *Remember Martin*'.[6]

Here we have two, what we might call, ground-breaking episodes, the second of which comes from Baxter. The similarities come from a similar mind-set: the products of a providential universe in

6 Richard Baxter, *Catholick Communion Defended Against Both Extremes* (1684), part II, pp. 32–3.

which wrongdoers receive their deserved come-uppance. Eternal hellfire would seem to beckon, alike for the woman of the tub and the refugee from rustic thunder. Bunyan, in his *A Few Sighs from Hell* of 1658, did not mince words when he speculated on what awaited the sinner:

> thy soul will fall into extreme torment, and anguish so soon as ever thou dost depart this world, and there thou shalt be weeping and gnashing thy teeth, *Matth.* 8. 11, 12. *And besides all this*, thou art like never to have any cure or remedy, never look for any deliverance, if thou die out of Christ; thou shalt die in thy sins; and be tormented as many years as there are stars in the firmament, or sands on the sea-shore.

That was bad enough, but worse was to follow:

> *and besides all this*, thou must abide it for ever (*MW*, 1: 301).

When quoting this passage, Roger Sharrock puts Bunyan on the 'extreme conservative' wing of debates on Hell, and who would quarrel with that? Sharrock then contrasts Bunyan explicitly with 'his Nonconformist contemporary, Richard Baxter, always a moderate voice'.[7] Always a moderate? A fellow contributor to the same volume of essays, Gordon Campbell, offers a different view: 'the humane Richard Baxter', as Campbell called him, actually shared with Bunyan what Campbell described as this 'blood-chilling enthusiasm' for Hell.[8] Campbell, not Sharrock, is right here. One thinks of Baxter's description of Hell as 'a rational torment by Conscience, according to the nature of the Rational Subject'. The elegance of such a definition is that 'to remember the wilfulness will feed the fire, and cause the horrors of conscience never to die'. Always there is 'an angry sin-revenging God above them'. Those who enjoyed their earthly pleasures now pay for it: 'those Ears which were wont to be delighted

---

[7] Roger Sharrock, '"When at the first I took my Pen in hand": Bunyan and the Book', in N. H. Keeble (ed.), *John Bunyan: Conventicle and Parnassus* (Oxford, 1988), pp. 73–4.

[8] Gordon Campbell, 'Fishing in Other Men's Waters: Bunyan and the Theologians', in Keeble (ed.), *Conventicle and Parnassus*, p. 141.

with Musick, shall hear the shrieks and cries of their damned companions'.[9]

Sharrock misses the parallel because of his conviction that Baxter is a 'moderate'; Campbell notes the parallel, but with surprise, because of his conviction that Baxter is 'humane'. The stereotyping may derive from preconceptions about doctrine. Moderation and humanity seem to sit well with a theology (like Baxter's) which is self-consciously distancing itself from its Calvinist roots, whereas predestination and eternal hell-fire seem to make the perfect fit for Bunyan. It is, however, important to grasp that Baxter does not see his views on Hell as a deviation from his revisionism of doctrine, but rather as their logical corollary. What, for Baxter, is particularly satisfactory about his views on Hell is that they give a knock-out blow to determinism. Now, he noted, 'sinners shall lay all the blame on their wills in Hell for ever'. No shuffling off blame on to God. It is what Baxter had against Edward Fisher's classic exposition of high Calvinism in his *The Marrow of Modern Divinity* of 1645. What Fisher was doing, according to Baxter, was an exercise in blame-shifting: he 'earnestly presseth believers not to look to their sins as making them lyable to God's everlasting wrath and Hell-fire, nor to crave pardon and forgiveness for them that thereupon they may escape that penalty'.[10] For Baxter the saint's assurance comes, not from the fact that he is offered unconditional assurance (the vulgar error of 'Marrow divinity'), but that he will meet those conditions which have been set. It was the message he was to put across with great success (he thought) to his Kidderminster parishioners in the 1650s. Eternal hell-fire awaited those who failed to know their catechisms.[11]

So it would have been no surprise to Baxter that Bunyan – a 'Marrow' man in his theology, if ever there was one – would make light of Hell as a sanction. For him the surprise was that he did not. Coleridge, always the best reader of Baxter, grasped the paradox. Calvinism he said was 'the lamb in the wolf's skin'; Arminianism was

---

9 Richard Baxter, *The Saints Everlasting Rest* (1650), pp. 338, 271.
10 Richard Baxter, *A Confession of his Faith* (1655), pp. 123–4.
11 On which, see Eamon Duffy, 'The godly and the multitude in Stuart England', *The Seventeenth Century*, 1 (1986), 32, 38–40.

'the wolf in the lamb's skin'. One doctrine condemned the race, but gave comfort to the individual; the other was more generous to the race, but cruel to the individual 'for fear of damaging the race by false hopes and improper confidence'.[12] It would not be too much of an exaggeration to say that Baxter's whole career was one crusade against Antinomianism:[13] the Calvinist predestinarian doctrine carried to the pitch where it liberates the individual from all deference to the Law. That was the theme of his first book, *The Aphorismes of Justification* of 1649, which he called his 'dying thoughts', and it would continue to be the theme of his cluster of writings in 1691 which really *were* his dying thoughts. Between 1649 and 1691, however, there is a significant difference, and Bunyan plays a part in that difference. Writing in 1654, Baxter had argued that, while Arminianism could be *taken up by* wicked men (how else to explain the phenomenon of Archbishop Laud?), Antinomianism, its opposite, was quite simply *the religion of* wicked men. When men spoke about conversion they were really talking about 'the cure of Naturall Antinomianism'.[14] Yet, by the later date, he had come to recognise that it was 'the Piety and Strictness of the lives' of many individual Antinomians 'which hath drawn many well-meaning ignorant persons to their Errors'. In manuscript he named names: men like Thomas Beverley (a fellow prisoner with him in 1686 and correspondent there about the millennium) and John Bunyan, whom he called 'an unlearned Antinomian', and yet one, he had to concede, who was also the type of an 'honest, Godly man'.[15] Perhaps that insight colours his response even to Bunyan's doctrinal quarrel with Edward Fowler's *Design of Christianity* in 1672. True, Baxter sides in the end with Fowler, but he simultaneously distances himself from Fowler's claim (in Baxter's perception, at least) that 'personal holiness' is Christ's

12   S. T. Coleridge, *Complete Works*, ed. W. Shedd, 12 vols. (New York, 1854), 5: 200.
13   See on this the excellent study, Tim Cooper, *Fear and Polemic in Seventeenth-Century England: Richard Baxter and antinomianism* (Aldershot and Burlington VT, 2001).
14   Richard Baxter, *Richard Baxter's Confutation of a Dissertation for the Justification of Infidels* (1654), p. 288.
15   Richard Baxter, *The Scripture-Gospel Defended* (1690), part II, p. 49.

only design.[16] Baxter and Bunyan remain apart in doctrine – it would be perverse to suggest otherwise – but they are *not that far apart*. Bunyan's stress on the need for repentance and the will in *Mr. Badman* and *The Holy War*, and his lack of stress on election and reprobation in *The Pilgrim's Progress*, might (argues Gordon Campbell) persuade the unwary reader of the view that they came from the pen of 'a free-willer'.[17] And what of the 'free-willer' Baxter? Samuel Young in 1699 had to attempt to destroy the rumour that, two days before his death, Baxter had said that the Antinomian champion, Tobias Crisp, was an orthodox man.[18] Similarly his literary executors, Matthew Sylvester and Daniel Williams, were at great pains to set aside doubts raised by his reported dying words: '*No works, I will leave out works, if he grant me the other*'. They were driven to publishing in 1697, that is to say six years after his death, an earlier manuscript on doctrine by Baxter, under the title, *The Protestant Religion Truely Stated and Justified*, to put an end to such stories.[19] Baxter and Bunyan were not soul-mates on doctrine, certainly, but Baxter was no more an Edward Fowler than Bunyan was an Edward Fisher.

A comparison between Bunyan's and Baxter's late meditations on the millennium should not, therefore, start from the premise that they spoke across an unbridgeable divide: the one representing the 'moderate', 'humane', 'respectable' wing of Puritanism, and the other the view from the 'world turned upside down' perspective. Bunyan's manuscript, *Of Antichrist and his Ruine*, was composed in the early 1680s,[20] although it was not published until 1692 (along with eleven other previously unprinted works) by his friend, Charles Doe. The main themes of his treatise are these. Antichrist first came in when

---

16 There is a good discussion of their debate in: Hans Boersma, *A Hot Pepper Corn: Richard Baxter's doctrine of justification in its seventeenth-century context of controversy* (Zoetermeer, 1993), pp. 306–10.
17 Campbell, 'Fishing in Other Men's Waters', pp. 149–50.
18 Samuel Young, *A New-Year's Gift for the Antinomians* (1699), p. 5.
19 Richard Baxter, *The Protestant Religion Truely Stated and Justified* (1697), preface by Daniel Williams and Matthew Sylvester.
20 W. R. Owens, 'The Date of Bunyan's Treatise, *Of Antichrist*', *The Seventeenth Century*, 1 (1986), 193–7.

church leaders flattered their Emperor, Constantine. Conversely, Antichrist will only fall when the Christian magistrate exerts his proper authority: '*Antichrist shall not down but by the Hand of Kings*' (*MW*, 13:462). No date can be given, nor should it be. There will be an initial period of persecution – the slaying of the Two Last Witnesses (this in marked contrast to Bunyan's expectation in 1665 of an imminent, if still unspecific, time of glory).[21] After the resurrection the physical destruction of Antichrist will be achieved by the armies of the Protestant Kings, but even less than full-blooded Protestant Kings – shall we say, a Charles II? – would have a role to play.[22] In Bunyan's manuscript, Artaxerxes is an example of a King who gives his subjects religious toleration, even if he does not share their beliefs. Louis XIV even might be used by God in the destruction of Antichrist. Dr Owens, an expert commentator on the treatise, concludes that – in the atmosphere of the 1680s – there was enough in the manuscript that was provocative to make it 'understandable that Bunyan should have left *Of Antichrist and his Ruine* in the safety of manuscript'.[23]

In Baxter's case, we do not have to speculate on the reasons why he might have wanted to suppress his millenarian thoughts in 1686. We know that he wanted them to be *concealed*. Even stronger than that, he left instructions that they should be burnt if an expert on the millennium examined them later on and found them wanting. Even if approved by a specialist in the field, they should remain 'utterly secret'; that is, until 'the Designe of papall prevalency be blasted by the providence of God'.[24] To understand this curious request, it must be put in its historical context. His millenarian researches were conducted in 1686, when the civil magistrate on the English throne was

---

[21] W. R. Owens, '"Antichrist must be Pulled Down": Bunyan and the Millennium', in Anne Laurence, W. R. Owens, and Stuart Sim (ed.), *John Bunyan and his England, 1628–88* (London and Ronceverte WV, 1990), pp. 88–9.

[22] 'Take heed in laying the cause of your Troubles in the badness of the Temper of Governours [...] *Good temper'd* Men have sometimes brought Trouble; and *bad temper'd* Men have sometimes brought Enlargement to the Churches of God' (*MW*, 13:428).

[23] Owens, '"Antichrist must be Pulled Down"', p. 94.

[24] Doctor Williams's Library, *Baxter Treatises*, vol. vii, fol. 296.

papist James II. The effect of his researches, as we shall see, was to enhance dramatically the authority of the civil magistrate. Therefore 'papall prevalency' would be strengthened, not weakened, if his conclusions went public. It would take the 1688 blast of God's providence to remove James II, and it would be in 1690 and 1691 that Baxter could draw upon these earlier researches – at last – to make the case for Protestant William III's accession. He could not have foreseen this turn of events in 1686, but it is what he had ardently prayed for.

As early as 1959 Roger Thomas had drawn attention to the importance of these neglected Baxter papers. He wondered then why Baxter had not published these ideas and could only speculate that age – he was then 71 – had 'prevented this sobering challenge to the wild men of his day'.[25] This will not do on several counts. First, as we have seen, much of the material would in the end make its way into his last published writings. His target never was the 'wild men of his day'. Thomas makes here the common mistake of lumping millenarians in one pigeonhole marked 'revolutionary', but Baxter is neither writing against Fifth Monarchists nor is he reading the proofs of Norman Cohn's masterpiece-to-be. His opponents in fact are conformists like Henry More, or personal friends like his fellow prisoner, Thomas Beverley. Were his targets to have been 'wild men', then the act of publicising their wildness could do nothing but good. He was in much more delicate territory, engaged with opponents whom he respected, and haunted by the unintended fillip he could give to Popery by premature publication. As he himself put it, 'even great Truths may be silenced when they will do more hurt than good'.[26] The hurtful 'Great Truth' of 1686 – all power to the civil magistrate – became the blessed 'Great Truth' of 1691.

In the neglected papers Baxter explained his own evolution. He had started his studies in Revelation from an agnostic base. As a young man, he had been dismayed, on reading commentators on Revelation, to discover how varied their findings were, but at the same

---

25   Roger Thomas, *The Baxter Treatises*, Doctor Williams's Library Occasional Paper 8 (London, 1959), p. 2.

26   Doctor Williams's Library, *Baxter Treatises*, vol. vii, fol. 296.

time he took that, in his own words, 'for truth which the pious adversaries of Popery agreed in, believing that they knew what I did not'. One such truth (to which Bunyan would also have subscribed) was that the Pope was Antichrist. However, in 1684, Baxter's friend John Humfrey had urged him to write a paraphrase on the epistle to the Romans. He found the work 'so pleasant' that he extended it to a paraphrase on the entire New Testament. He could not leave out from such a task a paraphrase of the Book of Revelation. Going back to re-read previous commentaries on the text only revived old misgivings. He did not like the way that Thomas Brightman 'Englished' the Apocalypse[27] (the very quality that had endeared him to countless 'root and branch' radicals in the 1640s).[28] Henry More's gloss on the history of the Church seemed to him to be equally suspect, but there was no personal vendetta here: he and More had after all shared an interest in spirits and ghosts, along with their mutual friend Joseph Glanvill.[29] When, however, Judge Jeffreys sent Baxter to prison for what was tendentiously read as subversive in his paraphrase of Scripture, More had launched a personal attack on him as 'a man of a wooden soul', a schismatic and a rebel. What had stung More (and others of Baxter's friends too) was Baxter's public statement of his disbelief in the thesis that Rome was Antichrist.[30] Yet More's counter-claim, that the episcopal Church of England was the purest in the world as the heir to the Christian church in the first four hundred years before Antichrist came in, drew a similarly vehement response from Baxter. What, the same church that had silenced and ejected two thousand preachers in 1662![31] More's assault only quickened Baxter's resolve to read Revelation more deeply than he ever had done before: and now (a typically caustic Baxter aside) he had the leisure to do so. Providence even decreed that a prisoner in an adjacent cell would be his friend Thomas Beverley, a considerable scholar of the millennium.

27 Doctor Williams's Library, *Baxter Treatises*, vol. vii, fol. 294v.
28 Lamont, *Godly Rule*, pp. 95–100.
29 Doctor Williams's Library, *Baxter Treatises*, vol. vii, fol. 295.
30 Richard Baxter, *A Paraphrase on the New Testament* (1684); Henry More, *Paralipomena Prophetica* (1685), preface.
31 Doctor Williams's Library, *Baxter Treatises*, vol. vii, fol. 295.

Their prison correspondence has survived. There was to be no shortage of messengers to transmit letters between them (and then to leak them to the authorities). They would provide a further arsenal for More's grotesque claim (in Baxter's eyes) that 'I had perfidiously in an Address *sought the favour of the Papists* by telling them how I understand the revelation'. Baxter called the study 'the last work (proposed) of my life', though all Baxter's works, including his first in 1649, were, as we have seen, his 'dying thoughts'. Whilst it could seem natural that his last thoughts should be on last things there is, in Baxter's case, an extra dimension. What More (and other hostile commentators) struck at were Baxter's core beliefs. As he himself put it, 'I am a dying man and would not have my hopes in Christ shaken, which they would be much, if I believed that as soon as his Church was delivered from Pagan captivity, it became Antichristian, as very many say; or before 400 years, as Dr. More saieth.'[32]

What did his researches add up to? First, a strengthening of his 1684 argument that there was no scriptural basis for the identification of Antichrist with Rome. He claimed – on Joseph Mede's testimony – that this false lead had been first given by the Albigensians.[33] Secondly, a preference for John Foxe's reading of the Turk, not Rome, as the greater Antichrist.[34] It would have been useful to Protestants to take the Albigensian line.[35] Similarly, it would have been useful for Protestants to believe in the historical existence of a Pope Joan,[36] but in neither case were Protestants justified in telling lies. Thirdly this insight does not let Papists off the hook (as More seemed to think that it did). Their crime was worse than that. What now was revealed in his researches was that Christ's Kingdom had been set up by 'Christian Emperors and Kings'. When Constantine was converted to Christianity, the millennium (a past one) had begun. Baxter followed Foxe in

32   Doctor Williams's Library, *Baxter Treatises*, vol. vii, fol. 295v.
33   Doctor Williams's Library, *Baxter Treatises*, vol. vi, fol. 357.
34   Doctor Williams's Library, *Baxter Treatises*, vol. v, fol. 96.
35   Doctor Williams's Library, *Baxter Treatises*, vol. vii, fol. 45.
36   Peter Stanford has argued for a 'truth' about the existence of a Pope Joan which is buried under the (admitted) myths: *The She-Pope: a quest for the truth behind the myths of Pope Joan* (London, 1998); but see the withering review of the book by Eamon Duffy: *Times Literary Supplement*, 4973 (24 July 1998), 27.

his five-stage periodization of history, as in almost every other aspect of his interpretation. For both men, the second period was the best (from 300 to 600 AD), when Christians were rescued from their first three hundred years of persecution. In Foxe's words, the 'suffering' time gave way to the 'flourishing' time. Both Baxter and Foxe believed that they were in the fifth and last period of history, the struggle between Christ and Antichrist. Revelation thus condemns Popery, not directly (by a dubious scriptural identification with Antichrist), but indirectly, *and much more tellingly*, by contradicting its false challenge to what Scripture unambiguously reveals: that National Churches are 'nothing but Christian Kingdomes ruled by the Magistrates Sword; and guided by confederated Pastors under him'. He goes on: 'this is the forme of Government that Christ expressly offered the Jewes, and owned and claimed in the world [...] which no part of Scripture more fully showeth than the Apocalypse, and former prophecies'.[37]

Where do such views place Baxter in relation to Bunyan? The overlap is considerable. To set up 'schismatic' Bunyan against 'moderate' Baxter does not work. Both men took stock of the Apocalypse near the end of their lives. Both men kept their thoughts to manuscript form. This was not because they were closet Fifth Monarchists – for both men, the Captain Venners of the world were abhorrent figures[38] – but because they were *loyalists*. Both men were actually happiest under the Cromwellian Protectorate. Although Bunyan had died by 1688, there can be little doubt that his welcome for William III would have been as unreserved as Baxter's. It is worth, however, staying for a moment with this notion of their shared 'happiness' in a Protestant ruler, for this will have an important bearing on our understanding of their shared 'unhappiness' with a Catholic ruler. If they shared 'hap-

---

37   Doctor Williams's Library, *Baxter Treatises*, vol. vii, fol. 299v.
38   Doctor Williams's Library, *Baxter Treatises*, vol. vii, fol. 299v contains Baxter's critique of the wrong-headedness of Fifth Monarchist interpretations; Richard Greaves, *John Bunyan and English Nonconformity* (London and Rio Grande OH, 1992), p. 57, notes Bunyan's repudiation of Venner's Fifth Monarchist rising in 1661, although (p. 143), he recognises that in the mid-1650s Bunyan may have been closer in sympathy to them, particularly in view of 'his close relationship to the Fifth Monarchist agent, John Child'.

piness' and 'unhappiness' in both of these cases, *it was not in the same way*. Setting aside all the (exaggerated) superficial differences between the two men, one profound difference remains. The clue is provided by their differing responses to Oliver Cromwell.

We are able to document Bunyan's commitment to Cromwell. His name appears on a document applauding Cromwell's decision to dissolve the Rump in 1653, and suggesting two names for the Barebones Assembly which succeeded it. Members of his Bedford congregation in 1657 signed a protest in favour of Commonwealth as against Monarchy and, two years later, agreed to set apart a day of prayer of thanksgiving for the defeat of Sir George Booth's royalist rising.[39]

On the face of it this is a much more convincing commitment than Baxter's. Baxter had declined the Engagement to the Commonwealth, had disapproved of the regicide, and was pretty lukewarm about Cromwell in the memoirs he wrote after the Restoration. This is, however, misleading. Baxter's commitment ran much deeper than would appear on the surface. A clue comes in his prison manuscripts, in his outrage at More's claim that the Church was *extinct* in the Interregnum. In reply, Baxter delivered this panegyric on Cromwell:

> When Oliver the usurper ruled in England, there was a policie that renounced Popery, and had thousands of ministers and people that earnestly desired and endeavoured such a concord in Apostolike doctrine as he mentioneth.

He went further still in going on to call this period of 'extinction' 'the time of the fall of Antichrist'.[40] It was easier to put these things in manuscript than in print, of course, but he had actually said much the same as this in his *A Holy Commonwealth* of 1659. The theme of that work had been that the catechising successes of his Kidderminster ministry, translated across the counties of England through the Ministerial Associations, was on the verge of achieving a national reformation when the army officers' coup removed Richard Cromwell.[41] In his later memoirs he would claim that 'England had been like in a

---

39 W. R. Owens, '"Antichrist must be Pulled Down"', p. 91.
40 Doctor Williams's Library, *Baxter Treatises*, vol. vii, fol. 299.
41 See Richard Baxter, *A Holy Commonwealth*, ed. William Lamont (Cambridge, 1994), pp. ix–xxi.

quarter of an Age to have been a land of saints, and a pattern of holinesse to all the World, and the unmatchable Paradise of the Earth'.[42]

One telling argument against a future millennium, which Baxter used against Beverley in their 1686 prison debates, was that the conversion of the Jews was a *sine qua non* for such a change. Most contemporaries (but not Bunyan, by the time he wrote *The Holy City*)[43] shared that premise. Baxter's brief was to show that the millennium was a past one, and he revelled in the implausibility of the mass conversion of Jews that a future millennium would have necessitated. Missionaries, he pointed out, would need a great deal of time to learn the language of conversion; in particular, to acquire the fluency which would persuade the uncommitted. He set out the problem with pedantic zest:

> Halfe the age must be spent in learning to speake, and when they have done, men would laugh at them for their ill accented broken language, as we do at foreigners and welshmen.[44]

Now contrast this with his mood of the 1650s, when such cavils are brusquely swept aside. In *The Life of Faith* he recounted what had been his dream project in the 1650s, of a College for Conversion, which would have been resourced by merchants and staffed by linguistic experts. Christians would have then not been dependent upon personal praying for the Jews' conversion; instead Baxter had told them to 'study what is within the reach of your power to do for their conversion'.[45] That 1650s apocalyptic mood would be revived after 1688. William III – called by Baxter 'a wise and godly King' – would take on the mantle of first Oliver, and then Richard, Cromwell. Baxter did not now speak of 'holy commonwealths' but he wrote about 'National Churches', which were the same thing. One tract of

---

42   Richard Baxter, *Reliquiae Baxterianae*, ed. Matthew Sylvester (1696), part I, p. 97.
43   W. R. Owens, '"Antichrist must be Pulled Down"', p. 82.
44   Doctor Williams's Library, *Baxter Treatises*, vol. ii, fol. 180v.
45   Richard Baxter, *The Life of Faith* (1670): though there were additions to the manuscript in this published version, the substance had been composed in 1660.

1691 was even called *The Glorious Kingdom of Christ*: a translation of his 1650s aspirations, reinforced by his millenarian researches in 1686, to the political scene in 1691 when they could now be acted upon.[46]

They could be acted upon, because the Glorious Revolution had given England another Constantine. Two polarised views of Constantine were available to seventeenth-century Puritans. The first was the old Tudor 'imperial' idea – propagated by, among others, Foxe, Jewel and Spenser – that Christianity (the millennium itself) took off with the Emperor's conversion to Christianity. The alternative view, argued most effectively by Milton in his *Of Reformation Touching Church Discipline* of 1641, was that Antichrist *came in* with Constantine; the Church was at its purest on the receiving end of the cosh. Bunyan plumped for neither, though he was closer to the second. In his 1682 manuscript he traced the rise of Antichrist to the time when church leaders 'so inveigled Constantine that he bestowed upon them much Rules and Honour'.[47] Some six years earlier, Marvell had broken off his knock-about polemic, *Mr. Smirke*, when he had reached page 43 with these words: 'But the printer calls: the Press in in danger. I am weary of such stuff [...] I would rather give the following essay'. 'The 'following essay', written in a quite different tone, was his learned treatise, *A Short Historical Essay Touching General Councils, Creeds and Imposition in Religions*. Marvell anticipates the Bunyan line: 'the good Constantine', as he called him, had brought his bishops 'the Fiddles' though he was soon 'weary of the Ball'. Constantine, too good-natured for his own good, had let himself be imposed on by the clergy, and realized his mistake too late. The bishops asserted themselves, not (the Italian way) by exalting the Pope, but (the French way) by exalting Councils.[48] Neither Bunyan nor Marvell would, therefore, seem to share in the extravagant claims that we have seen were made for Christian Empire in Baxter's 1686 manuscripts. However, neither would Baxter have himself, roughly between the years 1660 and 1676, when he was telling his fellow Nonconformists to

---

46 Richard Baxter, *The Glorious Kingdom of Christ* (1691).
47 W. R. Owens, '"Antichrist must be Pulled Down"', p. 84.
48 Andrew Marvell, *Mr. Smirke* (1676), pp. 43, 71.

offer passive obedience (no more) to the magistrate, nor again roughly between the years 1676 and 1682, when he was humming the same tunes as they were. What had changed in the late 1670s (Baxter would argue) were not the principles of Baxter himself, but those of Charles II and his bishops. The secret Treaty of Dover – combined with the willingness of key High Church clergymen to form alliances with their French counterparts, on the Gallican model of conciliar, not papal, supremacy – then set off the same alarm bells ringing in Baxter's mind, as they had in Bunyan's and Marvell's. In those years his response was the same as theirs: arguing in a number of political tracts *against* national churches as breeding-grounds for hypocrites;[49] debunking the claims of Constantine's Christian Empire;[50] ridiculing the idea that Church discipline needed the backing of the magistrate's sword;[51] exposing the bishops' 'Grotian' conspiracy.[52] Baxter's *The True History of Councils* of 1682 complements in every way Marvell's *Essay on Councils* of 1676.[53]

Therefore, in 1682, when Bunyan was writing up in private his views on Antichrist, he and Baxter were as close, in their historical and eschatological readings of Revelation, as they ever had been, or ever would be again. It was in the process of re-reading scripture that Baxter would be won back to his old imperial faith, even if there were now no Oliver, or Richard, Cromwell around to put it into practice. His prison enquiries completed the conversion process, begun with his 1684 publication. He now saw how right Foxe had been to exalt Constantine, and how (hopelessly) wrong More had been, in dating the decline of the Church from its very highest point, the Emperor's conversion to Christianity. Semi-sectarian temptations were now permanently banished. What England needed above all was a 'National Church'. In 1686 England was, to borrow a later definition of George Orwell, a family with the wrong members in control. Providence, or

---

49   Richard Baxter, *The Nonconformists Plea for Peace* (1679), dedicatory epistle.
50   Richard Baxter, *A Treatise of Episcopacy* (1681), p. 19.
51   Ibid, p. 195.
52   Richard Baxter, *The True History of Councils* (1682), dedicatory epistle.
53   Ibid, p. 15, for his revised view of Constantine: 'he foresaw not the evils that afterwards would follow [...] The Emperor also being a Christian, worldly men are mostly of the Religion of the Prince or highest powers'.

the Glorious Revolution (they are interchangeable), decreed that the right members should now take control. When that change came Baxter had prepared in secret for it, even if it might never have come in his own lifetime. When he wrote up in 1691 the case for William III's 'National Church' it was under the near-blasphemous title of *The Glorious Kingdom of Christ*.

Baxter had invested magistracy with apocalyptic expectations at various points in his writing career: in the last years of Oliver Cromwell's Protectorate, in the all-too-brief period of Richard Cromwell's Protectorate, in the accession to the throne of William III. We never do have such intimations in Bunyan. We saw certainly that he was committed to the Commonwealth, that he did not like the Restoration, and that he would have been (we may safely conjecture) very happy with the aftermath of 1688. In what way then is he different from Baxter (except, that is, the Baxter of 1676–82)? Dr Owens has an illuminating comment to make on the readiness of Bunyan and his congregation to take advantage of Charles II's Declaration of Indulgence in 1672: 'if all you were chiefly interested in was toleration, it made sense to look to the King, rather than Parliament, in Restoration England'.[54] When James II in 1687 offered *his* Declaration of Indulgence, he was able to play off nonconformists against their Tory Anglican oppressors (the 'Mr. Atheism' and 'Mr. False Peace' of Bunyan's *The Holy War*). James II found takers in William Penn's Quakers, and also in Bunyan's Baptists. As Professor Greaves has pointed out, six members of Bunyan's church went on to accept positions in the remodelled Bedford Corporation in the Spring of 1688.[55] And, to echo Dr Owens, if what you cared most about was toleration, this made as good political sense in 1687 as it had in 1672.

It did not, however, make sense to Baxter. He was not chiefly interested in toleration in Restoration England. He made it clear in his memoirs why no Puritan ever could be 'the introducer of the Papists Toleration': 'God do what he will with us, his way is best, but I think that this is not his way'.[56] Consistent with this belief, Baxter would

---

54 W. R. Owens, '"Antichrist must be Pulled Down"', p. 92.
55 Greaves, *Bunyan and English Nonconformity*, p. 69.
56 Baxter, *Reliquiae Baxterianae*, Part III, p. 36.

block any moves for toleration when hopes were high in 1668 to relax the disciplinary legislation of the Restoration Church. Bunyan, on the other hand, believed that Papist kings, offering toleration to their subjects from whatever motives, could be *used* by those same subjects. That went for Charles II, James II and even, as we have seen, in his *Of Antichrist* manuscript, for Louis XIV. Behind that belief lay more than expediency. Professor Greaves has brought out well Bunyan's belief in the positive virtues of suffering. He drew a distinction between the passive sufferings of victims and 'active suffering', that is, 'by the consent of the will'. Greaves points out 'as any reader of John Foxe's *Acts and Monuments* knew, it was also a telling pedagogical act'. He quotes from Bunyan this crucial passage: 'a man when he suffereth for Christ, is set upon a Hill, upon a Stage, as in a Theatre, to play a part for God in the World'.[57]

Professor Knott has drawn attention to Joseph Besse's *Collection of the Sufferings of the People Called Quakers* of 1753, and calls it a Quaker Book of Martyrs, influenced by Foxe, 'an overview of the persecution of Quakers in the period up to the Toleration Act (1650–89)'.[58] It is not pedantry to insist on the correct title for Foxe's great work – *Acts and Monuments* – not the popular (and early) *Book of Martyrs*. Scholars who do so, emphasise correctly that Foxe is concerned less with the martyrs' sufferings, than with the *point* of them, with how they fit into a wider pattern of history and eschatology. For Bunyan, however, as much as for Besse, the sufferings *are* the point. Bunyan in *Of Antichrist* only quotes Foxe on Constantine to make his thrust at power-hungry clergymen:

> he bestowed upon them much Riches and Honour; and then it was *cried* by an *Angel*, and the Cry was heard in the City, *Constantinople! Wo, wo, wo! this day is Venom poured into the Church of God* (as both My Lord *Cobham* and Mr. *Fox* witness in the book of *Acts and Monuments*) (*MW*, 13: 497).

---

57 Greaves, *Bunyan and English Nonconformity*, p. 182.
58 John R. Knott, 'Joseph Besse and the Quaker Culture of Suffering', in Thomas N. Corns and David Loewenstein (ed.), *The Emergence of Quaker Writing* (London, 1995), pp. 126–7.

The contrast with Baxter's apocalyptic interpretation of 1686 could not be more telling. Foxe's first period of history, 'the suffering time of the church', is not its best period; that distinction belongs to the second period – 'the flourishing time of the church' – under Constantine. A fruit of Baxter's prison researches is a chastened recognition, in manuscript, of the need to 'expiate my errors' in ever having thought ill of 'National Churches'[59] (as he certainly had done in the previous decade). John Foxe had put him back on the right track. There were three ways of reading prophecy – 'literal', 'cabbalistical' and 'conjectural' – which were as abhorrent to Bunyan as to Baxter. Baxter offered a fourth way which was acceptable. He called it 'rational', and described it as being 'fetch from the context of former prophecies'. Only one way was higher and that was 'by propheticall Inspiration or Vision': a claim which Baxter would not make for himself, but which he would for Foxe.[60]

To end with the question with which we began: how revolutionary was seventeenth-century Puritanism, and what light is thrown on the question by a comparison of two Puritans' wrestlings with Revelation at the end of their lives? When we have set aside stereotyping of either man, accepted the genuineness of their respect for the magistrate, and acknowledged their shared abhorrence of Fifth Monarchist activism, we are left with one extra dimension in 1686 Baxter: his apocalyptic claims for Christian empire and a national church. Does this make him, therefore, a more 'loyal' citizen than Bunyan?

It does, and it does not. Baxter gives to Oliver Cromwell (at the end of his Protectorate), Richard Cromwell and William III a reverence beyond anything we can find in Bunyan. Yet by the same token Charles I, Charles II and James II had more to fear from Baxter than they ever had to from Bunyan. The ideology of Protestant imperialism was a two-edged sword. If the Protestant magistrate abused his office to advance Popery, then on self-preservative grounds the subject must resist him. It is what Baxter said far too candidly about the origins of the Civil War in his *A Holy Commonwealth* of 1659, which he had to

---

59 Doctor Williams's Library, *Baxter Treatises*, vol. vii, fol. 296.
60 Doctor Williams's Library, *Baxter Treatises*, vol. ii, fol. 103v.

withdraw in 1670.[61] It was the case which he also mounted against James II in his 1691 work, *Against the Revolt to a Foreign Jurisdiction*. And, in that same year, he made in manuscript the crucial connection: that James II's perfidy had to be put in the context of 'the designe of K Charles I and 2nd' to ensure 'that Papists might come in'.[62] No surrender to a foreign jurisdiction: this meant, in the last analysis, more to Baxter than the pragmatic arguments for cohabiting with a Papist King who was offering toleration, or the theological arguments for embracing a doctrine of positive suffering, whereas for Bunyan the reverse was true.

This paradox is at the heart of English Protestantism, and it was finely captured in a recent essay by Jonathan Barry:

> The awareness of the need for a strong state to buttress Protestants helped to ensure the Erastian nature of English Protestantism and legitimate and enhance secular authority, whether that of monarch, parliament, civic elite or even paterfamilias. Yet the fear of betrayal from enemies within could *in the right conditions* turn religious conservatives into radical overthrowers of the intellectual order.[63]

Here we see how Collinson Man could *become* Walzer Man, and why Stuart Kings had more to fear from 'moderate, 'humane', 'respectable' Baxter than they ever had to fear from 'turbulent, 'subversive', 'plebeian' Bunyan.

---

61   Baxter, *A Holy Commonwealth*, pp. 211–30, for the candour of his last chapter, 'Of the late Warres', and pp. 251–2 for his retraction of these views.
62   Doctor Williams's Library, *Baxter Treatises*, vol. v, fol. 298.
63   Jonathan Barry, 'Bristol as a "Reformation city" c. 1640–1780', in Nicholas Tyacke (ed.), *England's Long Reformation 1500–1800* (London, 1998), p. 273.

3

W. R. Owens
Reading the Bibliographical Codes: Bunyan's Publication in Folio

> Lo! all in silence, all in order stand,
> And mighty Folio's first, a lordly band;
> Then Quarto's their well-order'd ranks maintain,
> And light Octavo's fill a spacious plain;
> See yonder, rang'd in more frequented rows,
> An humbler band of Duodecimo's ...
> George Crabbe, *The Library* (1783)

One of the most striking developments in textual scholarship over the last few years has been a growing recognition of the extent to which the physical format in which works are published may play a part in the construction of textual meaning. Two of the scholars most prominent in this development have been D. F. McKenzie and Jerome J. McGann. In his 1985 Panizzi Lectures, subsequently published under the title *Bibliography and the Sociology of Texts*, McKenzie argued that 'the material forms of books, the non-verbal elements of the typographic notations within them, the very disposition of space itself, have an expressive function in conveying meaning'.[1] Many authors, he argued, have been keenly aware of this, and have tried to influence how their works appeared in print. In an earlier article he took as an example the case of William Congreve. Congreve's plays originally appeared in separate quarto editions, but he later undertook a thorough revision of the texts for a three-volume collection of his *Works*, published in octavo in 1710. Influenced by the format of printed editions of neo-classical French drama, Congreve divided his

---

1   D. F. McKenzie, *Bibliography and the Sociology of Texts* (1986; rpt. Cambridge, 1999), p. 17.

own plays for the first time into numbered scenes separated by print ornaments. He provided many more stage directions to accompany the dialogue, and revised the texts in ways which made them conform to their more dignified presentation in octavo, but he was also attentive to the typographical appearance of the texts – the size and styles of type, the use of ornamental drop initials, capitals, italics, punctuation, the inclusion of elaborately decorated head- and tail-pieces – and he took great care over the layout of individual pages and the arrangement of contents within each volume. In McKenzie's view, it is 'quite impossible [...] to divorce the substance of [Congreve's] text on the one hand from the physical form of its presentation on the other. The book itself is an expressive means'.[2]

McKenzie's approach has been taken up and extended by a number of scholars, most notably by Jerome McGann, who has argued that bibliographers, editors and literary critics interested in recovering the meanings of texts need to pay attention not only to what he has termed 'linguistic codes' (that is, the words, punctuation, etc.), but also to what he calls the 'bibliographical codes' (that is, the format, typography, layout, paper, circumstances of publication, etc.). As he puts it: 'Every literary work that descends to us operates through the deployment of a double helix of perceptual codes: the linguistic codes, on the one hand, and the bibliographical codes on the other'. McGann calls for the bibliographical codes of texts to be made 'a major object of historical analysis' by literary and textual scholars. Such a study would represent, he says, 'a project of greater cultural significance for textual scholarship than anything we have seen since the [...] late eighteenth century'.[3]

Many of McGann's examples of the ways in which meaning is transmitted through bibliographical as well as linguistic codes are drawn from authors such as Blake, Thackeray, Morris and Pound, for whom the physical format and visual design of their works was of crucial importance. Clearly, however, whether or not authors take a

2   D. F. McKenzie, 'Typography and Meaning: the Case of William Congreve', in Giles Barber and Bernhard Fabian (ed.), *Buch und Buchhandel im Europa im achtzehnten Jahrhundert* (Hamburg, 1981), pp. 81–125.
3   Jerome J. McGann, *The Textual Condition* (Princeton, 1991), pp. 77, 85.

direct interest, or indeed any interest in the physical appearance of their works in book form, it is obvious enough that, in McGann's sense, every literary work is coded bibliographically as well as linguistically. While the chief, though not necessarily the only, authority over the linguistic features of a text will be the author, in most cases the chief authority over the bibliographical codes will be those who arrange for its initial and subsequent publication.[4] McGann sees the publication of a literary work as a social process, involving many more people than the originating author of the text, and those responsible for the physical format and appearance of a book contribute just as importantly to its meaning as those responsible for the words.

Whether or not one goes all the way with McKenzie and McGann in their view of the relationship between medium and message, it cannot be denied that the form in which a text is presented to readers may be significant, and in some cases extremely so. McKenzie cites Bunyan's *The Pilgrim's Progress* as an example of the significance of the physical form of books in such matters as portability, size of type and page layout. Apart from the first edition, which was a small octavo, all the early editions of *The Pilgrim's Progress* were small duodecimos, set in pica roman in short lines of 14 ems. These short lines, as McKenzie points out, would have assisted less literate readers, as would other features of the layout of the text, such as the use of marginal notes. We have no information as to whether Bunyan himself was involved in decisions about the physical form in which his allegory was presented, but his publisher, Nathaniel Ponder, clearly regarded *The Pilgrim's Progress* as an important publication. He had it licensed, as required by the Licensing Act of 1662, and registered his ownership of copy by entering the first edition in the Stationers' Register.[5] As McKenzie suggests, Ponder's decisions about the physical format of *The Pilgrim's Progress*, including such matters as page layout, typography, and, of course, the

---

4   McGann, *Textual Condition*, pp. 66–7.
5   See G. E. B. Eyre and C. R. Rivington (ed.), *A Transcript of the Registers of the Worshipful Company of Stationers, 1640–1708*, 3 vols (London, 1913–14), 3: 49.

number and price of copies printed, would not have been arbitrary, but would have been affected by the religious, cultural and political views of both author and bookseller, and by the literacy and economic level of the readers they aimed to reach.[6]

What I want to do in this essay is to consider what we might learn from a study of the bibliographical codes and publishing history of a very different work, the earliest folio collection of Bunyan's writings, published in 1692, four years after his death. This 'First Folio' is of enormous significance to Bunyan studies, not least because it provides us with the earliest extant texts of twelve works never published in Bunyan's lifetime.[7] As we shall see, a surprisingly large amount can be discovered about the circumstances of publication of this important book, and a consideration of its physical makeup and publication history, as well as its contents, can add significantly to our understanding of Bunyan's place within the culture of the late seventeenth century, and the way in which his works were received by contemporary, or near contemporary, readers. My argument will be that the publication of the Bunyan folio represents an attempt to make this unlearned Baptist preacher and prisoner of conscience respectable, so to speak, and to assert his right to an honoured place alongside the great Anglican, Presbyterian and Independent divines of the seventeenth century. Its appearance may even be seen as part of a wider effort to promote nonconformist texts and culture following the passage of the Toleration Act in 1689. As well as the Bunyan folio, the 1690s saw the posthumous publication of works such as Richard Baxter's *Reliquiae* in 1696, Milton's *Prose Works* in 1698, and Edmund Ludlow's *Memoirs*, also in 1698, all from the dissenting tradition.

The earliest known reference to plans for a collected edition of Bunyan comes in an advertisement in the newspaper *Mercurius Reformatus* for 11 June 1690. According to this advertisement, Bunyan's widow, Elizabeth, wanted to publish a number of manu-

---

6   McKenzie, 'Typography and Meaning', p. 103.
7   *The Works of that Eminent Servant of Christ, Mr. John Bunyan* (London, 1692);   hereafter referred to as *1692 Folio*. For an account of the editor, Charles Doe, and the circumstances of publication, see *MW*, 12: xvii–xxiv.

scripts which he himself had prepared for the press before his untimely and unexpected death. The publisher was to be Dorman Newman, one of the largest and most active bookseller/publishers of the later seventeenth century. A Presbyterian of strongly Whiggish views, Newman owned a number of shops in London, and is estimated to have brought out over 200 titles during his career.[8] Together with Benjamin Alsop, he had published Bunyan's allegorical work *The Holy War* in 1682, and a second edition appeared under his sole imprint in 1684. In 1688 he produced another Bunyan work, *The Advocateship of Jesus Christ*. The advertisement he placed in *Mercurius Reformatus* sought subscriptions for 'a Book of *10s* in sheets, in *Fol.*', which would include not only previously unpublished material, but other works of Bunyan's which were now out of print. It is possible that Bunyan himself had been planning such a collection before his death, or had given his permission for one, but he of course did not hold the copyright in his own published works, and it seems that the booksellers who did were either not prepared to grant permission for them to be reprinted, or demanded too much money for the rights. Ponder certainly had been involved in a number of legal disputes over unauthorized reprints of *The Pilgrim's Progress*, and would have been reluctant to relinquish his hold over such a valuable literary property.[9]

Elizabeth Bunyan died early in 1691, and responsibility for overseeing publication of the projected folio edition passed to a friend and disciple of Bunyan's, a comb-maker from Southwark named Charles Doe. At about the same time there was a change of publisher. For reasons that are not entirely clear, Dorman Newman pulled out. He may have been getting into financial difficulties, because only a year or two later, in 1694, he went bankrupt.[10] At any rate, his place as publisher of the folio was taken by William Marshall, a leading

---

8   For an account, see Elizabeth Lane Furdell, '"At the King's Arms in the Poultrey": the Bookshop Emporium of Dorman Newman 1670–1694', *London Journal*, 23 (1998), 1–20.

9   See Frank Mott Harrison, 'Nathaniel Ponder: The Publisher of *The Pilgrim's Progress*', *The Library*, 4th ser. 15 (1934), 257–94.

10 See the announcement in the *London Gazette*, 24–27 September 1694.

nonconformist bookseller and bookbinder who operated from premises at the Bible in Newgate Street from 1679 to 1725.[11] Marshall arranged for the printing and sale of many works of nonconformist divinity by authors including Benjamin Keach, Hanserd Knollys, John Owen, Thomas Delaune, and Samuel How. As far as I have been able to discover, however, the Bunyan volume was the only work in folio he ever published. Significantly, he did not finance publication of the book himself, nor did he enter into partnership with other booksellers. Instead, in 1691 he issued a sheet of subscription proposals for

> The Labours of John Bunyan, Author of the Pilgrims Progress, Late Minister of the Gospel, and Pastor of the Congregation at Bedford, Collected, and to be printed in Folio, by Procurement of his Church and Friends, and by his own Approbation before his Death, that these his Christian Ministerial Labours, may be preserved in the World.

The titles of ten manuscripts and ten previously published works to be included are listed, and subscribers are promised that the book will include an engraved portrait of Bunyan. They should send in five shillings, with a further five shillings to pay on delivery of the book, unbound. Once 300 subscriptions had come in the book would be printed.[12]

It is worth noting that the method of publishing large and expensive works by subscription was very largely an innovation on the part of nonconformist booksellers and printers. According to Sarah Clapp, from the early 1680s onwards subscription publishing became the leading means of promoting and publishing the collected works of nonconformist divines.[13] So successful did the method become that, as is well known, in 1688 it was exploited for the first time for a work of imaginative literature, when Jacob Tonson used it to finance the publication of a folio edition of *Paradise Lost*. Indeed the fortunes earned

---

11 Henry R. Plomer, *A Dictionary of the Printers and Booksellers who Were at Work in England, Scotland and Ireland from 1668 to 1725* (London, 1922), p. 198.

12 A copy of Marshall's subscription proposals is in the British Library, 816. m. 21(5).

13 Sarah L. C. Clapp, 'Subscription Publishers Prior to Jacob Tonson', *The Library*, 4th. ser. 13 (1932), 158–83.

by writers like Dryden and Pope would come about largely as a result of the system of subscription publishing.

Marshall's proposals for the Bunyan folio give us an interesting indication of the geographical spread of expected subscribers. In addition to Marshall himself, a long list was given of persons authorised to accept and give receipts for subscriptions:

> Mr. *John Strudwick* Grocer, at the *Star* at *Holborn-bridge*, Mr. *Charles Dow*, at the *Boar's-Head* in the Burrough in *Southwark*, Mr. *Chandler* Minister, and Mr. *William Nichols*, in *Bedford*, Mr. *Edward Den* of *Cranfield*, *Nicholas Mayland* of *Gamlygay*, Mr. *Luke Astwood* of *Potton*, Mr. *Samuel Hensman* of *Brantery*, Mr. *James Collidge* in *Cambridge*, Mr. *Pack* of *Exeter*, Mr. *John Clark* of *Gilford*, Mr. *Masey* of *Harborough*, Mr. *William Hensmon* of *Wellingborough*, Mr. *Sory* of *Lancashire*, Mr. *Chandler* of *Malborough*, Mr. *Grifeth*, and Mr. *Pool* in *Lanviling*. To the Churches of *Brostol* [sic] and *Canterbury*, the said *William Marshall*, the Undertaker, does promise, That the Subscribers shall have them well Bound in good Calves Leather, for Two Shillings a piece.

That Marshall was able to assemble such a considerable list of names from throughout England and Wales bears out N. H. Keeble's argument that a substantial and well-defined market for nonconformist texts existed in the Restoration period, served by an extensive and highly-organized distribution network.[14]

In addition to the formal proposals issued by Marshall, Charles Doe published a circular listing thirty *Reasons why Christian People should Promote by Subscriptions the Printing in Folio the Labours of Mr. John Bunyan*. What is perhaps most striking to a modern reader of this document is that not one of these thirty reasons refers to Bunyan's literary achievements. There is no mention of *The Pilgrim's Progress* or any of the other writings for which Bunyan was best known. Instead, Doe emphasises Bunyan's extraordinary reputation as a preacher, and in particular the fact that he gained this reputation despite being 'an illiterate poor Man' from a humble background. This goes to show, Doe says,

---

14 N. H. Keeble, *The Literary Culture of Nonconformity in Later Seventeenth-Century England* (Leicester, 1987), pp. 128–35.

> That God is not bound to Humane Means of Learned Education (though Learning may be useful in its place) but can, when he will, make a Minister of the Gospel without man's forecast of Education, and in spite of all the men in the World that would oppose it.

It is worth noting here in passing that Doe was by no means the first to defend Bunyan against charges that he lacked learning. Indeed two of Bunyan's earliest works had been furnished with prefaces vigorously defending his right, as an unlearned man, to preach and publish. In a preface to *Some Gospel-Truths Opened* (1656), John Burton, rector of St. John's in Bedford, advised Bunyan's reader not to be offended that the author has 'neither the greatness nor the wisdom of this world to commend him to thee; for as the Scripture saith, Christ (who was low and contemptible in the world himself) ordinarily chuseth such for himself, and for the doing of his work'. Bunyan, he says, 'is not chosen out of an earthly, but out of the heavenly University, the Church of Christ' (*MW*, 1: 11). Similarly John Gibbs, vicar of Newport Pagnell, in his preface to Bunyan's third work, *A Few Sighs from Hell* (1658), urges readers not to 'stumble at his [Bunyan's] meanness and want of humane learning', pointing out that Christ did not go 'to the schools of learning, to fetch out his Gospel Preachers, but to the trades, and those most contemptible too'. Gibbs does not speak against learning in itself, 'being kept in its place', but 'those that are learned should not despise those that are not' (*MW*, 1: 244). In his later writings Bunyan himself frequently asserted that human learning was of little value. For example, in the prefatory address 'To the Learned Reader' in his *The Holy City* (1665), he remarks that he finds 'such a Spirit of Whoredom and Idolatry concerning the Learning of this World, and Wisdom of the Flesh [...] that had I all their aid and assistance at command, I durst not make use of ought thereof' (*MW*, 3: 71).

What comes across most strongly in Doe's thirty *Reasons* is the sense that Bunyan, and, by implication, those who are being urged to subscribe for the Folio, are outside contemporary mainstream culture. Doe recalls that Bunyan had been 'a Christian Sufferer for above twelve years, by Imprisonment'. Likewise, it has only recently become possible to publish his works freely: 'By the late Act for Liberty of Conscience [i.e. the Act of Toleration of 1689], it is lawful now to print the works of Dissenters, though it was not so formerly'. The main aim of the projected Folio is to celebrate and memorialize the works of a great Dissenting hero: 'This preservation will preserve the Name of *John Bunyan*, a Champion of our Age, to future Ages; whereby it may be said in the Pulpit, The great Convert *Bunyan* said so and so'.[15]

As it turned out, Marshall and Doe were between them remarkably successful in their efforts to attract subscribers. According to Doe, there were *'about* 400 *Subscriptions, whereof about thirty are Ministers'*,[16] and the Folio was duly published in the late autumn of 1692.[17] It is worth pausing here to reflect on the significance of the folio as a format, and the fact that Bunyan appeared in folio so soon after his death. Folios were, of course, the largest and most imposing printed books, and throughout the sixteenth and seventeenth centuries folio had been the standard format for publication of the greatest and most highly valued works. Among the earliest substantial folio publications in England had been Richard Hooker's famous work *Of the Lawes of Ecclesiasticall Politie*, which appeared in 1593, and the *Workes* of King James, which appeared in 1616.[18] When the Imprimerie Royale was established in France by Richelieu in 1640, most of the works produced under its auspices were expensive, monumental folio editions, including the writings of the early Church Fathers, a collection of Church Councils in thirty-seven volumes, editions of

---

15 No separate copy of Doe's *Reasons* is known to have survived, but it was included in the *1692 Folio*, sig. 5T1v.

16 Charles Doe, *The Struggler*, in *1692 Folio*, sigs. 5T2–5U1r; reprinted in *MW*, 12: 453–60 (quotation from p. 458).

17 It was entered in the Stationer's Register for 3 August 1692, and an advertisement for it appeared in the *Athenian Mercury* for 13 December 1692.

18 On the significance of the format and typography of these early folios, see Mark Bland, 'The Appearance of the Text in Early Modern England', *Text 11*, ed. W. Speed Hill and Edward M. Burns (Ann Arbor, 1998), pp. 91–127 (pp. 120–1).

ancient and Byzantine authors in multi-volume sets, and a Polyglot Bible in ten volumes.[19]

Some modern authors of 'literary' works also achieved the accolade of publication in folio. Sir Philip Sidney's *Arcadia*, for instance, was published in folio in 1593. This was a posthumous honour, however; Sidney had died in 1586. A striking example of a living author choosing the folio format was Samuel Daniel, who published his collected *Works* in a folio volume in 1601, thereby, as Mark Bland has suggested, 'laying claim to be the foremost poet of his generation, in succession to Sidney and Spenser'.[20] The evolution of the format in which Montaignes *Essaies* apppeared was indicative of the growing esteem in which they were held. Early editions and reprints were small octavos and duodecimos, but the edition of 1588 was a quarto, and by the third edition of 1595, published just three years after Montaigne's death, the *Essaies* were thought worthy to appear in the prestigious format of the folio.[21] By contrast, as is well known, Ben Jonson was derided when, in 1616, he had the effrontery to publish his collected *Workes* in folio. In doing so, it was thought, he was equating mere plays with the great works of theology, philosophy and the classics for which the folio format had traditionally been reserved. Quite clearly, in choosing to publish in folio Jonson was making a significant statement about the literary value he attached to his plays. As Trevor Ross has put it, the 1616 folio *Workes* 'is the first self-consciously canonical edition of an author's works in English literature'.[22] The example Jonson set was followed by those who arranged for the publication in folio of Shakespeare's collected plays in 1623. It is important to note that in this period the act of collecting the works of an author was a crucial factor in ensuring the survival of their reputation. Gary Taylor has pointed out in his book *Reinventing Shakespeare* that in the later seventeenth century Jonson, Shakespeare

19 See D. C. Greetham, *Textual Scholarship: an introduction* (New York and London, 1994), pp. 101–2.
20 Bland, 'The Appearance of the Text in Early Modern England', p. 121.
21 See John McClelland, 'Text, Rhetoric, Meaning', in *Text 3*, ed. D. C. Greetham and W. Speed Hill (New York, 1987), pp. 11–26.
22 See Trevor Ross, *The Making of the English Literary Canon* (Montreal and London, 1998), pp. 108–15

and Beaumont and Fletcher were still the only dramatists honoured by having had folio collections of their works published, a testimony to their cultural prestige. The existence of the collected folio edition enabled readers to appreciate the range and scope of an author's achievement, whereas the achievement of authors who had not been collected was dispersed among individual editions, often long out of print or unattributed to them.[23]

It seems certain that behind the posthumous publication of Bunyan in folio lay a desire to assert and secure his status as a preacher and writer of national importance. The writings and sermons of the great Anglican and nonconformist divines were often collected in folio after their death. The works of the famous Royalist cleric Henry Hammond, for example, were published in four folio volumes in 1684; those of John Lightfoot appeared the same year in two volumes; Isaac Barrow appeared in four volumes between 1687 and 1692; John Tillotson, Archbishop of Canterbury, appeared in 1696, Ezekiel Hopkins, Bishop of Raphoe and Derry, appeared in 1701; Edward Stillingfleet's complete works were published between 1707–10, and John Scott, Canon of St. Paul's, appeared in two volumes in 1718. Leading Presbyterian and Independent ministers were similarly honoured. Stephen Charnock's works were published in two large folio volumes in 1683–84; five volumes of Thomas Goodwin appeared between 1681 and 1701; William Bates appeared in 1700; John Flavel in two volumes in 1701; Richard Baxter in 1707; John Owen in 1721; and John Howe in two volumes in 1724. It is worth noting, however, that the authors of these folios were (with the exception of Baxter) all university educated men, many of whom had held positions of influence during the Civil War and Cromwellian period. Very few Baptists or Quakers were ever published in folio, and those that were tended to be educated, like the Quaker Isaac Penington whose works were published in folio in 1680, or wealthy, like William Penn whose works appeared in two volumes in 1726.

---

23 Gary Taylor, *Reinventing Shakespeare: a cultural history from the Restoration to the present* (London, 1990), pp. 31–2.

The 1692 folio therefore represented a bold attempt to establish Bunyan's place alongside these worthies.[24] Several features of the volume testify to this intent. First of all, it opens with a dignified frontispiece portrait of Bunyan engraved by John Sturt.[25] It is not known who the artist was. Doe says merely that *'His Effigies was cut in Copper from an Original paint done to the life (by his very good Friend a Limner)'*.[26] Such author portraits were a standard feature of folio collections,[27] and indeed it seems that they were also designed to be sold separately. In an advertisement for other works printed and sold by Marshall included at the back of the Bunyan folio, there is a list of 'effigies' of famous Dissenting divines, each printed on 'large Paper' and costing sixpence. Bunyan is here, in company with Matthew Mead, Joseph Caryl, Dr John Owen, and Dr Tobias Crisp.

Turning to the title-page of the folio, we find that it gives prominence to the word 'WORKS', which is in very large capitals, and to the phrase 'The First Volume', which is in heavy black letter.[28] The main title runs: 'The Works of that Eminent Servant of Christ, Mr. John Bunyan, Late Minister of the Gospel, and Pastor of the Congregation at Bedford. The First Volume'. Once again, it is worth noting that Bunyan is identified not as the famous author of *The Pilgrim's Progress*, but as a Dissenting minister. Below the main title are two columns giving the titles of the ten 'Excellent Manuscripts prepared for the Press before his Death, never before Printed', and the ten 'Choyce Books formerly printed'. Below this there is a statement explaining that these works have been 'Collected and Printed by the

---

[24] This point is also made by John Barnard in what is, as far as I am aware, the only previous discussion of the significance of the physical format of the *1692 Folio*; see his 'Bibliographical Context and the Critic', in *Text 3*, ed. D. C. Greetham and W. Speed Hill (New York, 1987), pp. 27–46, esp. pp. 36–8.

[25] The engraving is reproduced as the frontispiece to this volume.

[26] *The Struggler, 1692 Folio*, sig. 5U1r; *MW*, 12: 458.

[27] On author portraits in works, see Roger Chartier, *The Order of Books*, trans. Lydia G. Cochrane (Cambridge, 1994), pp. 52–3. See also McKenzie, 'Typography and Meaning', who notes that the frontispiece portrait was expressive of the close identity of the author's body and his printed works, as suggested by the use of the term 'remains' for posthumous collections (p. 94).

[28] The *1692 Folio* title-page is reproduced as the frontispiece to *MW*, vol. 12.

Procurement of his Church and Friends, and by his own Approbation before his Death: That these his Christian Ministerial Labours may be preserved in the World' and that included in the volume is 'a Large Alphabetical Table, containing the Contents of the Whole'. Rather oddly, under the details of the imprint, there is an apology to subscribers for an error in calculating the size of the book:

> Whereas it was proposed to the Subscribers, that this Book would contain near a Hundred and Forty Sheets, they are hereby certified, that by reason of the smallness of the Writing of the Manuscripts, it could not be so exactly computed; so that it is now about 155 Sheets, which additional sheets advance the price to about 1s. 6d. more in a Book, of which only one Shilling more is Required of the Subscribers, with which it is hoped they will not be displeased.

It is not clear who made the mistake in underestimating the extent of the book, but it would seem likely that it was the editor Charles Doe rather than Marshall, who was an experienced publisher.

Immediately following the title-page comes a lengthy prefatory 'Epistle', addressed to the 'serious, Judicious, and Impartial Reader'. This is signed by its authors, Ebenezer Chandler and John Wilson. Both men were colleagues of Bunyan's. Chandler had succeeded him as minister of the Bedford congregation, while Wilson, a former member of the Bedford congregation, was minister of the Tilehouse Street church at Hitchin in Hertfordshire.[29] The purpose of collecting Bunyan's works, they explain, is *'that they may be preserved to future Ages, fearing that their continuing single, or the rest being Printed so, may hazard their being lost, and so our Posterity deprived of that Benefit which we now hope they may receive from them'*. They note that it has not been possible to include all Bunyan's works, partly because there were too many to include in one volume, but also because the copyright owners of Bunyan's more famous works 'were

---

29 For Chandler, see S. Hillyard, 'Memoir of the Late Rev. Ebenezer Chandler', *Evangelical Magazine*, 24 (1816), 497–500; John Brown, *John Bunyan (1628–1688): his life, times and work*, rev. edn. ed. Frank Mott Harrison (London, 1928), pp. 397–401. For Wilson, see G. E. Evans, *Come Wind, Come Weather: chronicles of Tilehouse Street Baptist Church, 1669–1969* (London and Tonbridge, 1969), pp. 6–9; Richard Greaves, *John Bunyan and English Nonconformity* (London and Rio Grande OH, 1992), pp. 96–7.

not willing to resign up their Right at reasonable Rates'. However, efforts are being made to obtain these rights, and a second folio volume is promised, as soon as this can be arranged.

Chandler and Wilson pay warm tribute to Bunyan as a '*great Saint*', one who had displayed exemplary courage under a twelve-year imprisonment for his faith, and whose ministry in and around Bedford had been '*blest to the Edification, Comfort and Establishment of the Saints, as well as in the Conversion of Sinners*'. They praise, too, his originality as a writer:

> The Author indeed had a peculiar Phrase to himself in expressing the Conceptions of his Mind; his Words were his own, as well as his Matter. [...] Like the Spider, all came from his own Bowels; what the Spirit of God gave in to him, by Prayer and Study, that he freely gave out, and communicated to others, cloathed in a familiar Style. [...] his Fancy and Invention were very pregnant, and fertile; the use he made of them was good, converting them to spiritual Objects: His Wit was sharp and quick, his Memory tenacious; it being customary with him to commit his Sermons to Writing after he had Preached them: His Understanding was large and comprehensive, his Judgment sound and deep in the Fundamentals of the Gospel, as his Writings evidence.

What is most striking about this preface, however, is that, like Charles Doe in his thirty *Reasons*, Chandler and Wilson feel it necessary to apologise repeatedly and at length for Bunyan's lack of formal education and lowly social position as a brazier. Here is an extract from their preface:

> It's evident, that many in his Life-time did despise him, and all done by him, for the meanness of his Education, and Calling [...]; and it's probable some may still be ready to have mean and contemptible Thoughts of his Works, for that reason; as also because he had not that acquired Learning, that others have. For the first reason, there is no manner of ground for it; to such as make the last their plea, we would say, That as Learning hath been too much trampled on, by them in whom Ignorance hath prevailed, (Ignoti nulla cupido,) so it hath been, and is too much Idolized by those that have been Proficients in it; as though none might, or ought to engage in the Work of the Ministry, or publishing Treatises of this Nature, but Persons under their Circumstances: Not considering, that at the same time the Eternal Spirit doth bless the Studies of those that have Learning [...] the same Spirit may, and evidently doth instruct the Unlearned (more humano) also, if gracious and painfull, in the deep things

of the Gospel, and give them great knowledge therein, and truly qualifie, and fit them both for Preaching, and Writing, and bless them in so doing. [30]

It is noticeable here that Chandler and Wilson are careful to establish their own academic credentials by including Latin tags, thus to some extent implying a reader who can understand Latin. The very fact that they feel such a pressing need to defend Bunyan against charges that he lacked education serves only to heighten a sense that they realized that it would be thought highly unusual for a man like Bunyan to be published in folio.

Several other aspects of the folio are worth comment. Although, on the whole, it cannot be said that the appearance of the book is especially handsome, and there are various errors in running heads and pagination, some typographic features characteristic of the dignified folio format have been included. For example, the first work, *An Exposition on the Ten First Chapters of Genesis*, has an ornamented initial capital for the first word of the text, though later works only have dropped initials. In the second half of the book, which includes the previously published works, a number are provided with an ornamental headpiece.

Perhaps more importantly, at the end of the volume there is an account by Charles Doe of Bunyan's life, including some information about his own activities as editor of the folio. The heading of this address to the 'Christian Reader' runs: *The Struggler (for the preceding Preservation of Mr. John Bunyans Labours in Folio) thinks it may answer the Desires of many to give the following Relation* (*MW*, 12: 453–60). Once again, a prominent feature of *The Struggler* is its defence of Bunyan's abilities in the face of complaints that he lacked education. Doe is more vigorous in his defence than were Chandler and Wilson. As far as he is concerned, the fact that Bunyan, while preaching, also '*worked at his tinkering Trade for a Livelihood*' places him in line of succession to '*the Apostles, and other of the eminent Saints of old, most of them Tradesmen.*' In his remarkable conversion and subsequent writings from prison Bunyan may even be compared with the Apostle Paul himself. Doe enthusiastically praises

---

30 'Epistle to the Reader', *1692 Folio*, sig. A1r.

The Pilgrim's Progress, at which, he says, '*none but Priest-ridden people know how to cavil*', declaring that it has been printed '*in* France, Holland, New-England, *and in Welch, and about a hundred thousand in* England', making its author famous. He records his experience of hearing Bunyan preach to packed congregations in London, and recounts how Bunyan got the better of learned opponents in public disputations. He also describes his own labours as editor of the Folio, including the provision of running titles and the compilation of an extensive index. Perhaps the most valuable of his contributions, however, was 'A Catalogue-Table of Mr. Bunyan's Books, and their Succession in Publishing, most according to his own reckoning'. By including this bibliography, Doe enabled readers to see at a glance the remarkable extent of Bunyan's literary output. He lists sixty works, including the twelve manuscript works first published in the Folio.[31] The final four items on the list were described as manuscripts not yet printed. Two of these, 'A Christian Dialogue' and 'A Pocket Concordance', remain unknown. A third was purchased by Doe from Bunyan's son, and subsequently published by him as *The Heavenly Foot-Man* (1698); while the fourth, described here as 'An Account of his Imprisonment', was eventually published in 1765 as *A Relation of the Imprisonment of Mr. John Bunyan*.

Right at the end of the main text of Doe's folio there was a brief note saying that another volume of Bunyan's works would be printed a speedily as possible, and hoping that subscribers would come forward when notice of this was given. However, there were clearly difficulties over copyright, and it was not until fifteen years later that an attempt was made to raise subscribers for this second volume. In the *Daily Courant* for 21 October 1707, William Marshall placed an advertisement which read as follows:

> There is a 2*d* Volume of Mr. Bunyan's Works intended to be Publish'd by way of Subscription, by Wm Marshal at the Bible in Newgate-street, Bookseller, who Printed his 1st Volume in Folio; those that will promote so good a Work may have Proposals in a Fortnights time, which will have most of the following

---

31 See *1692 Folio*, sig. 5T1r. An expanded version of this bibliography was included by Doe as an appendix to his edition of *The Heavenly Foot-Man* (1698).

Books put in [and here Marshall lists thirty works]. This is to give notice, That if any one have a better Right to any of these Books then the said Wm Marshal, let them produce it to prevent any difference for the future, and they shall be left out of this 2nd Volume.

It is noticeable that the list of thirty works given by Marshall did not include *The Pilgrim's Progress*, *The Life and Death of Mr. Badman*, or *The Holy War*. Of the four manuscripts listed as unpublished in Doe's 'Catalogue-Table' the only one to be included was *The Heavenly Foot-man*, which Doe had already published in 1698.

Somewhat surprisingly, however, it turns out that Marshall's attempt to bring out this second volume did not have the support of Charles Doe, who had done so much to bring about the publication of the first. It seems that Doe had not been happy with Marshall's work on the first volume, and he saw Marshall's call for subscribers as an attempt to wreck his own quite separate plans for a second volume. A couple of months after Marshall's advertisement, Doe inserted a counter-advertisement in Daniel Defoe's *Review* for 9 December 1707. This remarkable document seems not to have been known to previous Bunyan scholars, and so is perhaps worth quoting in full.

> I *Charles Doe*, say that Mr. *Marshall's* Advertisement is a needless Thing, (and seems a Design to cross the Work of 155 Sheets, at 10*s*. *per* Book, and the 7*th Gratis*, in my Hands, and so puts me upon Publishing this Advertisement.) For I have been encouraged to do the Work some Months, by several principal Persons both at *London* and *Bedford*, who are raising Subscriptions for me; especially Mr. *John Bunyan*, the Eldest Son of our Author: For I have made some Progress to do the Work, and all the Well-wishers to it, that I know of, have, for some Reasons, refused Mr. *Marshall*, and chosen me. And as to his Title to the Books he mentions in his Advertisement, I have Reason to believe, that I have a better Title to them than he. And I may say that there was no Probability of his ever Printing the first Part, if I had not, besides my putting it into his Hands, raised him most Part of his Subscriptions; but my Subscribers, were not pleased with him, and he may despair of doing this without my Assistance. I live at the *Boar's-Head* in the *Burrough*, between *London-Bridge* and St. *Thomas's Hospital*, where Encouragers of the Work may have my Proposals, wherein the first Book is the *Pilgrims Progress*, and I take no Money, but a Promise in Writing, until I put the Work in the Press.
>
> *Postscript*. I have, and do resolve to have nothing to do with Mr. *Marshall* in this Work, tho' to colour his Pretensions he hath, without my

> Knowledge, put my Name into his Proposals, and I believe, the rest of the Persons mentioned, knew nothing of it.
>   *NOTE*, That when I put the Work in the Press, I shall give publick Notice in the Paper called the *Postman*, or in the *Review*; and as my further Good-Will to the Work, I propose, that he that subscribes for four Books, shall have a Fifth *Gratis*.

In the event, despite all Doe's efforts, no second volume of his folio edition of Bunyan ever appeared. In 1724 the bookseller John Marshall, William Marshall's son, tried to raise subscriptions for an octavo collection of Bunyan's works, but evidently support for this was not forthcoming, for no such edition was published.[32] A second folio edition in two volumes was published in 1736–7, edited by Samuel Wilson, a Baptist minister in London, and grandson of John Wilson who had been joint author of the preface to the 1692 Folio.[33] Although not quite complete, this was the best edition of Bunyan's works to appear in the eighteenth century. A third edition was published in 1767–8, with a 'Recommendatory Preface' by George Whitefield, and there was a further edition in folio in 1771.

The chequered history of Bunyan's publication in folio prompts reflection on the extent and nature of his popularity as a writer in the period following his death. There is no doubt that *The Pilgrim's Progress* was a publishing phenomenon. More than twenty editions were published before the end of the seventeenth century, representing sales of over 30,000 copies.[34] Nathaniel Ponder, its first publisher, was nicknamed 'Bunyan Ponder' by his envious fellow-booksellers, and he went to great lengths to try to protect his copyright from pirates.[35] It is not so certain, however, that Bunyan himself was highly regarded as a writer. Indeed, in the late seventeenth and early eighteenth centuries, references to Bunyan which have survived in print are more likely to be mocking, if not outrightly hostile. Samuel Wesley (father of the more famous John and Charles Wesley) provides a telling

---

32 'Advertisement' in *The Heavenly Foot-man*, '8th' edition (1724), sig. B6r. For John Marshall, see Plomer, *Dictionary*, p. 198.
33 A brief account of Wilson is included in John Gill, *A Sermon Occasioned by the Death of the Revd. Mr. Samuel Wilson* (London, 1750), pp. 43–50.
34 See Keeble, *Literary Culture*, p. 128.
35 See Harrison, 'Nathaniel Ponder: The Publisher of *The Pilgrim's Progress*'.

example. Although brought up as a Dissenter, he later conformed, and became rector of Epworth in Lincolnshire. He recalled how, as a student at Charles Morton's famous Dissenting Academy, he and his fellow-students were taken to hear '*Friend Bunnian*, when he preached at *Newington-Green*'. For Wesley this was a reason to condemn Dissenters who, though 'careful to distinguish themselves in Mr. *Baxter's* Style from the *wild Sectarians*', were nevertheless prepared to listen to preachers like Bunyan, 'who have no *Form* of *Ordination*'.[36] Similarly, the anonymous author of a pamphlet produced in 1711 during the Sacheverell controversy referred sarcastically to 'the Works of the *Learned Bunyan*'.[37] In 1720, the Anglican clergyman Thomas Cox described Bunyan as the 'author of *The Pilgrim's Progress*, and several other little books of an antinomian spirit, too frequently to be met with in the hands of the common people'.[38] In such a hostile context, it is perhaps not surprising that plans for a complete edition of Bunyan in folio should have run into difficulties.

---

36 Samuel Wesley, *A Defence of a Letter Concerning the Education of Dissenters in their Private Academies* (London, 1704), p. 48.

37 *A Vindication of the Reverend Dr. Henry Sacheverell* (London, 1711), Introductory 'Letter', unpaginated.

38 Cited in Christopher Hill, *A Turbulent, Seditious, and Factious People: John Bunyan and his church* (Oxford, 1988), p. 348. See further, N. H. Keeble, '"Of him thousands daily Sing and talk" Bunyan and his Reputation', in N. H. Keeble (ed.), *John Bunyan: Conventicle and Parnassus* (Oxford, 1988), pp. 241–63, esp. pp. 246–8; W. R. Owens, 'The Reception of *The Pilgrim's Progress* in England', in M. van Os and G. J. Schutte (ed.), *Bunyan in England and Abroad* (Amsterdam, 1990), pp. 91–104, esp. p. 98.

4

TAMSIN SPARGO
Bunyans Abounding, or the Names of the Author[1]

Who was the author of *The Pilgrim's Progress*? Of all the questions we might ask about seventeenth-century literature, this might seem to be one of the silliest. This essay is not, therefore, an attempt to provide an answer but to justify asking the question. A survey of title-pages of the seventeenth-century editions of the texts which bear the name of John Bunyan reveals not one name of the author, but many different names. There are variations in the spelling of the name: *John Bunyan*, *John Bunnyan*, *John Bunian*.[2] Whilst these differences may be read as examples of relatively non-standardised spelling in seventeenth-century writing and publishing, they also alert us, quite literally, to the instability of authorial identity.

It is some time now since we pondered, after Coleridge, on whether or not 'the Bunyan of Parnassus had the better of the Bunyan of Conventicle'.[3] Few today would deny that this opposition is the product not of a conflict or contradiction in the consciousness of the writer, but of a Romantic taxonomy anachronistically applied to the different world of seventeenth-century nonconformity. Much stimulating critical work on the writing of John Bunyan has stemmed from the explicit challenging of Coleridge's formulation, and from the exploration of the complex interrelationship of literary and religious strategies, contexts and drives in seventeenth-century nonconformist

1   This essay has been developed from work in my study *The Writing of John Bunyan* (Aldershot and Brookfield VT, 1997).
2   'John Bunnyan' appears in *Some Gospel-Truths Opened* (1656; *MW*, 1: 5), 'John Bunian' in *A Discourse Upon the Pharisee and the Publicane* (1665; *MW*, 10: 106).
3   Roberta Florence Brinkley (ed.), *Coleridge on the Seventeenth Century* (New York, 1955), p. 475.

writing that this binary opposition had occluded.[4] However, while I want to acknowledge the importance of the research that has enriched our understanding of nonconformist writing practices, I would like to attempt something different. Perhaps perversely, I want to return to the question of authorship and to the Romantic conception of the author as inspired and inspiring source and guarantee of meaning that has for so long been treated as the false idol, marked for demolition, of modern literary criticism. I want to suggest that in Bunyan's later writings we glimpse a figure of the author whose implicit ambitions exceed even the most confident formulation of the Romantics, but that it is a figure whose con-struction is fundamentally unstable.

In this essay I will suggest that Bunyan is created as an author, practically, by his publisher's exploitation of the success of *The Pilgrim's Progress*, and promoted as an author in his own later writings. In supplementary material published with *The Holy War*, it is possible to identify a version of the author that prefigures, and contributes to the development of, a model of the author as origin and owner of the text, a model that has little place for inspiration, whether divine or mundane. Finally, however, in the very act of establishing a position as the source of the text that comes perilously close to displacing the divine, Bunyan's writing startlingly reveals the limits and instability of any claim to control meaning.

We know Bunyan was a writer, but is it appropriate to think of him as an author? The most obvious answer is that he while he is considered an author today he was not so classified in his own lifetime; but is this true? It is easy to identify certain actions that consolidated the modification of writer to author after his death, notably the published collections of his writings, from the first attempt to produce a volume of collected works in 1692[5] to the first publication of a scholarly edition of the complete miscellaneous works in the 1980s. Is the birth of the author only made possible at the death of the writer, however? I would suggest that it is possible to identify publication strategies that exploited connections between texts, and

---

[4] See N. H. Keeble (ed.), *John Bunyan: Conventicle and Parnassus* (Oxford, 1988) for examples of the 'first wave' of such explicit critical engagements.

[5] See on this W. R. Owens' essay in the present volume.

between texts and the name *John Bunyan*, during the writer's lifetime, strategies that began to establish him as an author figure who anticipates the Romantic and post-Romantic model. I would certainly acknowledge that this is only one of the models of writing in mid and late-seventeenth-century culture. However, as we explore the complexity of non- conformist writing and publication, we should not overlook the signs of the history of the model of authorship that continues to haunt us today.

A survey of the descriptions of the author on title-pages of the seventeenth-century editions of Bunyan's writings may be a useful way of discovering some of the textual and discursive strategies which were employed to establish the name during Bunyan's lifetime and how these relate to broader issues of authorship and authority. It is, of course, important in this context to note that we cannot be sure who chose or wrote the descriptions which are the subject of this analysis. In the absence of any copyright legislation which named the writer as owner of his or her writing, published texts were the property of the publishers and there is considerable evidence that the division between publishers, printers and writers was not the same as it is today. Whilst the current understanding of the different roles played by those who are involved in the production of texts is in part an effect of the legislation introduced in 1710, it is also reinforced by the Romantic notion of the author as specially responsible, as creator in a unique sense of text and meaning, with publisher and printer relegated to positions as facilitators with economic rather than creative powers within cultural production. However, when we read the title-pages of Bunyan's texts written over two hundred years ago we cannot be sure who was responsible for them.

Some Gospel-Truths Opened, in 1656 the first text to be published as the work of John Bunyan, is described on the title-page as 'Published for the good of Gods chosen ones, by that unworthy Servant of Christ, *John Bunnyan*, of Bedford, By the grace of God, Preacher of the Gospel of his dear Son' (*MW*, 1: 5). This description, the longest to appear on the title-page of any seventeenth-century text ascribed to Bunyan, introduces several key phrases or titles which are used to qualify or situate the name *John Bunyan* in later texts. In *A Vindication of the Book Called Some Gospel-Truths Opened* (1657) and *A Few Sighs from Hell* (1658) the writer is described as 'John Bunyan, Preacher of the Gospel of CHRIST' (*MW*, 1: 121) and 'that Poor and Contemptible Servant of Jesus Christ, JOHN BUNYAN' (*MW*, 1: 230). *The Doctrine of the Law and Grace Unfolded* (1659) is 'Published by that poor and contemptible Creature, *John Bunyan* of *Bedford*' (*MW*, 2: 9) and *Profitable Meditations* (1661) bears the inscription 'By *John Bunyan*, Servant to the Lord JESUS' (*MW*, 6: 3).

The majority of texts published from 1656 to 1666 are either combative texts, treatises in which Bunyan attacks the theological precepts or religious practices of different sects, notably the Quakers who had gained a considerable following in Bedford, or texts which are offered as written sermons. In both cases a stress on the writer's pastoral authority, on his status as minister, would seem to be of paramount importance in establishing the authoritative status of the texts. The descriptive titles on the early works emphasise the dual status of the writer as abject sinner or contemptible subject and as divinely authorised minister. The often repeated word 'servant' suggests both positions, indicating at once a lowly status in relation to God and an active role in his service. References to Bedford, the location of Bunyan's ministry, reinforce the identification of the writer as minister, providing the reader with precise information about the geographical location of his ministry to support the implicit claim to a broader pastoral mission. Bunyan is located in Bedford, but 'God's chosen ones' may, like his readers, be elsewhere. The reader is thus assured that the hitherto unknown John Bunyan is a figure of some authority. The conventional assertions of unworthiness, the references to divine grace and claims to pastoral intent all imply that the writer is immersed in, and authorised by, what could be called a discourse of salvation. He and his texts are components in a divine strategy of addressing and enlisting sinners, a strategy which is described by deploying the familiar figures, terms and locations of pastoral ministry.

An exception to the deployment of this form of description can be found on the title-page of *Christian Behaviour* (1663), a guide to Christian conduct within the family unit. This text was published by Francis Smith, the radical Baptist printer who published almost all of Bunyan's writings up to 1678, including *Profitable Meditations*, a verse dialogue between Christ and a sinner.[6] Even though this text departed from the treatise form, it bore the conventional pastoral description of 'Servant to the Lord Jesus'. Two years later, however, *Christian Behaviour* was described as written by '*John Bunyan*, a Prisoner of *Hope*' (*MW*, 3: ii). A new label is introduced here by Bunyan's imprisonment in November 1661 for preaching without a licence. Where in earlier examples Bedford, his pastoral location, reinforced his status as minister, here it is his status as prisoner which is emphasised. The description can be read as foregrounding his relationship to the representatives of the law and of the episcopal church who had denied his legitimacy as a preacher of the Word. Bunyan here is not preacher but prisoner, his authority paradoxically that of one denied authority. The prisoner/writer's '*Hope*' signals a possible end to his present situation, whether interpreted in a limited and specific sense as an end to his incarceration or as the freedom from worldly troubles afforded by ultimate re-incorporation in divine being through salvation. In either case, the presence of this description on the title-page, and the publication of the text itself, constitute a direct challenge to the power of the persecuting authorities to silence its author.

The use of this description signals a clearly political dimension in the functioning of the name of John Bunyan, produced in response to the change in his relationship with those in authority and of his own circumstances. The description of Bunyan as a prisoner was repeated in *Prison Meditations*, a short poem which was first published as an appendix to *Christian Behaviour*, but other texts published during the early and mid 1660s still describe the writer as servant of Christ, including the two texts published by Joan Dover in 1665, *The Holy City* and *The Resurrection of the Dead*. The fact that these two forms of

---

6   There are examinations of Francis Smith's activities as a printer during this period, including his work with Bunyan, in N. H. Keeble, *The Literary Culture of Nonconformity in Later Seventeenth-Century England* (Leicester, 1987), pp. 60, 97, 98, 113, 118, 121, 122, 305 and Christopher Hill, *A Turbulent, Seditious, and Factious People: John Bunyan and his church* (Oxford, 1988), pp. 123, 238, 284–8. Both texts also offer useful information about Bunyan's other printers and about the context and activities of radical and dissenting publishing in this period.

description coexisted while Bunyan was imprisoned points to the impact on publishing and textual strategies of a range of struggles for pastoral authority. In 1656 Bunyan was competing with rival ministers, many of whom had either official positions in the Cromwellian church or longer histories of nonconformist ministry, but from 1661 he was also in direct conflict with the representatives of state authority who had denied him a voice. The contemporaneous use of the figures of servant/minister and of prisoner indicate that we cannot think of discrete phases or stages in the construction of Bunyan as author, but rather of different forces at work on and in that construction. Although he had been active as a preacher up to his arrest, Bunyan was not appointed as pastor of the Bedford congregation until January 1672, three months before his release from prison. However, as his account of his calling to the ministry indicates, Bunyan's sense of pastoral duty predated his appointment. In this context the need to claim a position of pastoral authority evident in the earliest texts is not displaced but rather given an additional impetus by his im-prisonment.

Bunyan's enforced separation from his congregation affected his construction as an author in another way. In silencing an unlicensed preacher, those who arrested and imprisoned Bunyan contributed to his transformation into a writer. Deprived of the ability to minister to the Bedford congregation, being, as he wrote in *Grace Abounding*, '*taken from you in presence*', the preacher can only maintain sustained contact through the written word (*GA*, p. xliv). The enforced use of the written word as a supplement or alternative to an oral ministry has profound effects from the 1660s onwards on the production of both texts and author.

The pastoral form of the name of the author outlined above was last used on the title-page of *Grace Abounding*, first published in 1666. Here a subtitle describes the text as 'A Brief and Faithful RELATION of the Exceeding Mercy of God in Christ, to his poor Servant *JOHN BUNYAN*' (*GA*, p. 1). The title of the text and the name of the author are interwoven in a structural prefiguration of the avowed intent of the author, outlined in the preface, to publish this narrative in order that readers may be reminded of God's grace by '*reading his work upon me*' (*GA*, p. 2). The author who has written this text 'by his own hand' and published it 'for the support of the weak and tempted People of God' is an active agent of the text's production (*GA*, p. xliv). However, as a subject produced by the workings of divine Grace, he is both the subject of this text and a text in his own right. In one textual moment three main techniques of nonconformist teaching – pastoral ministry, reading one's own life as an example of divine intervention, and writing – are held together in a balance that cannot be sustained.

Grace Abounding stands as the culmination of the first stage in a ministry in which the production of author and texts has been firmly located within a predominantly pastoral framework of reference. The meanings of both the name *Bunyan* and the texts published under that name are signalled as decidable only by reference to the pre-existing theological and pastoral formations of nonconformist teaching and preaching, which are in turn largely derived from Puritan beliefs and practices of the earlier seventeenth century. The significance or meaning of Bunyan's status as 'author' of the texts written during this period is clearly to be read as being of no greater importance than his status as minister or preacher and as exemplary subject of divine authority. The claim that *Grace Abounding* is written 'by his own hand' indicates that the fact that this is a personal account matters but writing is not itself an activity which can confer authority on the writing subject. It is, rather, just one facet of a wider ministry, albeit one which, under certain circumstances, such as imprisonment, appears to offer a greater potential for communication than speech. The idea that writing could be viewed as a simple extension or continuation of oral ministry was, however, regarded as problematic within Puritan and nonconformist movements. The threat posed by writing as a supplement to divine truth, embodied in the Logos, is ever present to those ministers who attempted to represent that truth through the medium of the written word.

The complexity of nonconformist attitudes to the role of writing in the dissemination of divine truth has been explored in detail by N. H. Keeble in *The Literary Culture of Nonconformity in Later Seventeenth-Century England*. Keeble's work has largely displaced the somewhat reductive reading offered by Lawrence A. Sasek, but Sasek's study does consider one intriguing exception to what he perceives as the general marginalisation of writing and authorship within the pre-Restoration Puritan tradition. Prefaces and introductions to *posthumous* publications, he notes, frequently emphasised not only the value of the written works as a means of communicating divine truth, but also the value of the writer. In Sasek's words, 'the emphasis on the man himself, almost as a personality, in the prefaces tended to elevate some writers into classics, into important literary figures, and to sanction within the framework of puritanism a genuinely literary fame'.[7]

It is certainly possible to identify the mobilisation of the name *John Bunyan* within a near approximation to a framework of authorial (perhaps a better term than *literary*) repute in the publication of his writings immediately after his death. The publication in 1692 of 'A Continuation of Mr. Bunyan's Life', to accompany *Grace Abounding*, would certainly appear to fit into the pattern of celebration of the author's 'personality', suggested by Sasek. The prospectus for publishing Charles Doe's edition of the complete works of Bunyan was accompanied by a printed list of thirty *Reasons why Christian People should Promote by Subscriptions the Printing in Folio the Labours of Mr. John Bunyan* (*MW*, 12: xxi). This similarly foregrounds Bunyan's eminence as preacher and writer, with particular emphasis on his status as author of *The Pilgrim's Progress*. The list includes the suggestion that 'Not to preserve his labours and name, which are so great, is a disingenuous slighting or despising them, and serving them no better than a wicked man's that rots'. The publication, to be illustrated with engravings of the author's image, is, significantly, presented as being prompted by an 'extraordinary' case: 'The chief reasons we argue from are not common rules, that therefore every good minister's endeavours ought to be printed in folio. But this case is extraordinary, as an eminent minister, made so by abundance of gospel grace, who has also writ much, which hath gone off well'.[8]

The success of Bunyan's writing is thus cited as one of the reasons for this publication. In an address to the Christian reader of his 1692 folio edition of Bunyan's *Works*, headed 'The Struggler', Doe

---

7   Lawrence Sasek, *The Literary Temper of the English Puritans* (Baton Rouge, 1961), pp. 27–8.
8   George Offor (ed.), *The Works of John Bunyan*, 3 vols. (Glasgow, Edinburgh and London, 1860–62), 3: 764, 765.

gave an account of Bunyan's life and 'labours' which included a section on the writing of *The Pilgrim's Progress*. This book, it argues,

> *hath done the superstitious sort of men and their practice, more harm, or rather good, as I may call it, then if he had been let alone at his Meeting at* Bedford, *to preach the Gospel to his own Auditory, as it might have fallen out [...] and hath been printed in* France, Holland, New-England, *and in* Welch, *and about a hundred thousand in* England, *whereby they are made some means of Grace, and the Author become famous, and may be the cause of spreading his other Gospel-Books over the* European *and* American *World, and in the process of time may be so to the whole Universe* (*MW*, 12: 456).

Here one text is presented as both conferring fame on its author and creating interest in his other texts. *The Pilgrim's Progress*, it seems, is pivotal in evangelical marketing strategies. It is the supreme success story in nonconformist attempts to harness the power of the written word, and the printing press, to extend an evangelical ministry beyond the geographical constraints of the author's physical location. Doe stresses the effects of the text on its readers throughout the world but also acknowledges its effect on the author who has 'become famous'.

It is this section of 'The Struggler' that I find most interesting. While the celebration of Bunyan's good works may be a key component in the posthumous establishment of his fame as an author, it alerts us to the effect of one of his works in his lifetime. I want to suggest that if we trace the impact of the publication of *The Pilgrim's Progress* on the marketing of the author even before his death, we may find evidence of some of the ways in which the processes of writing and publication not only confer fame on the author but also begin to destabilise the relationship between Bunyan as writer and God as original author, and to upset the balance between the intended communication of singular truth and the dissemination of uncontrollable meaning.

First editions of eight texts attributed to Bunyan published after *Grace Abounding* and before *The Pilgrim's Progress* are extant, including *Light for Them that Sit in Darkness* (1675), *Instruction for the Ignorant* (1675) and *Come & Welcome, To Jesus Christ* (1678).[9] Of these, six bear the simple name 'John Bunyan' on the title-page; one, *Come & Welcome, To Jesus Christ*, is offered as the work of 'J. Bunyan'; and another, *A Confession of my Faith* (1672), has no author's name on the title-page, but bears the initials 'J. B.' at the end of the prefatory letter. *The Pilgrim's Progress* (1678, known as 'Part I' after the publication of Part II in 1684) is attributed to 'John Bunyan', with no reference to the author's position either as sinner or minister. Only three texts published after *Grace Abounding* make any reference on the title-page to Bunyan's pastoral activity, two describing the author as 'JOHN BUNYAN of *Bedford*' (*MW*, 11: 2; *MW*, 6: 273), and the third, published the year after his death, as 'that Eminent Preacher, and Faithful Minister of Jesus Christ, Mr. JOHN BUNYAN of *Bedford* ' (*MW*, 12: 2). All three texts, *The Jerusalem Sinner Saved, or Good News for the Vilest of Men* (1688), *A Discourse of the Building, Nature, Excellency and Government of the House of God* (1688) and *The Acceptable Sacrifice* (1689) were published by George Larkin, publisher of *Grace Abounding*. No title-page makes reference to Bunyan as author of *Grace Abounding*, whereas after the publication of *The Pilgrim's Progress*, four texts published by three different booksellers all describe the work as written by the author of *The Pilgrim's Progress*.

9   Other texts are thought to have been written and may have been published during this period, including *The Heavenly Foot-Man* and *Saved by Grace*, but I have chosen to refer only to those of which editions published between 1666 and 1678 are extant and which offer evidence of the form of the author's name used in this specific period. These are: *A Defence of the Doctrine of Justification by Faith* (Francis Smith, 1672); *A Confession of My Faith and A Reason of My Practice in Worship* (Francis Smith, 1672); *Differences in Judgment about Water-Baptism No Bar to Communion* (John Wilkins, 1672); *The Barren Fig-Tree* (Jonathan Robinson, 1673); *Light for Them that Sit in Darkness* (Francis Smith, 1675); *Instruction for the Ignorant* (Francis Smith, 1675); *The Strait Gate* (Francis Smith, 1676); *Come, & Welcome, to Jesus Christ* (Benjamin Harris, 1678). Charles Doe records the publication of an edition of *Peaceable Principles and True* in 1674, but the only extant copy, in the collection of the American Baptist Historical Society in Rochester, New York, lacks the title-page, and so evidence of the form of the name of the author used is missing.

In 1680 *The Life and Death of Mr. Badman*, published, like *The Pilgrim's Progress*, by Nathaniel Ponder, is the first text to be attributed to Bunyan as author of the latter text. Two years later, *The Holy War*, the next text to be published, this time by Dorman Newman, is similarly attributed. Whilst both of these texts share the fictional or narrative model employed in *The Pilgrim's Progress*, two other texts which bear this form of the name of the author are treatises: *A Discourse upon the Pharisee and the Publicane*, published in 1685 by Jo Harris, and *The Advocateship of Jesus Christ*, published in 1688 by Dorman Newman.

Whilst Newman, as publisher in partnership with Benjamin Alsop of the first edition and, by himself, of the second edition of *The Holy War*, might be seen as attempting to capitalise on the success of the earlier text he had published, Harris had published no other Bunyan texts. The form of the name of the author in this context would seem to suggest that the market potential of 'John Bunyan' could be established by the name of the text. The authority or worth of the author of new texts is here guaranteed by reference to an earlier text. A new name of the author is thus produced through the discursive procedure of linking two texts, of conferring on the later text the established authority of the earlier text. The Bunyan who stands as author of the texts written after 1678 is in a sense the product of the success of *The Pilgrim's Progress*. There is, however, no evidence on the title-pages that the name 'John Bunyan' in and of itself is being offered as guarantee of these texts, as it has been in conventional literary studies. The name of the author still requires a suffix in the form of the name of one text, *The Pilgrim's Progress*. No suggestion is made that the texts have a shared origin in a figure of the author, represented by his name.

In textual material accompanying one of these texts there is, however, evidence of an attempt to establish an intimate connection between the form of the name of the author, *John Bunyan*, the Author of *The Pilgrim's Progress*, and the writing subject. This text can be read as a claim to authorial authority and is a clear example of the type of text identified in a recent study by Kevin Dunn as being at the heart of the development of the figure of the author.[10] Dunn examines the institution of authorship which emerged from authoritarian models of textuality that developed through and with humanism. He argues that it is in the Renaissance and, more particularly, in the Reformation, that the authority of the author is first established and institutionalised within what became the highly developed market culture of the seventeenth century. He offers a useful revision of Michel Foucault's argument that texts, books and discourses began to have authority when authors became subject to punishment and discourses are perceived as transgressive.[11] Dunn argues that since discursive transgression and its punishment antedate the development of authorship as an institution in the European tradition

> texts, books, and discourses begin to need authors when their transgression itself seeks institutionalization. In other words, it is when the subversive discourse finds itself on the brink of empowerment, of articulating something more than a negative critique of the reigning orthodoxies, that the authority of the author becomes necessary.[12]

This revised model can be productively applied to Bunyan whose punishment, his lengthy incarceration, was indeed for discursive transgression, but of a spoken rather than written kind. His enforced separation from his Bedford congregation may have contributed to his development as a writer, to the production of texts which bore his name, but the construction of John Bunyan, author, cannot be simply attributed to the punitive actions of the state.

Dunn is particularly interested in the moment when

> the writer attempts an ideological separation of himself and his work from the market that created both in order to establish the work as inimitable artifact rather than commodity and himself as author rather than craftsman or chapman.[13]

---

10 Kevin Dunn, *Pretexts of Authority: the rhetoric of authority in the Renaissance Preface* (Stanford, 1994).
11 See Michel Foucault, 'What is an Author?', in Donald F. Bouchard (ed.), *Language, Counter Memory, Practice* (Oxford, 1977).
12 Dunn, *Pretexts of Authority*, p. 10.
13 Dunn, *Pretexts of Authority*, pp. 10–11.

The terms employed here might seem to fit overtly literary or fictional writing or the texts of humanism more closely than the didactic, combative or 'saving' texts of religious writing in the period. Dunn himself, however, focuses on texts which he locates at the 'edges' of the institution of authorship, on the writings of Luther and Milton as well as of Descartes and Bacon, refusing to accept the exclusive model of humanism as a separate tradition.

Whatever their misgivings about the effects of writing, Puritan and later nonconformist groups exploited the oppor-tunities offered by the press, as N. H. Keeble has argued, both to overcome the isolating and, literally, silencing effects of persecution by ecclesiastical and civil authorities and to reach a wider audience in the form of a readership. Keeble quotes Richard Baxter's succinct formulation of the role that written publication might have in nonconformist strategies, '*Preachers* may be silenced or banished, when *Books* may be at hand', but he notes that this knowledge was shared by those who wished to deprive radical and dissenting religious groups from any means of communicating with each other or with wider audiences.[14] In the mid- and late- seventeenth-century nonconformist writing, like any other type, was implicated in the market and in the processes of regulation that were instituted after the Restoration in the form of censorship and licensing of publications. There is not enough space here to chart the changing conditions, the periods of harsh repression interspersed with those of greater leniency, in the publishing industry during the period of Bunyan's career. It is interesting to note, however, in the light of Dunn's argument that authorship becomes important when subversive discourses are on the brink of empowerment, that *The Pilgrim's Progress*, the text which seems to have contributed most to the construction of Bunyan as author, was granted an official licence, which is noted on the title-page, and could thus be seen as having been given in some sense a seal of approval by those who censored written discourse. Whilst the granting of a licence does not in itself constitute a singularly important moment in the construction or production of Bunyan as author, it would certainly have

---

14   Keeble, *Literary Culture*, p. 93.

enabled the book to be printed and sold in quantities that would have been out of the question for an unlicensed text.

Dunn's examination of the work of Martin Luther, whose influence on Bunyan's theological position and self-presentation has been firmly established, focuses on the interrelationship in his 'self-authorizing personal narrations' between a pull towards a Medieval corporate voice and the subversive individualism of Renaissance humanism. This Dunn connects with the attempted resolution of the bifurcated forces of divine inspiration and personal agency in St. Paul.[15] In the work of both writers theological and material contexts are interconnected in the rhetorical attempt to negotiate an authoritative position which will communicate rather than challenge the ultimate authority of God. Dunn's reading reveals that both writers deployed an image of the body of the writer in this attempt. Paul, writing to embattled early Christians, employs the image of his own, irreducibly human, suffering body, marked by the visible traces of martyrdom, produced through battles with his persecutors, to establish a position of authority which imitates Christ's suffering without threatening to efface it. Luther, writing in the mid-sixteenth-century context of the struggles between Reformed and Roman Catholic positions, presents himself, as Bunyan will later in *Grace Abounding*, as a text written by God, a body of writing, but also as a writer forced through the exigencies of his own material circumstances to add to this divinely authored *corpus* his own narrative which negotiates the contradictions of inner and outer experiences.

The rhetorical strategies employed later by Bunyan can be read as displaying continuity with those of both Paul and Luther beyond the explicit parallels acknowledged by Bunyan himself in his earlier writing.[16] Written in the contexts of a different struggle for authority within a competing network of religious groups, and of a more fully developed publication market, the otherwise parallel situation of

---

15 Dunn, *Pretexts of Authority*, p. 15.
16 See the evident Pauline borrowings in the title and prefatory address of *Grace Abounding*. There is a fuller analysis of Bunyan's address to his congregation / readership at this stage in his ministry in chapter 2 of Spargo, *Writing of John Bunyan*, pp. 43–67.

Bunyan's text is inflected by a further, and more troubling or destabilising, force unleashed by a stress on writing in a literal or graphic sense.

When *The Holy War* was published in 1682, the association of its author with *The Pilgrim's Progress*, signalled on the title-page, was reinforced by '*An ADVERTISEMENT to the READER*' defending Bunyan's authorship of the earlier text, printed at the end of the new book. The text also takes a cue from *The Pilgrim's Progress* by including a visual depiction of the author. Later editions of *The Pilgrim's Progress*, published before *The Holy War*, had included a portrait of Bunyan as the sleeping man, presumably dreaming the dream which became the narrative of the text. In the reading that concludes this essay, I shall suggest that in '*An ADVERTISEMENT to the READER*' Bunyan constructs an image of the writer's body that strikingly departs from the figures of the author's body in Luther and Paul and has profound implications for the relationship between writing and faith. On a more mundane level, however, the inclusion of portraits in *The Pilgrim's Progress* and *The Holy War* suggests that, the physical appearance of the author was assumed to be of interest to readers.

In *The Holy War* two portraits are included in the first edition. One engraving, placed after the prefatory address to the reader, depicts Bunyan as a type of Mansoul, with his figure standing between Shaddai's army and Diabolus' force. This resembles the device of the engraving in *The Pilgrim's Progress*, placing a image of the body of the author within a depiction of the narrative of the text. In both engravings a suggestion at the real appearance of the man is made, but the figure is locked within the world of the text. The other engraving, facing the title-page, shows the author without the context of the text. All three engravings, in *The Holy War* and *The Pilgrim's Progress*, have been reliably attributed to Robert White, and are evidently based on his pencil drawing of Bunyan.[17] The inclusion of this portrait of Bunyan 'as himself' can, I think, be seen as the most confident assertion of his authorial identity and marks *The Holy War* as the culmination of a process of consolidating his image. It is surely a

---

17　For additional information on these engravings, see *HW*, pp. xliv–xlv.

precursor of the modern author photograph. Even here, however, a touch of instability is evident: the engraving is described as being a portrait of 'John Bunnyon' while the facing page attributes the text to 'John Bunyan'. The difference in spelling of the names of the author on title-page and engraving may seem trivial, but read in the light of '*An ADVERTISEMENT to the READER*', it may be seen to be of considerable significance.

The advertisement is undersigned by the author, here written as 'JOHN BUNYAN'. Presented, like the text's prefatory address to the reader, in verse form, this stands not only as a refutation of implied accusations that Bunyan has profited by other writers' labours but also as a claim to a position as originator of the text's 'matter in this manner' (*HW*, p. 251). This contrasts with his earlier arguments about the nature of his position as writer both in the early treatises and in *The Pilgrim's Progress* whose allegorical mode itself marked a departure from the 'simplicity' claimed for Bunyan's previous experiments with written ministry.

In the preface to *The Pilgrim's Progress* the defence of allegorical method as a means of contributing to the '*advance of Truth*' implies a position for the author which is almost passive (*PP*, p. 5). The author '*fel*' into allegory and '*things*', which might be interpreted as ideas or words, of unspecified origin, '*multiply*' in the writer's '*crown*' and are '*set down*' (*PP*, p. 1). This preface has long been regarded as the supreme articulation of a model of inspired writing which marks Bunyan as a predecessor of the Romantics. However, the privileged position which would be given by the Romantics to the imagination is here occupied by 'things' which as yet lack a name and which Bunyan treats with some caution: '*Nay then, thought I, if that you breed so fast,/ I'll put you by your selves, lest you at last/ Should prove ad infinitum, and eat out/ The Book that I already am about*' (*PP*, p. 1). If this is inspiration as we have learned to recognise it through the lens of Romantic models of writing and of post-Romantic literary criticism, it is, as yet, a troubling force for a nonconformist writer when faced with the task of transmuting it into text.

The writer here is presented as a channel for divine truth and the text's didactic potential as its ultimate justification. His mode of writing is authorised by scriptural precedent, as had already been signalled on the title-page by the citation of Hosea xii. 10: 'I have used Similitudes'.[18] Authorial intent is, however, less clearly defined. The description of the writer's decision to '*set down*' the breeding '*things*', whose appearance interrupted the writing of another book, is followed by a passage in which the initial emphasis on the passivity of the writer is modified: '*I did it mine own self to gratifie./ Neither did I but vacant seasons spend/ In this my Scribble; Nor did I intend/ But to divert my self in doing this,/ From worser thoughts, which make me do amiss*' (*PP*, p. 1). In this passage, the writing of *The Pilgrim's Progress* is presented as a means of self-gratification which is also a method of self-government. Writing is thus an activity which displaces '*worser thoughts which make me do amiss*' but involves occupying a position, or positions, which are not entirely under the control of the writer. In the interaction between text and reader, the 'I' of the writer, whose domination of the passage quoted above catches the eye of the reader, may eventually challenge the singularity and transcendence of God as sole origin and guarantor of meaning.

An examination of the advertisement to the reader which accompanies *The Holy War* may indicate, however, that this is not such a smooth transition from one figure of ultimate and absolute authority to another as the development of a humanist approach to issues of cultural production and the Romantic model of authorship might imply. The advertisement begins by relating accusations that *The Pilgrim's Progress* 'is not mine':

> Some say the *Pilgrim's Progress* is not mine,
> Insinuating as if I would shine
> In name and fame by the worth of another,
> Like some made rich by robbing of their Brother.
> Or that so fond I am of being Sire,
> I'le father Bastards: or if need require,
> I'le tell a lye in Print to get applause.
> I scorn it; *John* such dirt-heap never was,
> Since God converted him. Let this suffice
> To shew why I my *Pilgrim* Patronize (*HW*, p. 251).

---

18 Hosea xii. 10 also appears on the title-page of *The Holy War*.

The conjunction of 'name' and 'fame' here immediately introduces the concept of reputation as bound up with the establishment of the name of the author. Bunyan is accused of claiming the name and fame of an author, which is not legitimately his, being rightly the property of a 'Brother'. It is important to note that there is no suggestion that he is seeking to usurp the position of God as universal Father, but the generating, creating force of the divine is certainly occluded or effaced here by the struggles for the right to claim legitimate paternity by the rival Brothers writing and publishing in the seventeenth-century market.

The initial refutation of these accusations foregrounds the name of the author on a literal level: 'I scorn it; *John* such dirt-heap never was,/ Since God converted him' (*HW*, p. 251). The shift from first person to third in this sentence would appear to objectify the name of the author, to introduce a distance between the writing subject and the subject written about, an effect reinforced by the fact that the name is printed in italics. Yet the use of the forename alone simultaneously suggests a relationship of familiarity between writer and name, which reduces the distance between subject and object without collapsing the difference. The combined impact of these textual strategies may serve to designate the name as a distinct object, but one which can be claimed by a rightful owner.

The central claim of this address to the reader is an apparently confident assertion that *The Pilgrim's Progress* is the product of Bunyan's 'own heart':

> It came from mine own heart, so to my head,
> And thence into my fingers trickled;
> Then to my Pen, from whence immediately
> On Paper I did dribble it daintily (*HW*, p. 251).

The text is presented here as originating in the core of the writer's corporeal being and as following a progress through other parts of his body, 'head' and 'fingers', through 'my Pen' and onto paper. Head, fingers and pen are all links in a chain which leads from heart to paper, from point of origin to destination, a chain in which bodily parts and inanimate object are all bound to their owner, the dribbling author. Ink thus becomes a secretion of the body of the author, a fluid channel for the transmission of the text from the innermost part of the body, the heart, to the external surface of the paper. The body of the author stands here as the point of origin of the text rather than as a channel for the transmission of material which has its origin in the divine being. Through the use of the metaphoric chain of heart to paper, the process of literary production from conception to inscription has been internalised, located in the operations of the body of the author, which stands defined against exterior and anterior forces, both divine and worldly. There is a striking connection here with the rhetoric of the writer's body traced by Dunn, but the crucial difference is that this is not a suffering body as in the case of Paul or of the historically situated body of Luther, but emphatically a *writing* body.

There is an oblique qualification of the apparent exclusion of divine input in the process of the production in the next section:

> Manner and matter too was all mine own,
> Nor was it unto any mortal known,
> 'Till I had done it. Nor did any then
> By Books, by wits, by tongues, or hand, or pen,
> Add five words to it, or wrote half a line
> Thereof: the whole, and ev'ry whit is mine (*HW*, p. 251).

The assertion that no 'mortal' knew of the substance or style of the text may signal divine knowledge of the writer's intentions, but agency here is clearly both human and individual. If there is a divine input in the creative process it has been transmuted into human activity: the breath of divine presence must be transformed into writing by the human body. Whereas, in the opening section, divine agency in the production of Bunyan as a subject is located in the past, when 'God converted him', here the possibility of divine agency in the production of the text is subsumed within a model of creation/creativity which foregrounds the process of writing in order to guarantee the authorship, the authority, of the writer. This strategy is in marked contrast to the earlier texts such as *Instruction for the Ignorant* and *Light for Them that Sit in Darkness* which deployed metaphors of speech and hearing in order to privilege divine truth and to differentiate between divinely sanctioned and 'fallen' texts. It can be read as a response to the changed context of later seventeenth-century writing and publishing practices: in the earlier texts Bunyan defended himself, his own writings, and the Scriptures against those who challenged their veracity; here he defends his own status as author.

In the advertisement the text is presented as the product and, in a sense, the property of the author, who later reinforces his claims to ownership of *The Pilgrim's Progress* by a parallel statement of his relationship to the text which the reader is in the process of reading:

> Also for *This*, thine eye is now upon,
> The matter in this manner came from none
> But the same heart, and head, fingers and pen,
> As did the other. Witness all good men;
> For none in all the world without a lye,
> Can say that this is mine, excepting I (*HW*, p. 251).

The repetition of the pattern, heart, head, fingers and pen, once more locates the origin of the text in the writing body of the author. Writing is, in a sense, like getting something out of the writer's system. This text, like *The Pilgrim's Progress*, is claimed as the sole product and property of the writing subject, but has the gap between the writing subject and the name of the author opened up in the original accusations been bridged?

In a final move to close that gap, the writer may be read as attempting to guarantee the legitimacy of the writing subject, the name of the author and the text, by presenting them as being inextricably linked in a system of mutual reciprocity. Just as the passage opened with a double move which both objectified the name of the author and claimed kin on the part of the writing subject, so this text ends with the writing subject recreating the name of the author, quite literally. The verse is presented to the reader as a text which offers a succinct formulation of his claims to be the legitimate source of the works which bear this name and of the legitimate right of those texts to bear that name:

> I write not this of any ostentation,
> Nor 'cause I seek of men their commendation;
> I do it to keep them from such surmize,
> As tempt them will my name to scandalize.
> Witness my name, if Anagram'd to thee,
> The Letters make, *Nu hony in a B* (*HW*, p. 251).

The writer writes his own name differently, playing with its capacity to be something else. This self-advertisement may be read as the culmination of a series of claims to transcendence on the part of the writing subject, in which the dismissal of counter-claims by rival writers is paralleled by an implicit displacement of God as sole source and guarantee of meaning. Yet the textual play, by means of which this apparently confident assertion of control over the meaning of the name of the author is achieved, foregrounds the fragility of this imaginary moment of resolution. '*Nu hony in a B*' is a rearrangement of the ten letters which, on the title-pages of *The Pilgrim's Progress* and *The Holy War* and at the foot of this advertisement, are arranged as 'John Bunyan', the established name of the author. The apparent control of the meanings of the name of the author by the writing subject, who dismantles and reconstitutes his own graphic identity, is displayed in an attempt to master and limit the arbitrary system of differences by which the name is formed and reformed. The temporary displacement of 'John Bunyan' by '*Nu hony in a B*' may be read as a move which paradoxically reinforces the imaginary identification of the writing subject with the 'real' name, 'John Bunyan'. Yet this apparent mastery of difference is at the level of the grapheme: the re-placement of 'John Bunyan' as '*Nu hony in a B*' demands the substitution of the letter 'i' for the letter 'j'. The typographic interchangeability of these two letters is itself culturally contingent; even though decades earlier the two letters were indistinguishable typographically, by this time they were only rarely interchanged. The spelling of 'Nu' and 'hony' is eccentric even by seventeenth-century standards. Bunyan's inscription of an imaginary identity is achieved precisely at the level of written signification: a name, a subject, is formed and re-formed by an assemblage of graphic fragments. Difference thus establishes the possibility of identity: it acts as a hinge which both connects and separates units of signification, temporally and spatially.

The graphic construction of '*Nu hony in a B*' as a different meaning of the name of the author may serve to reinforce other meanings ascribed to 'John Bunyan' in this advertisement, such as creative writing subject, but it also raises the possibility of other meanings, other positions. The writing subject's apparent mastery of the written subject is thus exposed as itself an effect of linguistic difference at the level of the grapheme and of historical contingency in the production of meaning.

The author or writer, however, is not the only source of meaning implicitly constructed and deconstructed by writing in Bunyan's later work. Four years after the publication of *The Holy War* and its troublesome supplement, Bunyan cast his net wider than ever in the attempt to catch the attention of readers and in so doing presented a text that threatened radically to undermine the entire basis of his project. *A Book for Boys and Girls* (1686) presents a collection of poems to a readership of men and women as well as boys and girls. The poems themselves can be read as fairly conventional depictions of the work of God in the created world, representations of divinely-ordained and pre-existing meaning, but in an addition to the text Bunyan returns once more to the question of writing in a literal sense. He prefaces the poems with a spelling guide, announcing his intention to teach children 'their A,B,C' because 'All needs must there begin, that wou'd be wise' (*MW*, 6: 193).

The brief spelling and reading guide is, on one level, a neat example of the nonconformists' commitment to literacy as a vital part of a redemptive process: it is described as being 'enough for little Children to prepare themselves for Psalter, or Bible' (*MW*, 6: 196). However, the method employed to teach the construction of words suggests rather an organizational linguistic principle which has little direct relationship to divine authority. Words in the section are printed with breaks to mark each syllable, Bunyan states that 'e-ve-ry word or syl-la-ble (tho ne-ver so small) must have one vow-el or more right-ly placed in it', and a list of non-words is offered: 'sl, gld, strnght, spll, drll, fll' (*MW*, 6: 194). The suggestion that words exist on the basis of meeting internal, systematic or structural criteria is not tempered by any reference to divinely-ordained meaning, indeed to meaning at all.[19]

One of the sections in this guide is, quite touchingly, given the diverse spellings of the name of the author on his own title-pages, a chart 'To learn Chil-dren to spell a-right their names' (*MW*, 6: 195). While for Bunyan, endeavouring to convey God's Truth, the impossibility of finally controlling meaning in writing may have been a source of anxiety, for his later readers it has guaranteed that his works have enjoyed a life long after the death of the author. We might say, in conclusion, that, unwittingly and to our benefit, 'the writing Bunyan has the better of Bunyan the author'.

---

19   For a fuller analysis of the spelling guide, see my 'The Purloined Postcard: Waiting for Bunyan', *Textual Practice*, 8 (1994), 79–96.

5

MICHAEL DAVIES
'Stout & Valiant Champions for God':
the Radical Reformation of Romance in
The Pilgrim's Progress

In his millenarian tract *The Holy City* (1665), John Bunyan discourses at one point upon the 'Altar-men' who have so far contributed to the construction of the 'New Jerusalem', an allegory for the 'true Church'. '[T]hese men in their Altar-work', he states,

> did figure-out for us our famous and holy Worthies, that before us have risen up in their place, and shook off those Reliques of Antichrist that intrenched upon the Priestly Office of our Lord and Saviour, even worthy *Wickliff, Hus, Luther, Melancton, Calvin,* and the blessed Martyrs in Q. *Maries* dayes, &c. with the rest of their companions: these in their day were stout & valiant Champions for God, according to their light, and did upon the Altar of God, which is *Christ* our Lord, offer up many strong cries, with groans and tears, as every day required, for the compleat recovering of the Church of God; the benefit of whose Offering we have felt and enjoyed to this day (*MW*, 3: 134).

Clearly, this passage is important for a number of reasons. On one level, it offers some insight into Bunyan's somewhat Foxean concept of Protestant historiography, and of the Bedford Church's continuation both of and within it: Bunyan is, it seems, positioning himself and his nonconformist congregation in a distinguished and unquestionably authentic Protestant genealogy, that of leading English and Continental reformers, as well as of the Marian martyrs revered so deeply in *Actes and Monuments*. As Stuart Sim and David Walker note, here Bunyan acknowledges 'the immense courage and fortitude displayed by such men in the face of overwhelming pressures', and it is in the image of such heroism that Bunyan presents himself too 'as one of an elect minority destined by God to safeguard the faithful'.[1] On another level, however, what is so remarkable about this writing is the style of Bunyan's presentation of the Reformation. The great Protestants of the past are, after all, given to us as 'our famous and holy Worthies', a phrase which displays not only Bunyan's admiration, but also his typical propensity for punning. The term 'worthy', as the *Oxford English Dictionary* usefully illustrates, develops a particular usage in the seventeenth century: it denotes a specifically Protestant scholar or theologian. Hence, Luther, Calvin, and the others within Bunyan's list are indeed notable 'worthies' in precisely this sense.[2] At the same time, though, such a word cannot fail to conjure somewhat less scholastic and more heroic associations. With 'our famous and holy Worthies' we are also being asked to recall, it would seem, the 'Nine Worthies' of Medieval chivalric legend (most memorably celebrated, of course, in Caxton's preface to Malory's King Arthur romances, and paraded forth in Shakespeare's *Love's Labour's Lost*).[3] That Bunyan specifically wants his Protestant saints and sufferers to be considered a chivalric pageant of the faithful in *The*

---

[1] Stuart Sim and David Walker, *Bunyan and Authority: the rhetoric of dissent and the legitimation crisis in seventeenth-century England* (Bern, 2000), p. 83.

[2] See the entry for 'worthy' in *The Oxford English Dictionary*, prepared by J. A. Simpson and E. S. C. Weiner, 2nd edn (Oxford, 1989), esp. entries C. sb. 1. b, c, and d, which offer definitions of 'worthy' as 'A hero of antiquity', as one of the Nine Worthies, or as 'A prominent scholar or theologian' respectively. The earliest examples of the latter usage are dated 1603, 1607, and 1611 in the *OED*, and all relate specifically to Protestant scholars and theologians. This sense of 'worthy' is also evident in John Milton's *Areopagitica* (1644) when he describes England as a nation 'approaching Reformation' through the heroic activities of its Protestant scholars: 'What wants there to such a towardly and pregnant soil, but wise and faithful labourers, to make a knowing people, a Nation of Prophets, of Sages, and of Worthies?' (John Milton, *Prose Writings*, ed. and intro. by K. M. Burton (1927; rev. edn. London 1958), p. 177).

[3] See William Shakespeare, *Love's Labour's Lost*, ed. by H. R. Woodhuysen, Arden Shakespeare 3rd ser. (London, 1998), V.i.109–47 and V.ii.485–710, and Caxton's preface to Malory's *Works*, ed. by Eugène Vinaver, 2nd edn. (Oxford, 1971), pp. xiii–xv. For further reference to the Nine Worthies, see M. Y. Offard (ed.), *The Parlement of the Thre Ages* (Oxford, 1959), lines 300–53. (I owe thanks to Dr. David Salter of the Department of English at the University of Leicester for kindly providing these references to the Medieval 'Worthies'.)

Holy City is, moreover, reinforced by another prominent phrase: these men, like the 'Nine Worthies' alluded to, are nothing less than 'stout & valiant Champions', albeit 'for God' rather than for chivalry, and for whom they have heroically 'risen up [...] and shaken off those Reliques of Antichrist' in the course of their renowned lives.

Such language is, of course, supremely relevant for Bunyan's later and most famous work, *The Pilgrim's Progress*, a text which also presents its protagonist as a 'stout & valiant' champion, and which narrates its Christian's quest in the form of an allegory the structure, motifs, and episodes of which are clearly akin to (if not indistinguishable from) chivalric romance, replete with giants and monsters, castles and dungeons, battles and enchantments. Not surprisingly, illustrations for *The Pilgrim's Progress* have long reflected this dimension of Bunyan's story: from the earliest woodcuts to the more sumptuous pictures and engravings of nineteenth- and twentieth-century editions of the text, Christian has been presented as the image of the knight errant confronting his trials in radiant Arthurian fashion. For all that such romancing has made *The Pilgrim's Progress* an enduring literary classic, however, it is not exactly an unproblematic mode of representation in either *The Holy City* or indeed the later allegory. In *The Holy City*, for instance, the rhetoric of chivalry might heroicise Bunyan's 'Worthies', but it also threatens to undermine the very authority with which Bunyan presumably intends to imbue his 'stout & valiant Champions for God'. In presenting the Reformation as a romance of Protestant valour, Bunyan could be accused of enchanting Protestant history into something profoundly and uncomfortably (if not perilously) close to the non-historical: the unreal and mythical stuff of mere legend. As such, Bunyan seems to be in danger not only of making a fable out of history, but of weakening his own identity and authority as a Protestant nonconformist, both being profoundly and necessarily bound-up with the actual (and not merely mythical or legendary) historicity of the original reformers and martyrs.

In *The Holy City*, though, this problem is largely solved for us. As we read on, it becomes quite clear that Bunyan can indeed invoke the 'Champions' of the Protestant past as 'legendary' owing largely to his view of ecclesiastical history as a whole. Although the early reformers performed crucial roles in establishing Protestant doctrine and liturgy, nevertheless the 'Foundation' of the true Reformed Church, Bunyan states, 'was *not yet laid*' by them. Rather, the real basis for the 'Holy City' is finally being constructed in the present, he asserts, and only by separating nonconformists, like Bunyan himself, whose ecclesiology simply outstrips that of Luther and Calvin in terms of 'having the Church *a select company of visible Believers*' set apart '*from the unconverted and open prophane*', independent, that is, from the kind of churches which, as Bunyan puts it, 'every where like Locusts and Maggots craul up and down the Nations' (*MW*, 3: 135). Behind Bunyan's strategy of relegating the great reformers to a more distant and romantic past, therefore, lies the millenarian desire in *The Holy City* to promote the present Bedford congregation as a manifestation of the one and only eternal and true Church.

With *The Pilgrim's Progress*, however, the problem of Bunyan's romancing cannot be brushed aside so easily. Far from performing a momentary rhetorical trick conjured only to be discarded, as in *The Holy City*, in *The Pilgrim's Progress* romance provides, it would seem, the formal and structural blueprint for Christian's entire journey. Indeed, it is the very extent of this romantic influence that has long caused problems for the text's readers and critics. After all, what we must negotiate in *The Pilgrim's Progress* is something of a paradox in Puritan culture: a work of imagination, of feigning and fable, which is the product of a discourse of 'Truth' anathema to it. Although Bunyan's apologetic preface to his allegory strenuously defends such fabling ('*grave* Paul [...] *no where doth forbid/The use of Parables*', he asserts), it is hardly surprising that amidst the immediate and general success of Bunyan's book some nonconformist contemporaries were offended by its imaginative and chivalric style (*PP*, p.5). Most famously, Bunyan's General Baptist counterpart, Thomas Sherman, published his own *Second Part* of *The Pilgrim's Progress* not only out of doctrinal disagreement with Bunyan's 'useful tract', but in order to remedy the fact that, for Sherman at least, Bunyan's book is largely indistinguishable from other 'novels, romances, and plays' currently debauching the 'vain and frothy minds' of the nation's otherwise godly readers. Such dangerously deleterious reading matter, the horrified Sherman claims, is not only being consumed

The Radical Reformation of Romance in The Pilgrim's Progress 107

at 'a strange and prodigious rate', but 'to the sensible discouragement and decay of piety and religion', and the vitiation of 'people's minds'. For this reason, Sherman's *Second Part* proves to be nothing less than a radical rewriting of Bunyan's *The Pilgrim's Progress* with 'lightness and laughter' being replaced by 'serious and spiritual phrases', the imaginative indulgence and surface froth of Bunyan's book being septically treated and sceptically scraped away.[4]

What seems even more problematic, though, is that Bunyan himself would hardly have disagreed with Sherman on the personal and national detriments of reading romances and frothy fables. In *A Few Sighs from Hell* (1658), Bunyan can be found raising very similar concerns, ventriloquising at one point the voice of a damned soul who confesses to having fatally rejected Scripture for 'a ballad, a newsbook, *George* on horseback, or *Bevis* of *Southampton*', all 'old fables' echoes of which (as many scholars have noted) are clearly (if not paradoxically) to be found within the pages of *The Pilgrim's Progress* (*MW*, 1: 332-3). Nor does Bunyan ever moderate his traditional Puritan rejection of such seventeenth-century pulp fiction. The lost soul of *A Few Sighs from Hell* takes on the more corpulent form of Bunyan's later Mr. Badman, a reprobate equally unwilling to repent of pernicious reading habits, of indulging in 'all the bad and abominable Books that he could, as Beastly Romances, and books full of Ribbauldry, even such as immediately tended to set all fleshly lusts on fire' (*MB*, p. 40). Surpassing even this condemnation, however, is Bunyan's memorable attack on the 'odious, nasty' and 'lascivious' 'beastliness' of Mr. Filth's writings in *The Holy War*, works designed to poison the minds of Mansoul's inhabitants, and which become marginalised in the text, quite literally, as 'Odious Atheistical Pamphlets and filthy Ballads & Romances', all again 'full of baldry' (*HW*, pp. 31–2).[5]

4 T.[homas] S.[herman], *The Pilgrim's Progress from this Present World of Wickedness and Misery, to an Eternity of Holiness and Felicity – The Second Part* (1682; repr. in *The Pilgrim's Progress* (Glasgow, 1736), this edition of *The Pilgrim's Progress* being in three parts with Sherman's text as Part II), from 'The Author's *Apology* for his Book', pp. viii–ix.

5 Bunyan's comments on romances and ballads can be compared with the great English Calvinist William Perkins' attitude to such reading matter. For Perkins,

There can be little doubt, then, that for Bunyan chapbook-fables and romances were both socially and spiritually damaging: they were crude and prurient distractions from the more important readings of Scripture, and of the self, in relation both to one's salvation and to one's community. This, however, again begs the obvious question: why has Bunyan, who evidently felt an overwhelming hostility to the stuff of romance, presented his allegory of salvation by grace in exactly these terms? Although this is a mouldy issue in itself, one that has been addressed and explored in a number of literary studies of Bunyan, I am not convinced that this matter has been dealt with either fully or satisfactorily. Many scholars (including Northrop Frye, Paul Salzman, and Roger Pooley) have emphasised *The Pilgrim's Progress*'s deep structural kinship with folk-tale and romance, and as far back as the 1920s Harold Golder was making similar comparisons with potential sources for the likes of Giant Despair and other romance features apparently adopted by Bunyan.[6] Recognising

> it is a sign of the great ignorance and degeneracy of the English people 'That merry ballads and books as *Scoggin, Bevis of Southampton* etc., are good to drive away the time and to remove heart qualms' (*The Foundation of Christian Religion Gathered into Six Principles* ([1590]), in Ian Breward (ed.), *The Works of William Perkins* (Abingdon, 1970), p. 143). Similarly, Richard Baxter was, in his youth, 'extremely bewitched with a love of romances, fables and old tales, which corrupted my affections and lost my time', before discovering reading matter spiritually more edifying (N. H. Keeble (ed.), *The Autobiography of Richard Baxter*, abridged J. M. Lloyd Thomas (London, 1974), pp. 5–7). For further accounts of hostility towards romances and chapbook fiction in the sixteenth and seventeenth centuries, from both Roman Catholic and Protestant writers and moralists, see Arthur Johnston, *Enchanted Ground: the study of Medieval romance in the eighteenth century* (London, 1964), pp. 32–7. Alternatively, John Milton claims to have found 'lofty fables and romances' far from 'the fuel of wantonness and loose living' but, rather, a source of 'incitements [...] to the love and steadfast observation' of 'chastity' (*An Apology for Smectymnuus* (1642), in Burton (ed.), *Prose Writings*, pp. 69–70). It must be remembered, however, that Milton also rejects outright the 'tinsel trappings' of romance in Book IX (ll. 1–47) of *Paradise Lost*, a poem in which Christian heroism is figured in terms not of chivalry but of 'the better fortitude/ Of patience and heroic martyrdom/ Unsung'.
>
> 6   See Harold Golder, 'John Bunyan's Hypocrisy', *North American Review*, 223 (1926), 323–32, 'Bunyan's Valley of the Shadow', *Modern Philology*, 27

conventions and then explaining *how* and *why* Bunyan is using them are, however, different matters altogether. In wondering why such an anti-romantic Puritan as Bunyan falls into romance in *The Pilgrim's Progress*, Golder, for instance, offers a somewhat less than ingenious solution: Bunyan was, Golder suggests, simply a benign hypocrite who, while he 'outwardly abhorred romance [...] secretly lived in a romantic world', unable and unwilling (like some kind of romance addict) to exorcise 'the memories of the old, sinful, and pleasant reading' of his youth 'out of his mind'. According to Golder, in fact, Bunyan read the Scriptures as a substitute for secular fiction: for him, we are told, the Bible itself 'was a romance'.[7]

The absurdity of this proposition, of Bunyan treating the Word in the same way as fiction, fable, or imaginative story, hardly needs to be emphasised. Nevertheless, there have been few convincing explanations since. Even U. Milo Kaufmann's classic study of *The Pilgrim's Progress and Traditions in Puritan Meditation* reconciles the imaginative basis of Bunyan's allegory with the Puritan emphasis on *logos* only by suggesting that in the Restoration a 'distinct carry-over of attitudes from secular to sacred texts' was occurring, a process

---

(1929), 55–72, and 'Bunyan's Giant Despair', *Journal of English and Germanic Philology*, 30 (1931), 361–78; Henri Talon, *John Bunyan: the man and his works*, trans. by Barbara Wall (London, 1951), pp. 172–7; Paul Salzman, *English Prose Fiction: a critical history* (Oxford, 1985), pp. 243–4; Margaret Spufford, *Small Books and Pleasant Histories: popular fiction and its readership in seventeenth-century England* (London, 1981), pp. 6–8; Roger Pooley, 'The Structure of *The Pilgrim's Progress*', *Essays in Poetics*, 4 (1979), 59–70; Northrop Frye, *Anatomy of Criticism: four essays* (Princeton, 1957; repr. Harmondsworth, 1990), pp. 144–5, 194–5, 305–07, and more generally *The Secular Scripture: a study of the structure of romance* (Cambridge MA, and London, 1976); N. H. Keeble, *The Literary Culture of Nonconformity in Later Seventeenth-Century England* (Leicester, 1987), pp. 154–5; Roger Sharrock, 'Life and Story in *The Pilgrim's Progress*', in Vincent Newey (ed.), *The Pilgrim's Progress: critical and historical views* (Liverpool, 1980), pp. 49–60; Nick Davis, 'The Problem of Misfortune in *The Pilgrim's Progress*', in Newey (ed.), *Pilgrim's Progress: critical and historical views*, pp. 182–204; Johnston *Enchanted Ground*, pp. 203–4.

7   Golder, 'John Bunyan's Hypocrisy', p. 31; 'Bunyan's Valley of the Shadow', pp. 66, 68.

which placed a new accent upon the imagination and upon 'biblical *mythos*' in Puritan Scriptural traditions.[8] Kaufmann's thesis thus suggests a compatibility between story and doctrine, fable and truth that we find in *The Pilgrim's Progress*, but it still does not explain what Bunyan is doing with romance conventions specifically. Alternatives become rather bland and well trodden at this point. Either Bunyan is simply sugaring his doctrinal pill to make his interesting but tough theology more palatable for his readers (but using the conventions of a mode of fiction of which he blatantly disapproved?), or he is just elaborating imaginatively upon those Biblical passages that lend themselves to the idea of the Christian as a warrior-hero, one who dons the Pauline armour of faith and brandishes the sword of the spirit (but which would still have some difficulty in explaining Bunyan's use of giants, castles, and enchanted lands).

Evidently, the one thing needful here is something of a reassessment of Bunyan's use of romance motifs and structures in *The Pilgrim's Progress*, and in a way compatible with his attitude towards chapbook fiction as well as with his nonconformist faith. This essay is an attempt to do just this. Far from adopting or even celebrating romance as an imaginative means of conveying spiritual truths, in *The Pilgrim's Progress* Bunyan is, I suggest, to be considered as wholly intent upon converting romance both formally and doctrinally, and re-forming (as well as reforming) it through a manipulation of its generic conventions in order to give precedence to the more profound theological truths of Bunyan's reformed faith, over and above any 'story'. In other words, *The Pilgrim's Progress* should not be considered as romance at all (Puritan or otherwise) but, rather, a rewriting of romance, one that deconstructs the genre, its features and its forms, and reconstructs them within the frame of Bunyan's own theology. By showing that *The Pilgrim's Progress* finally offers a dismantling of the fleshly seductiveness of chivalric tale-telling within the compass of Bunyan's doctrines of law and grace and of justification by faith, it becomes possible to view *The Pilgrim's Progress* as offering a radical reformation, rather than just a meek rehabilitation, of 'the fiction-

---

8   U. Milo Kaufmann, *The Pilgrim's Progress and Traditions in Puritan Meditation* (New Haven and London, 1966), p. 162.

reading impulse', through a reconstruction of seventeenth-century popular fictional modes and reading habits which amounts to little less than a form of narrative, if not cultural, iconoclasm.[9] As the title of this essay suggests, this is a radical process indeed, and not only in terms of Bunyan's overturning of story-telling conventions and expectations: it is also politically radical in that Bunyan's romancing, as we shall see, reflects and encodes nonconformist issues of persecution and liberty of conscience.

These claims can best be substantiated by reference to the three most obviously romantic episodes in *The Pilgrim's Progress*: the pilgrims' crossing of the '*Inchanted ground*', their imprisonment by Giant Despair within Doubting Castle, and Christian's battle with the dragon-like Apollyon.[10] The Inchanted ground is, of course, that most typical of folk-tale or romance motifs, and in *The Pilgrim's Progress* (as in its later counterpart *The Wizard of Oz*) it presents the final obstacle facing the pilgrims prior to entering the far more enchanting land of Beulah, and from there onwards to the Celestial City. Naturally, the introduction of a landscape which threatens to cast one into a deep and deadly slumber would seem to indicate quite clearly Bunyan's indebtedness to chapbook fiction, and the kind of story driven by such an obviously make-believe convention. Despite the

---

9   Leopold Damrosch, *God's Plot and Man's Stories: studies in the fictional imagination from Milton to Fielding* (Chicago and London, 1985), p. 174.

10 Bunyan's sources for these kinds of romance episodes (which are structurally and thematically derived from Medieval and early modern romance fiction) are, on a very specific level, uncertain. They are clearly the kinds of features we would expect to find in folk-tales generally, and especially in popular chapbook fiction of the seventeenth century. Margaret Spufford's scholarship on the subject makes this very clear. However, the romance motifs and details that Bunyan draws upon in *The Pilgrim's Progress* are akin to those included in the longer versions of Medieval romances, but which are often absent from the seventeenth-century, 'popular' chapbook versions. This raises the question of which versions of romances, like those found in *The Seven Champions of Christendom* or *Bevis of Southampton*, Bunyan is likely to have read and known, the implication being that Bunyan may have been aware of the longer and fuller as well as of the shorter, 'popular' varieties of romance. I owe this point entirely to Anne Dunan of the Université Paul Valéry, Montpellier, whose research on this subject has yet to be published.

outward indications, however, crossing the Inchanted ground becomes something quite different from an adventure of the imagination. In fact, what is so remarkable about this episode is that it actually serves to frustrate rather than to enhance narrative interest: at the moment when Bunyan's allegory suddenly becomes most like a romance (the pilgrims must keep awake or else fail in their quest), it is simultaneously and conspicuously transformed into one of the most theologically didactic parts of the whole book.

What ensues, of course, is a spiritually edifying dialogue which will, as *'The Dreamer's note'* kindly informs us, *'keep ope'* the *'drowsie slumbring eyes'* of saints on their way, a lengthy conversation in which Hopeful recounts not only his conversion but all the tenets of Bunyan's doctrine of salvation by grace, a topic which then develops into the pilgrims' uncharacteristically hostile altercation with the soteriologically erroneous Mr. Ignorance (*PP*, pp. 137–54). While the pilgrims are crossing the Inchanted ground, then, Bunyan's reader is similarly forced to traverse some eighteen pages or so of enumerated, unadulterated, and certainly unromantic doctrinal instruction. What we learn from Hopeful's conversion account (aside from its being, as Kaufmann puts it, a *'Grace Abounding* in miniature')[11] is that *'All our righteousnesses are as filthy rags, By the works of the Law no man shall be justified'*, and that *'Christ Jesus [...] is the end of the Law for righteousness to everyone that believes. He died for our sins, and rose again for our justification: He loved us, and washed us from our sins in his own blood: He is Mediator between God and us'* (*PP*, pp. 139–43). This is far from any folk-tale discourse, therefore; as Bunyan is at pains to stress elsewhere, it is one which is certainly to be distinguished from anything like the lies or fables that an *'Inchanted ground'* suggests. In *The Doctrine of Law and Grace Unfolded* (1659), for example, Bunyan recounts his religious conversion for exactly the same reason that Hopeful re-tells it again in *The Pilgrim's Progress*: 'so that thou mayest not think these things [his points of doctrine] are fables.' 'I lye not', Bunyan states emphatically in this early tract: 'these things be not fancies', for

---

[11] Kaufmann, *Pilgrim's Progress and Traditions in Puritan Meditation*, p. 228.

he would preach no 'cunningly devised fables, in telling you of the blood of Christ' (*MW*, 2: 156–60).

At the same time, however, Hopeful's words about law, grace, and the way of salvation while passing through distinctly Inchanted territory do more than school the reader in some serious spiritual truths. That Bunyan's allegorical narrative has turned into one of the baldest statements of justification by grace, and not by the law, in all his works points, in fact, to an ulterior didactic function of this episode. Such doctrinal lesson-learning is evidently needed if the reader is to appreciate exactly why the likeable and reasonable Mr. Ignorance, who fortuitously reappears in the narrative just as Hopeful is recalling 'the sence of mine own Ignorance', must finally face damnation (*PP*, p. 144). After Hopeful's conversion account, and the theological lectures on law and grace that go with it, the reader can be left in no doubt why Mr. Ignorance, a character who believes in salvation through church 'Duties' and 'obedience' to the 'Law', is thrown into hell 'even from the Gates of Heaven' at the allegory's end (*PP*, pp. 123–4, 147, 163). With its legalism emphasised in his every word, the only truly fabulous or 'Fantastical' feature to emerge from the Inchanted ground finally turns out to be nothing other than Ignorance's fatally 'False *Faith*' (*PP*, pp. 147–8).

It is precisely because Bunyan's story-telling comes to be underpinned (if not wholly subsumed) by the theological points it is necessary for him to make here that any reader's interest in the narrative-as-fable must ultimately give way to something far more doctrinal. As a consequence, Christian and Hopeful's conversation might serve to keep them awake but, as C. S. Lewis puts it, it does 'not prevent drowsiness on the part of many readers'. Indeed, he identifies this episode as one of those 'long dialogues' in *The Pilgrim's Progress* 'where we get bogged down in doctrine', surpassed only by Faithful's dialogue with Talkative which, for Lewis at least, is '[w]orse still'.[12] In saying this, however, Lewis seems to be missing Bunyan's point: it is precisely the aim of the Inchanted ground episode to discourage any reader who wishes to engage merely

---

12 C. S. Lewis, 'The Vision of John Bunyan', in Walter Hooper (ed.), *Selected Literary Essays* (Cambridge, 1969), pp. 146–53 (p. 146).

with the story of *The Pilgrim's Progress* and, as Bunyan himself puts it in the allegory's 'Conclusion', to prevent anyone from '*playing with the* out-side *of my Dream*' alone (*PP*, p. 164). What Hopeful's explicitly theological discourse does, and at the point when the narrative seems to be becoming most like a romance too, is to awaken the reader to the doctrinal import not only of this episode but of the text as a whole: it reminds the spiritually drowsy reader of the purpose of *The Pilgrim's Progress* beyond the kind of overt romancing embodied in the fabulous Inchanted ground itself. Hopeful's conversation thus functions far more significantly than as just 'an accessory to the unfolding of the plot', the means by which the pilgrims stay awake. Rather, the episode offers a clear example of Bunyan's narrative practice throughout *The Pilgrim's Progress* in preventing the reader from foregrounding fable over doctrinal lesson.[13]

With the Inchanted ground, the process of introducing a romance convention in order to discard it for a much less imaginative and much more doctrinal matter is, then, transparent. After the initial conversing, there is little at all to remind us that the pilgrims are still walking on dangerous territory: the motif, like the danger it represents, simply evaporates. In the case of Giant Despair, however, the palpable form of fable seems to be far more in danger of dominating the whole narrative, just as Despair himself easily overwhelms the captured pilgrims. Unlike the Inchanted ground, it would seem that the wayfarers' imprisonment in Doubting castle has a real potential for tearing the doctrinal fabric of the spiritualising allegory, with the reader surely and most sorely tempted at this point to respond to the 'outside' of the dream only, and to indulge in the fictive suspense and terror this most harrowing Giant provides, rather than to stop and consider anything overtly theological or doctrinal.

---

13 As Kaufmann puts it, Hopeful's dialogue with Christian at this point exemplifies an 'earmark' of Bunyan's narrative procedure as 'the arresting of the forward thrust of the action while experience is reviewed not for entertainment but for the edification of the listener' (*Pilgrim's Progress and Traditions in Puritan Meditation*, pp. 230, 231). In this case, as ever, the listener is not merely another allegorical character but the reader him- or herself.

Responding to this part of *The Pilgrim's Progress* can, therefore, be particularly problematic. Though traditionally read as evidence of the profound influence on Bunyan of chapbook romances such as *Bevis of Southampton* and *The Seven Champions of Christendom*, and consequently viewed as exemplary in terms of what makes *The Pilgrim's Progress* a unique 'Puritan folk-tale', Christian's encounter with Giant Despair (like Bunyan's allegory as a whole) is nevertheless informed by more than the desire to make harsh doctrine imaginatively pleasing. Although Christian's escape from Doubting Castle is quite memorably one of the most fabulous scenes in the narrative, Bunyan cannot allow it simply to be so. On the contrary, rather than simply making a fairy-tale out of doctrine, or marrying evangelism with romance, Bunyan, in his translation of Despair into a typical folk-story monster, is far more intent upon actively deconstructing the conventions of romance narrative than making them doctrinally agreeable, and he does this again by purposefully reconstructing them within the specifically theological framework of grace. In the case of the pilgrims' trespass along '*By-Path-Meadow*', therefore, we have the most obviously folk-tale elements (a giant, a grim castle, bone bestrewn dungeons for the captured trespassers, and a semi-comic, though conventionally malicious, gigantic spouse) reformulated to represent arguably the most important theological point of the whole text: that is, to escape from Despair one must simply apply the graceful promises of Scripture to oneself.

It seems important to note, then, that Christian's decision to follow the false way of '*By-Path-Meadow*' (an action upon which despair follows hard for this pilgrim) becomes simultaneously a decision to enter the world of romance narrative, Bunyan thereby implying that the pilgrim-reader is similarly capable of trespassing not only upon the theological territory of doubt and despair in his or her life, but upon a way of reading *The Pilgrim's Progress* itself that seems far more 'easie' (as '*By-Path-Meadow*' appears to Christian) than the 'rough' and arduous path of the text's doctrinal message (*PP*, p. 111). Along with Christian at this point, the reader of *The Pilgrim's Progress* must decide which path of interpretation to choose – the by-path of romance or the way of doctrine. It must be noted, however, that Bunyan does not make such a decision straightforward for the reader. His revisions of this episode, from the second edition onwards, involve almost four additional pages in which the 'story' is not restrained but elaborated. In introducing the character of Giant Despair's wife (a somewhat faithless and evil '*Diffidence*'), Bunyan inaugurates narrative suspense and a more conventional romance structure to this episode (both of which are missing from the original first edition) by having the dialogue between Despair and his mistress, about how to force the pilgrims into self-murder, develop gradually over a definite period of time (from '*Thursday*' to the '*Saturday*', as the marginal notes indicate (*PP*, pp. 114–17)). This additional material thus allows Bunyan to develop Christian's encounter with Despair more precisely as a story, one in which a plot is literally being hatched (to scare or to persuade the prisoners into suicide), and for which embellishment with detail becomes paramount: Despair wounds his victims with 'a grievous Crab-tree Cudgel', we are told, with the Giant now acting not autonomously but, rather, on the advice of a partner who counsels her inept husband (in the stereotypical manner of the scheming wife) while 'in bed' after a hard day's torturing (*PP*, pp. 114, 117).

Given Bunyan's own re-construction of this episode, it is easy to see how the reader could indeed, or at least to some degree, blatantly ignore the theological import of the scene and simply enjoy the tale for its own imaginative, if not comedic, sake. For all his fictively indulgent revisions, however, Bunyan clearly aims to curb such a reading nonetheless. The additions, while creatively fulfilling, afford Bunyan a new opportunity to explore despair in terms of any consequent temptations to suicide, as exemplified in the incarcerated pilgrims' discourse. Hence, Hopeful's counsel to the Christian who can only bring damning Scriptures to bear on his desperate situation ('*My soul chuseth strangling rather than life*', he cries) comes in a form reminiscent of Bunyan's pastoral address in the preface of *Grace Abounding*. Hopeful not only argues against suicide according to the fact that '*all the Law is not in the hand of* Giant Despair', but he encourages Christian to remember '*how valiant thou hast been heretofore*', in order to '*bear up with patience as well as we can*' (*PP*, pp. 115–17). Here, Bunyan's fleshing-out of the story offers him a discursive space in which he can present some very practical advice to potentially despairing wayfarers tempted '*to commit murder*' upon their '*selves*'.

At the same time, though, whole-hearted absorption in the romance of Christian's daring deliverance from Doubting Castle is in any case actually prevented by Bunyan through the fact that this is a story pivoted finally upon an anti-climax: Christian and Hopeful escape neither through guile, cunning, nor the bravery that Hopeful, at one point, resolves to '*pluck up*' should the Giant suffer from one of his '*fits*' again. Rather, they exit in a moment almost of narrative bathos, Christian suddenly remembering that he has had the means of release upon him all along: '*What a fool, quoth he, am I, thus to lie in a stinking Dungeon, when I may as well walk at liberty?*' (*PP*, p. 118).[14] This breakout is, therefore, both narratively conventional and yet unconventional simultaneously. On the one hand, Christian and Hopeful flee from Doubting Castle through a typical romance strategy: via the agency of a key that almost magically releases them from a doomed fate. On the other, however, this single means of liberation performs a role far from solely narrative, turning (quite literally) upon a more important doctrinal premise: the '*Key*' is nothing less than Scriptural '*Promise*' constantly present for the backsliding pilgrim and always available throughout his journey, despite any trespass committed (*PP*, p. 118). Whereas desperate romance heroes may typically effect their escape through the means of some enchanted artefact, Bunyan's deconstruction of romance's mythical

---

[14] Critics have long puzzled over the anticlimactic nature of Christian's and Hopeful's escape from Doubting Castle, and the detrimental effect it has upon the 'story'. For Roger Sharrock, the theological significance of Christian remembering the 'promise of faith' allows Bunyan to emphasise 'a principle of Puritan psychology' only 'at the expense of narrative plausibility' (*John Bunyan* (London, 1954; repr. 1968), pp. 85–6). For different reasons, Brian Nellist too has described this moment as the 'most outrageous of all the fractures of narrative probability' within Bunyan's allegory ('*The Pilgrim's Progress* and Allegory', in Newey (ed.), *Pilgrim's Progress: critical and historical views*, pp. 132–53 (pp. 148–9)). For other readings of this anticlimax, see Stanley E. Fish, *Self-Consuming Artifacts: the experience of seventeenth-century literature* (Berkeley, Los Angeles, and London, 1972; repr. 1974), pp. 256–8, and Vincent Newey, 'Bunyan and the Confines of the Mind', in Newey (ed.), *Pilgrim's Progress: critical and historical views*, pp. 21–48 (pp. 22–7).

conventions here comes in the form of a magic key that is nothing less than the saving Word.

It is at this point, then, that Bunyan pulls the rug from beneath any narratively vain-confident reader's feet. Far from any romancing, the encounter in Doubting Castle presents simply another comforting lesson in law and grace for Bunyan to offer his reader.[15] In these terms, the point Bunyan seems to be making here is actually one of disenchanting myths, not of creating them, as this episode serves largely to demystify that other horrendous emblem of despair in *The Pilgrim's Progress*: the Man in the Iron-Cage, shown to Christian in Interpreter's House. What Christian and Hopeful's escape from Doubting Castle effectively demonstrates is that, through the remembrance of the promises of Scripture, the narrative of that Man's incarcerating despair actually need dominate neither Christian's own soterial story nor his faith. Despair is, therefore, finally presented in *The Pilgrim's Progress* in the recognisably folk-tale form of the Giant not to present a harsh aspect of Bunyan's theology in an easily acceptable way, but in order to reinforce a de-mythification of hopelessness all along: far from being an irremovable iron-cage after all, Despair becomes a bogey-man of children's stories that can be left crippled and impotent (suffering from 'his fits') through the efficacy of the promises of the Word (*PP*, p. 118).

In order truly to understand the doctrinal significance of Christian's spiritual backsliding into despair and his release from it, the reader seems to be being asked to discard wholly the shell of folk-tale conventions in which Bunyan encases this episode in order to read the doctrine within. *The Pilgrim's Progress* hence offers not so much a sanitisation of romance within a doctrinal frame (as is often suggested of Bunyan's narrative art) as it does the complete reformation of the stuff of vulgar chapbooks – even to the extent that the folk-tale conventions Bunyan adopts are ultimately to be abandoned by any reader serious in matters of salvation. In this way, not playing with the 'out-side' of the dream, not reading for the story, does indeed seem to

---

15 For a more pessimistic doctrinal reading of Giant Despair, see John Stachniewski *The Persecutory Imagination: English Puritanism and the literature of despair* (Oxford, 1991), pp. 193–206.

be an inherent part of Bunyan's reconstruction of his reader's interpretative habits, especially at those points when that reader may feel most inclined to indulge in *The Pilgrim's Progress* as romance fiction rather than as theological allegory.

Whereas the Inchanted ground and Doubting Castle are invoked to encapsulate the most significant of theological issues in *The Pilgrim's Progress*, that other great appropriation of chivalric romance, Christian's battle with Apollyon, presents a more complicated, if not intriguing, use of fable, one which offers a similar sense of the subversion of folk-tale conventions but, interestingly, not simply in terms of a solely doctrinal reading this time. Apart from Stanley Fish (whose interpretation of this episode in Christian's journey is typically both idiosyncratic and ingenious), most commentators view the fight with Apollyon as the externalisation of a spiritual battle in Christian's soul. Read almost autobiographically, then, Apollyon can be seen as representing the temptations Bunyan describes suffering after conversion in *Grace Abounding*, albeit cast, this time, within the style of chivalric romance.[16] Because Apollyon is a common seventeenth-century type for both the Devil and for sin, as well as a figure in a story evidently known by Bunyan – *Bevis of Southampton* – it is quite easy to read this scene as an example of Bunyan's artful fusion of folk-tale narrative with spiritual instruction: in facing Apollyon, Christian becomes a knight who must overcome the temptations of his own pride clothed in the whole armour of Ephesians and armed with the sword of the spirit.[17]

---

16 See Fish, *Self-Consuming Artifacts*, pp. 235–6; Roger Sharrock, 'Spiritual Autobiography in *The Pilgrim's Progress*', *Review of English Studies*, 24 (1948), 102–20 (p. 118); John R. Knott, *The Sword of the Spirit: Puritan responses to the Bible* (Chicago and London, 1980), pp. 147–8; William York Tindall, *John Bunyan, mechanick preacher* (New York, 1934; repr. 1964), p. 40.

17 Apollyon ('Apoline' or 'Apolyn') is a demi-god worshipped by heathens in the romance *Bevis of Southampton*, as well as the 'angel of the bottomless pit' in Revelations ix.11. Alternatively, 'sin is the Apollyon, the destroyer', Jeremy Taylor, *Holy Dying* (1651), p. 25 (cited by Sharrock in *PP*, p. 322). Similarly, N. H. Keeble notes how in Benjamin Keach's *The Travels of True Godliness* (1683) and *The Progress of Sin* (1684), Apollyon represents the 'cursed prince

Such a reading is understandable, moreover, given the stylistic similarities between *The Pilgrim's Progress* and chapbook chivalry at this point. While Apollyon is undoubtedly the biblical dragon of Revelations, he also takes the unmistakable shape of a typical folk-tale 'Monster [...] hideous to behold': whereas the 'Dragon' that St. George slays in *The Seven Champions of Christendom* has 'burning winges', 'scales' which 'glistered brighter than siluer, but farre more harder than brasse', and a 'belly of the coloure of gold, but more bigger than a Tun', Apollyon is similarly 'cloathed with scales like a Fish', and has 'Wings like a Dragon, feet like a bear', 'the mouth of a Lion', and 'Fire and Smoak' pouring from his 'belly' (*PP*, p. 56).[18] It is, though, Christian's actual combat with this beast which elicits an even closer proximity to chapbook romance, having been structured, it seems, according to strict fictional conventions. We are given, for example, a prose which conveys the melee of battle through a series of clausal blows and counter-blows, with short, sharp sentences vying antithetically for dominance – Apollyon 'threw a flaming Dart', but Christian 'caught it' with his 'shield'; Christian draws 'for he saw 'twas time to bestir him; and *Apollyon* as fast made at him'. Typically, this is a style which creates suspense by having the prose mirror the thrusts and parries of mortal combat. More crucial, though, is the shape the battle takes after these initial skirmishes. Like St. George and Bevis of Southampton in their conflicts with dragons, Christian too receives a pounding at one point which, and with some obvious narrative tension, places his success against Apollyon in jeopardy: Christian suffers not only wounds to 'his *head*, his *hand* and *foot*', but 'a dreadful fall' in which his 'sword flew out of his hand', causing him 'to despair of life'. True to chivalric fashion, however, and again like George and Bevis before him, Christian 'nimbly' recovers (albeit without the aid of a holy well or an enchanted fruit-tree, as in these earlier tales) in order to give his adversary 'a deadly thrust' which,

---

of darkness', 'the Old Serpent, the Devil and Satan' (*The Pilgrim's Progress*, ed. N. H. Keeble (Oxford, 1984), p. 271).

18 Richard Johnson, *The Seven Champions of Christendom* (1596), pp. 14–18, and cited in Jennifer Fellows, 'St. George as Romance Hero', *Reading Medieval Studies*, 19 (1993), 27–54 (pp. 48–51).

The Radical Reformation of Romance in The Pilgrim's Progress

though not as 'mortal' as it sounds, nevertheless suitably vanquishes him (*PP*, pp. 59–60).[19]

However, for all that Christian's encounter with Apollyon bears even more strongly the traits of the folk-tale influence that we find in Giant Despair and the Inchanted ground, Bunyan's adoption of romance motifs here seems distinctly different from their use elsewhere in the text. Here, the fictive element cannot be so easily or straightforwardly discarded in favour of a reading of the battle as synonymous with either a doctrinal truth or the kind of spiritual trials the believer may go through during (or shortly after) conversion. Unlike the episodes with Doubting Castle and the crossing of the Inchanted ground, Christian's victory over Apollyon does not elucidate any specific theological lesson or any obvious point of doctrine that Bunyan wishes to raise (other than that, as the marginal note to James iv. 7 suggests, if you resist the devil, he will flee from you). This is not simply because the episode so effectively imitates chapbook heroism, either. Rather, the reason why this battle has a different significance from Bunyan's rewriting of romance elsewhere in *The Pilgrim's Progress* is largely because Christian's encounter with Apollyon has an index beyond the more mystical kind of spiritual temptations Bunyan describes facing in *Grace Abounding*. In fact,

---

19   In the St. George battle in Johnson's *Seven Champions* and in the Medieval romance of *Bevis of Southampton*, the heroes are saved respectively by an enchanted 'Orringe tree' (which offers St. George protection from the dragon and thus time to recover) and a holy well (into which the injured Bevis is smote and becomes healed). In some chapbook versions of the St. George story, the magic tree offers the warrior fruit which, upon his eating, restores him to full strength before continuing the fight. In Bunyan's doctrinal reworking of this motif, Christian is regenerated only after the battle by the 'hand' offering 'some of the leaves of the Tree of Life, which *Christian* took [...] and was healed immediately' (*PP*, pp. 60). For the similarities between St. George in *Seven Champions* and *Bevis* see again Fellows, 'St. George as Romance Hero' (esp. pp. 48–54), and Sharrock's note in *PP*, pp. 322–3. Compare Christian's fight with Apollyon also with other chapbook battles given in, for example, John Simons (ed.), *Guy of Warwick and Other Chapbook Romances: six tales from the popular literature of pre-industrial England* (Exeter, 1998), esp. p. 85. This edition contains a useful introduction, including a discussion of chapbook versions of Johnson's *Seven Champions* and other popular romances.

rather than just a spiritual temptation, it seems that Apollyon more precisely represents a political danger in *The Pilgrim's Progress*. This monster appears to figure forth not only persecution by the Devil or by one's own sins but, in a more controversial sense, the tyranny of conformist Restoration authorities which had imprisoned Bunyan himself and which tested nonconformist faith in a different but equally harrowing way.[20]

Despite the fact that critics as militant as William York Tindall and Christopher Hill have remained uncommonly silent about this episode, such a politicised reading of Christian's fight with Apollyon is signalled quite clearly by the verbal surface of the episode from the outset: this is a battle over loyalty in service, Christian being claimed by Apollyon as one of his own '*subjects*', while Christian's refusal to submit to this Prince's domination is couched in the overtly political terms of 'Government', 'Company', and 'Countrey' (*PP*, pp. 56–60). Moreover, although it is Christian's physical conflict with Apollyon which seems to have taken imaginative precedence in literary responses to this encounter, what is less commonly recognised is that the more important struggle between these two antagonists is actually discursive in nature, taking place in words long before any corporal combat ensues. Apollyon seems, in fact, far from willing to smite Christian at their first meeting. Instead, he attempts to 'perswade' the pilgrim to turn away from the way, with violence being an ever-present option to be used only when such rational means of persuasion fail. In this way, Apollyon appears to be adopting a distinctly Anglican strategy of attack, here: his carefully reasoned rhetoric of loyalty, possession, and mercy is one which (as the historian Mark Goldie has recently illustrated) was frequently employed in Restoration Anglican polemics to justify the coercion of separatists into the established church, to draw them in from 'the highways and hedges' (an Anglican gloss on Luke xiv. 23) by marrying 'force' with 'edification and

---

20 For a different kind of historical/political reading of this episode, see E. P. Thompson, *The Making of the English Working Class* (Harmondsworth, 1963; rev. edn. 1972), pp. 32–8.

argument'.[21] This is precisely what Apollyon (unwilling to '*lose his Subjects*' '*lightly*') seeks to do with Christian. This articulate beast offers a reasoned argument to draw the pilgrim from his way, before the latter's unreasonableness finally both compels and justifies the use of force.

It is for this reason that Apollyon at first seems so giving: '*that Countrey is mine; and I am the Prince and God of it*', Apollyon states, before addressing Christian's treachery ('*How is it then that thou hast ran away from thy King?*'), while simultaneously promising that '*all shall be well*' if Christian would only forsake his quest and '*yet turn again, and go back*' (*PP*, pp. 56–7). Christian's response is, however, nothing but an astute answering of Apollyon's own politic stratagem. This pilgrim justifies his rebellion (as any good Restoration nonconformist would) by referring his obedience to the higher authority of the divine: 'I have let myself to another, even to the King of Princes', he claims. Any turnaround now would, therefore, involve an act of treason which, for Christian at least, would be punishable on a much more profound level than that threatened by Apollyon: 'how can I go back from this, and not be hanged as a Traitor?', he asks. Christian's profession of loyalty to God's greater government naturally renders both Apollyon's more earthly promises of clemency, and his ever present and typically Anglican threat of violence ('*I would strike thee*

---

21   Mark Goldie, 'The Theory of Religious Intolerance in Restoration England', in Ole Peter Grell (ed.), *From Persecution to Toleration: the Glorious Revolution and religion in England* (Oxford, 1991), pp. 331–68 (pp. 337–8, 350). Goldie makes clear why Anglican intolerants adopted this strategy of arguing before persecuting. By raising the issue of 'whether the conscience is adequately informed, and whether we have true beliefs' (p. 353), Anglican divines could justify the coercion of nonconformists using a 'severity' which, they could argue, did not amount to persecution at all: because (for Anglicans) one could suffer persecution only for 'the true religion' (that is, for Anglican Protestantism, and not for any nonconformist, extreme, and therefore mistaken beliefs), using force on behalf of the 'true religion' is (according to the Anglican) not only 'by definition not persecution' but justifiable given that anyone unreceptive to arguments of reason and intellect in matters of religion (in this case, Christian) is necessarily incapable of judging on matters of conscience and worship, and consequently needs to be coerced 'as an act of the greatest charity' (pp. 358–9, 347–8).

now at one blow to the ground), wholly impotent. In fact, Apollyon's persuasions can offer Christian nothing at all: his promise that '*I will deliver thee*' from the '*shameful deaths*' suffered by other similarly foolhardy pilgrims is met with derision by a Christian who believes that the 'ill end' of such stout and valiant martyrs 'is most glorious in their account', and that 'their Glory' shall be made manifest at the Apocalypse 'when their Prince comes in his, and the Glory of the Angels' (*PP*, p. 58). It is perhaps not surprising, then, that when Christian confidently claims that 'the Prince whom I serve and honour, is merciful, and ready to forgive', and moreover that Christian has 'obtained Pardon of my Prince already', Apollyon 'broke out into a grievous rage': such words, it would seem, evidently and inevitably lead to blows (*PP*, pp. 58–9).

That the language of rebellion here is being set against a rhetoric of rational coercion, and that it is the dissenter's pride and humiliation which are being tested by an Anglican attempt to persuade before persecuting, seems clear to see in Christian's battle with Apollyon. That *The Pilgrim's Progress* has suddenly turned into a political (if not apocalyptic) allegory at this point can be evinced further, however, by reference to Bunyan's other writings on persecution and political authority. On one level, for example, and as Richard Greaves has noted, Christian's contest with Apollyon in *The Pilgrim's Progress* seems to be something of a reworking of Bunyan's own exchanges over loyalty and faith while on trial by Restoration authorities before his incarceration in Bedford gaol.[22] In Bunyan's *Relation of My Imprisonment* we see him, like Christian against Apollyon, not only steadfastly refusing to flee from imminent persecution ('I will not stir', he asserts) but, when arrested, having to defend his faith in contests over the interpretation of Scripture and accusations of sedition. Accused by '*Mr Cobb*' of encouraging the kind of 'insurrection' presented at the time by the Venner Rising, and which apparently 'intended no less than the ruin of the kingdom and commonwealth', Bunyan responds in a way that is both patriotic and yet, potentially at least, profoundly radical. As in Christian's verbal fray with Apollyon,

---

22 Richard L. Greaves, '"Let Truth Be Free": John Bunyan and the Restoration Crisis of 1667–73', *Albion*, 28 (1996), 587–605 (p. 590).

in which the political language of kings and government refers ambiguously both to the spiritual rule of God and the tyranny of temporal governors, here Bunyan's retort is couched in a similarly equivocal rhetoric. Like Christian, when questioned about loyalty and service, Bunyan simply professes: 'I will look upon it as my duty to behave myself under the King's government, both as becomes a man and a Christian; and if an occasion was offered me, I should willingly manifest my loyalty to my Prince, both by word and deed' (*GA*, pp. 105, 110–11, 114–15, 119–21). To which 'King' and 'Prince' Bunyan is ultimately professing loyalty here – whether to the 'King' of Christian's highway or Restoration England's Charles II – is, however, finally unclear.[23]

Such a politicised reading of Christian's encounter with Apollyon as the representative of Restoration persecution is supported, moreover, by Bunyan's particular references to this 'Monster' elsewhere in his writings. Apollyon is, for example, clearly the many-

[23] For a number of reasons, Bunyan's nonconformity is not necessarily incompatible with any profession of loyalty to Charles II. Firstly, until 1675 at least, Charles II seemed to show support for freedom of conscience, that is for the liberty of English subjects to worship separately from the Church of England. This is shown in the Declaration of Breda (1660) and, of course, in the Declaration of Indulgence made in 1672, through which Bunyan himself was released from gaol. Equally, though, Charles II would himself advocate a policy for the vigorous persecution of nonconformists in the 1680s. Secondly, however (and as Aileen Ross, Richard Greaves, and W. R. Owens have all shown), Bunyan's millenarianism envisaged a positive role for monarchs (no matter how persecutory) in bringing about the Apocalypse. This, along with Bunyan's many statements of pacifism and loyalty to the English monarchy, suggests that Bunyan's criticisms of Restoration persecution are aimed more at intolerant local magistrates and Anglican bishops and ministers than at Charles II *per se*. See Bunyan's tracts *The Holy City* (1665), *Seasonable Counsel* (1684), *Of Antichrist, and His Ruine* (1692), and also W. R. Owens '"Antichrist must be Pulled Down": Bunyan and the Millennium', in Ann Laurence, W. R. Owens and Stuart Sim (ed.), *John Bunyan and His England, 1628–1688* (London and Ronceverte WV, 1990), pp. 77–94; Aileen M. Ross, 'Paradise Regained: The Development of John Bunyan's Millenarianism', in M. van Os and G. J. Schutte (ed.), *Bunyan in England and Abroad* (Amsterdam, 1990), pp. 73–89; Richard Greaves, *John Bunyan and English Nonconformity* (London and Rio Grande OH, 1992).

headed monster of Revelations which, in *The Holy City* at least, is identified by Bunyan as a figure for the persecution of the true Church. Such an identification becomes even more pertinent, though, given that in Bunyan's *Exposition on the Ten First Chapters of Genesis* (1692), Apollyon is cited by name as being specifically aligned with the political oppression of the nonconformist faithful. According to Bunyan's typology, in this tract, true and faithful saints (such as those of Bunyan's own congregation) are figured forth in Genesis both by Abel and by his successor, Seth, the latter facing continued persecution from 'the Brood of *Cain*'. 'Observe', Bunyan therefore notes,

> That when Seth maintains his Brother's Lot, you hear no more of the Brood of *Cain*. And indeed, the way to weary out God's Enemies, is to maintain, and make good the Front against them: *Resist the Devil, and he will flie*. Now if the Captain, their King *Apollion*, be made to yield, how can his Followers stand their ground? The *Dragon*, the Devil, Satan, he was *cast out into the earth*, and his Angels were cast out with him. But how? It was by fighting: *Michael and his Angels fought with the Dragon*, and overcame him by the *Blood of the Lamb*, by the *Word of their Testimony*, and by *not loving of their lives unto the death*. (*MW*, 12: 179–80)

'Let this, in the last place', Bunyan states ominously, 'serve for Persecutors':

> That when you have cast down many Ten thousands, and also the Truth to the Ground, there is yet a *Seth*, another Seed behind, that God hath appointed to stand in the stead of his Brethren, by whom you will certainly be put to flight, and made to cease from oppressing the Truth. (*MW*, 12: 180)

What is so impressive about Bunyan's prose here is not only the forcefulness of his conviction that persecutors will be vanquished, and in a manner so reminiscent of Christian's battle with Apollyon, but also the vertiginous complication of Biblical and typological references into which Bunyan leads us. Arguing that, when faced with persecution the faithful church will be replenished just as Seth took the place of the murdered Abel, Bunyan suddenly asserts that, as evinced by Christian, 'the way to weary out God's Enemies, [...] is to maintain, and make good the Front against them', with particular reference to 'the Captain, their King *Apollion*'. With this in mind, Christian's clash with Apollyon in *The Pilgrim's Progress* evidently has its allegorical index not only in the cosmic Scriptural battles occurring in heaven before the creation of man and again at the Apocalypse, but also in the figure of Seth, the successor to the murdered Abel who will make persecutors 'cease from oppressing the Truth'. Bunyan's point is, of course, as plain as can be: only 'by fighting', he affirms, were the '*Dragon*' and 'his Angels' cast out of heaven by '*Michael and his Angels*' through 'the *Blood of the Lamb*, by the *Word of their Testimony*, and by *not loving their lives unto death*'. Because Bunyan explicitly wishes this to 'serve for Persecutors', Christian's battle with Apollyon in *The Pilgrim's Progress* can now be seen as framed by the same distinctly political (if not radical) Scriptural typology. After all, Bunyan's victorious Christian, recovering from his combat with Apollyon, gives thanks (and with much significance for persecuted Nonconformists too) that he has not only been delivered 'out of the mouth of the Lion', but, as the concluding verse states a little more apocalyptically, that '*blessed* Michael *helped me*' in the battle (*PP*, p. 60).[24]

Reading Christian's struggle with Apollyon as an allegory of the attempted coercion and suppression of nonconformity during the Restoration would not only be absolutely congruous with the kind of socio-political comment on corrupt authority Bunyan is making in his depiction of the trial at Vanity Fair: it would also support a growing critical sense that *The Pilgrim's Progress* actually has a 'more radical' dimension even than the later *The Holy War*, addressing itself specifically to the crisis over conscience evident in the late 1660s and early 1670s.[25] However while Richard Greaves has more than adequately

---

24   On the political implications of Bunyan's posthumous works see Christopher Hill, *A Turbulent, Seditious, and Factious People: John Bunyan and his church 1628–1688* (Oxford, 1988), pp. 323–334, and Richard Greaves, 'The Spirit and the Sword: Bunyan and the Stuart State', in his *Bunyan and Nonconformity*, pp. 101–26 (pp. 118–25).

25   This was the subject of a plenary lecture by Richard Greaves, '"Let Truth Be Free": John Bunyan and the Restoration Crisis of 1667–73', delivered at the International John Bunyan Society Conference at the University of Alberta in October 1995, and since published in *Albion*, 28 (1996), 587–605. Here,

illustrated that Bunyan's attitude towards persecution was one of absolute 'passive resistance', in which the saint must *actively* suffer for righteousness by willingly accepting affliction' within the compass of an 'ethic of suffering', and through which Bunyan 'insisted that this spiritual war is not offensive, but defensive', it seems that in Christian's warfare with Apollyon distinguishing between a defence of faith and a call to arms against one's persecutors, between 'Political quietism' and 'slumbering Radicalism', becomes far more difficult.[26] Although Christian's fighting is overtly out of self-defence, clearly illustrating that for Bunyan 'fidelity to the Gospel outweighed obedience to the state', both his valour and his victory nevertheless smack of something a little more radical and distinctly non-passive.[27] In the battle with Apollyon, in fact, we see the astute Christian 'draw' only at an opportune and decisive moment: 'for he saw 'twas time to bestir him'. The martial struggle that follows, therefore, bears not only the suspense and syntactical tension of a chivalric trial-by-combat, along with the cut-and-thrust of spiritual conflict, but, moreover, all the implications of a carefully timed and innately radical (if not apocalyptic) taking-up of arms (*PP*, pp. 59–60).

> Greaves suggests that 'Bunyan intended *The Pilgrim's Progress* in part to reiterate in dramatic fashion the basic case for Protestant freedom of conscience and the right of assembly that he had been espousing since 1660', concluding that '*The Pilgrim's Progress* may be more radical than *The Holy War*' in this respect (pp. 590, 604). My reading of Christian's battle with Apollyon takes Greaves's approach further. For Greaves's discussions of Bunyan's politics and the persecution of Nonconformity in relation to *The Holy War*, see '*The Holy War* and London Nonconformity' and 'Amid *The Holy War*: Bunyan and the Ethic of Suffering', in his *Bunyan and Nonconformity*, pp. 155–67 and 169–83. See also Gary S. De Krey's stimulating article, 'Rethinking the Restoration: Dissenting Cases for Conscience, 1667–1672', *Historical Journal*, 38 (1995), 53–83, and Sim and Walker, *Bunyan and Authority*, esp. pp. 89–106, 131–53. Of related interest is Barrie White, 'John Bunyan and the Context of Persecution', in Laurence et al. (ed.), *Bunyan and his England*, pp. 51–62.

26 Richard Greaves, 'The Spirit and the Sword', in his *Bunyan and Nonconformity*, pp. 110, 116, 121–5. Thompson, *Making of English Working Class*, p. 33.

27 Greaves, 'The Spirit and the Sword', in his *Bunyan and Nonconformity*, p. 102.

Bunyan's adoption of a typical folk-tale structure and language in this episode thus serves a purpose beyond the transformation of romantic reading habits that we see elsewhere in *The Pilgrim's Progress*. Here, the chivalric mode provides an ideal narrative cover for the delineation of a political battle over nonconformist faith and its practice by opportunely utilising the conventions of romance literature: knights questing for 'Truth', tyrannical Princes, and spectacular battles all offer Bunyan a certain amount of representational indeterminacy through the disguise of which he can depict a political war of conscience. Should the fictive vehicle be discarded here completely, as it must with the doctrinal Giant Despair, we could only be left with an unbending and unsettling political implication: persecution must be met with fighting. Consequently, the chivalric model, at least as it is adopted in the case of Apollyon, offers Bunyan perhaps the only way of representing the issue of the oppression of dissenting churches (and of any resistance to it) allegorically. While Christian's combat with Apollyon is potentially the most radical episode in the whole text, Bunyan is astute enough to make it excusable simply as fable.

Bunyan's appropriation of romance conventions and folk-tale structures in *The Pilgrim's Progress* should, then, be seen in terms far more complex than either the influence of his supposedly youthful indulgence in chapbook fiction or his intention to construct a 'profitable tension' between romance and doctrine.[28] Indeed, reading *The Pilgrim's Progress* as a radical reformation of romance bears more important implications for how we read and understand Bunyan's writings more broadly. On one level, Christian's chivalric encounter with Apollyon suggests an alternative to Bunyan's purely passive and pacifist response to persecution which (though confirmed in the excellent work of scholars such as Aileen Ross and Richard Greaves) seems to be in danger of becoming somewhat monolithic and unbending in current depictions of the political Bunyan.[29] While Bunyan's

---

28 Pooley, 'The Structure of *The Pilgrim's Progress*', p. 65; Roger Sharrock, 'Life and Story', pp. 56, 62; Salzman, *English Prose Fiction*, p. 243; see also Keeble, *Literary Culture of Nonconformity*, pp. 154–5.

29 See Ross, 'Paradise Regained', pp. 73–89, and Greaves, *Bunyan and Nonconformity, passim*.

passivism cannot be doubted (certainly in the early 1680s), perhaps Bunyan should be credited with less absolute inflexibility in such matters. After all, if Richard Baxter can be viewed as revealing complex and often extremely changeable radical views about the role of the magistrate and religious conscience during the Restoration, then why not Bunyan too?[30] Certainly in *The Pilgrim's Progress*, Christian's battle with Apollyon seems to have as much right to be claimed as an expression of Bunyan's attitude towards religious intolerance as the far more passive paradigm of Faithful's martyrdom at Vanity Fair.[31]

Reading Bunyan's narrative practice as a reformation, both theologically and politically, of the genre of romance fiction carries other significant ramifications for the way we perceive Bunyan's aims and methods as a writer. In presenting folk-tale episodes in *The Pilgrim's Progress* that serve largely to undo themselves before our very eyes (as with the Inchanted ground and Giant Despair), Bunyan can be viewed as an author with a highly sophisticated concept of what narrative can and should do. Bunyan is concerned, quite arguably, with aspects of narration which we might otherwise consider distinctly modern or even postmodern: Bunyan seems to be interested in anti-narrativity, in constructing stories which are difficult to enjoy as stories, rather than simply marrying popular fictive modes to a Puritan moralism. The reason for this, however, is always pastoral and theological. Because Bunyan's doctrine of salvation by grace is clearly the be-all and end-all of his works, any interest in 'story' must come second to this. Bunyan's narratives deliberately discourage any reading for the 'historical part' because they seek instead to teach the reader about a faith which is far from 'historical', but saving.[32]

---

30 This was the subject of William Lamont's plenary lecture given at the Second International John Bunyan Society Conference at the University of Stirling in September 1998, now published as the second essay in this volume.

31 Greaves in particular stresses Faithful's martyrdom as exemplary of Bunyan's ethic of passive suffering: see Greaves, 'Let Truth Be Free', pp. 601–5.

32 In *Grace Abounding*, Bunyan's pre-conversion legalism and unregeneracy is conveyed, at one point, by his way of reading the Bible just for the stories: 'I betook me to my Bible', he explains, 'and began to take great pleasure in reading, but especially with the historical part thereof: for, as for *Pauls* Epistles,

None of this, however, is unproblematic. The fact that *The Pilgrim's Progress* has been adopted within the literary canon (presumably because it is all too *easy* to read just for the story) must say something about Bunyan's failure to rewrite romance adequately enough in this instance. Given Thomas Sherman's criticisms of Bunyan's book being too 'frothy', and given also Bunyan's evident sensitivity to such opprobrium (incorporated in the prefaces of his later works), it is not surprising that Bunyan's own sequels to his allegory of the pilgrim are very different types of books indeed. Difficult to read, overtly doctrinal, anti-narrative, and distinctly non-romantic, it is hardly conceivable to think of *The Life and Death of Mr. Badman* or *The Holy War* as ever being or becoming children's classics. Equally, although Part II of *The Pilgrim's Progress* may seem at times little more than an explosive exaggeration of the romance of its original (with countless giants and monsters being slain with an almost jovial ease by Great-heart and his crew), nevertheless the purpose of this sequel is evident: it is to make clear the doctrinal import of the first, to defend the first part's romancing by confirming its popularity (despite any criticisms of its style), and to remind the reader (first and foremost) of its forerunner's theology.[33] The 'valiant Worthies' of Part II (such as Great-heart and Valiant-for-Truth) are thus, more than anything, followers of Christian's Christian example: they re-enact his spiritual journey, making good the front against Apollyon in the same heroic, chivalric fashion.[34]

and Scriptures of that nature, I could not away with them, being as yet but ignorant either of the corruptions of my nature, or of the want and worth of Jesus Christ to save me' (*GA*, § 29). Similarly, Richard Baxter too delighted in 'the historical part of the Scripture' in his ungodly youth, having 'neither understood nor relished much the doctrinal part and mystery of redemption' (Keeble (ed.), *Autobiography of Baxter*, p. 5). For Bunyan on 'historical faith', see *MW*, 2: 134.

33 On this subject see especially N. H. Keeble, 'Christiana's Key: the Unity of *The Pilgrim's Progress*', in Newey (ed.), *Pilgrim's Progress: critical and historical views*, pp. 1–20.

34 Great-heart and the others, we should not forget, at one point dispatch a particularly Apollyon-like '*Monster*', which repeatedly terrorises the reformed town of Vanity Fair in 'his certain Seasons' (surely a reference to the continued persecution of the saints in the 1680s): *PP*, pp. 277–8.

Perhaps not all the blame, however, should be placed upon Bunyan's failure to reform romance enough in his first allegory. The consequent reception of Part I of *The Pilgrim's Progress* as a precursor to the novel and as an imaginatively didactic children's story says as much about its subsequent de-radicalisation as a nonconformist text as it does about the cultural climates in which such misreadings have been authorised since the text's initial publication.[35] It seems crucial, therefore, to ask why, in the literary history of *The Pilgrim's Progress* so far, readings of it simply as romance or Puritan folk-tale have served to erase both its textual complexities and its political subversiveness. The relationship between Bunyan's 'sweet truth' and his 'sweet fiction' is narratively more sophisticated and politically more important than such traditional approaches would have today's reader of *The Pilgrim's Progress* believe.

---

35   For accounts of this cultural appropriation of *The Pilgrim's Progress*, see Michael A. Mullett, *John Bunyan in Context* (Keele, 1996), pp. 191–2. For a more detailed study of the reception of *The Pilgrim's Progress* and its social implications see also Barbara A. Johnson, *Reading Piers Plowman and The Pilgrim's Progress: reception and the Protestant reader* (Carbondale and Edwardsville, 1992).

6

Vera Camden
'That of *Esau*': Hebrews xii.16, 17 in *Grace Abounding*

G. B. Harrison observes that John Bunyan's life was spent trying to achieve self-expression. I would go further to say that Bunyan's life was spent trying to achieve a self through expression – trying to find a language sufficient to render his soul.[1] Bunyan's autobiography chronicles the process by which he discovers and takes possession of his being through the appropriation of the divine *Logos*. He inscribes himself as the product of God's Word: he measures his life in terms of his conformity with God's Word. The Word of God alone gives the Puritan autobiographer's language meaning, endurance and even existence itself.

I have argued elsewhere how the drama of Bunyan's youth derives from his frantic dependence on the false props offered by the languages of heresy he encounters in the 'world turned upside down' of seventeenth-century England; and how, in particular, Bunyan recognizes that his youthful profanity was a search for authority: 'I knew not how to speak unless I put an Oath before, and another behind, to make my words have authority ' (*GA*, §28).[2] Here, I take as given that there is a troubled homology between Bunyan's early blasphemy, his later Bibliolatry and his ultimate, mature belief. The Word which exists negatively in the inversion of blasphemy becomes a plausible, positive threat when Bunyan encounters the women of the

---

[1] G. B. Harrison, *John Bunyan: a study in personality* (1928; repr. North Haven CT, 1967), p. 27.

[2] Vera J. Camden, 'Blasphemy and the Problem of the Self in *Grace Abounding*,' *Bunyan Studies*, 2 (1989), 5–22; Christopher Hill, *The World Turned Upside Down* (London, 1972).

church at Bedford whose use of Scripture in their conversation precipitates his conversion and throws his narrative into the dark and frantic record of his attempt to bring himself into conformity with the Word of God. (*GA*, §37). His record of this conversion is notoriously neurotic, the writings of 'a sick soul' in the words of William James, but the dynamics of his obsessions have not sufficiently been discussed to explain how and why his text locks into patterns of unrelenting redundancy.[3] I want, then, to confront the central dynamic of repetition in Bunyan's prose in *Grace Abounding*, taking as a point of departure, Bunyan's obsessive temptation to 'sell his Saviour' which becomes so all-consuming that he claims he had almost no other thought than this (*GA*, §134). This temptation 'lay upon me for the space of a year, and did follow me so continually, that I was not rid of it one day in a month, no not sometimes one hour in many dayes together, unless I was asleep' (*GA*, §133). At the same time, Bunyan links this most 'grievous and dreadful temptation [...] to sell and part with this most blessed Christ' with the figure of Esau who is transported from the Old Testament account of his rivalry with Jacob into the new typology established in Hebrews xii.[4] Esau, as we recall, sold his birthright for 'a mess of pottage.' Bunyan has sold his Saviour. The attack of Bunyan's conscience over selling Christ ('You have sold your Saviour!') and the attack from the Hebrews verse ('for that Scripture did seize upon my Soul, *Or profane person, as Esau, for one morsel of meat sold his Birth-right; for you know how that afterwards, when he would have inherited the blessing, he was rejected*' (*GA*, §141)) provide the two notes for Bunyan's tortured refrain – one which in fact consumes the bulk of his narrative in *Grace Abounding*. I will focus on this problem of Bunyan's attachment to the Hebrews xii.16, 17 verses about Esau and make meaningful his own linkage of this 'selling' of the Saviour to these verses, suggesting that the Calvinist soteriology which plunges

---

[3] William James, *The Varieties of Religious Experience* (New York, 1919), p. 154.

[4] See Genesis xxvii; for a discussion of Bunyan's understanding of typology and the definitions of the Baptist preacher Benjamin Keach, see Charles W.. Baird, *John Bunyan: a study in narrative technique* (Port Washington NY, 1977).

Bunyan into the obsession with these Scripture verses is only worked through in *Grace Abounding* by a revelation of Biblical context which Bunyan comes to, ironically, through repetition.

In his introduction to *Grace Abounding* Bunyan's editor, Roger Sharrock, emphasizes that while Bunyan's narrative follows the broad conventions of seventeenth-century spiritual autobiography (1. Early providential mercies 2. Unregenerate life: sin and resistance to the Gospel 3. Conversion 4. Calling 5. Account of the ministry), Bunyan stands out from among his contemporary autobiographers by protracting the conversion stage of his account into virtually two-thirds of his text, effectively capitalizing on his terrified anxiety over his election (*GA*, p. xxi).[5] It is during his conversion stage, a period he calls his tribulation, that the verses from Hebrews xii.16, 17 run through Bunyan's mind like a song that is playing incessantly, to be picked up midstream in the narrative. While Bunyan never in fact quotes the full passage from Hebrews xii, I will cite it here in its entirety – the sentence begins with verse 14 and ends with verse 17:

> 14 Follow peace with all men, and holiness, without which no man shall see the Lord;
> 15 Looking diligently lest any man fail of the grace of God; lest any root of bitterness springing up trouble you, and thereby many be defiled;
> 16 Lest there be any fornicator, or profane person, as Esau, who for one morsel of meat sold his birthright.
> 17 For ye know how that afterward, when he would have inherited the blessing, he was rejected: for he found no place of repentance, though he sought it carefully with tears.

It is the last two verses of this passage which Bunyan fragments into pericopes to fall like 'hot thunderbolts' upon his conscience: concluding all of his 'thoughts, fears, and cogitations'. Harrison describes them running like 'dull tom-toms [...] through his brain'.[6] They exact their demands on his body as well as his soul. 'All this while I was tossed to and fro, like the Locusts, and driven from trouble to sorrow;

---

5   See also Vera J. Camden, '"Most Fit for a Wounded Conscience": the Place of Luther's "Commentary on Galatians" in *Grace Abounding*', *Renaissance Quarterly*, 50 (1997), 819–49.
6   Harrison, *John Bunyan*, p. 20.

hearing always the sound of *Esau*'s fall in mine ears' (*GA*, §158). Bunyan's temptation over selling Christ takes on an equivalent incantatory flavour. He attempts, for instance, in his various revisions of later editions of the text to rhythmically reiterate those words which haunt him: '*Sell Christ for this, or sell Christ for that*' (*GA*, §135). And lest his readers not feel the audible impact, Bunyan adds in a later revision of this passage, '*sell him, sell him*' – even though he had already included this exact refrain in the very next paragraph: 'Sometimes it would run in my thoughts not so little as a hundred times together, Sell him, sell him, sell him' (*GA*, §136). Writing thus merges with memory.

Bunyan's telling and re-telling of his battle with this crime of selling Christ and Esau's fall is often tedious. Boyd Berry charts Bunyan's 'turmoil of regression and despair' within five pages, demonstrating that Bunyan thrice constructs lists of sinners to whom to compare himself and thrice repeats the same conclusion which he had in fact reached six pages earlier. Bunyan's arrangement 'brilliantly records the motions of a mind going around in the circles of despair'. He regresses and relapses,

> He dithers for thirty seven pages over the possibility of 'selling Christ,' a metaphor which, if it clearly articulated his fascination with Judas, does not very clearly suggest precisely what Bunyan wanted or feared to do. At the end of the second section he remarked: 'Now I shall go forward to give you a relation of other of the Lord's dealings with me' ... He is right; for all these pages he has not gone forward at all. He has teetered. Occupying such a substantial portion of the middle of the book, this section blunts our sense of Bunyan's progress monumentally, blurs his conversion [...] and the resultant inconclusiveness eddies out into the whole of his work.[7]

Brainerd Stranahan similarly notes that the verses about Esau's reprobation become to Bunyan a personal 'thorn in the flesh'; he counts at least thirty repetitions of this text, most of which occur within the

---

7   Boyd Berry, *Process of Speech: Puritan religious writings and Paradise Lost* (Baltimore, 1976), pp. 198–200.

range of some ten pages.[8] Berry and Stranahan rightly recognize the brilliance and the boredom evoked by this account and that this is the problematic centerpiece of Bunyan's autobiography. Yet neither critic attempts to analyze why Bunyan's obsession with selling Christ and the Hebrews verse do so precisely 'eddy out' into his apprehension of the whole of Scripture.

Henri Talon, an early biographer of Bunyan, does attempt such an explanation and in so doing makes a challenging observation about Bunyan's remarkable victimization by Scripture texts. Writes Talon,

> The truth is that Bunyan was possessed of the spirit and natural disposition of the mystic, but these could not expand because his religious convictions stultified their growth. Protestantism, by harnessing faith to the Scripture, usually puts a check on the introversive movement of the soul, and deflects religious feeling into other channels. The individual, aware that he had no role of his own in justification but that the drama is *played* out outside him, lays the main emphasis on the sacred texts whence he draws his convictions; he inclines his flight toward external ends.[9]

Talon here attempts to explain briefly and simply Bunyan's obsession with certain Bible verses, and with the Esau verse in particular. He develops insight into Bunyan's undermining of his own introversion through the external structure of Scripture. And this is a valuable insight insofar as it faces the extent to which this introverted autobiography does at the same time have a tenacious feeling of inhibiting human, let alone mystic, release. Bunyan's autobiographical language writhes under the control exerted by periphrases and his repeated invocation of the Scriptures. Bunyan's movement toward Biblical texts does not, however, finally signify a flight outside the self – or at least not a successful one. On the contrary, the bulk of Bunyan's musings over the Scriptures do *themselves* take on an *inward* cast. If Bunyan's expression of his Scripture-based Protestantism shows us nothing else, it reveals how determined by his own subjectivity the believer's experience of the Scriptures may be, how deeply intro-

---

8   Brainerd P. Stranahan, 'Bunyan and the Epistle to the Hebrews: His Source for The Idea of Pilgrimage in *The Pilgrim's Progress*', *Studies in Philology*, 79 1982), 280.

9   Henri Talon, *John Bunyan: the man and his works* (London, 1951), p. 306.

spective the Puritan mind became under the guardianship of the Word. For Bunyan, the figure of Esau becomes sedimented with the weight of private association. When verses of certainty and promise 'bolt in upon' him, enabling him to make 'a stand in his spirit,' the encouragement of the revelation may last only for the space of two or three hours. The word of hope 'tarries not' because it is consumed,

> chiefly by the aforementioned Scripture, concerning *Esaus* selling of his Birthright; for that Scripture would lie all day long, all the week long; yea, all the year long in my mind, and hold me down, so that I could by no means lift up my self; for when I would strive to turn me to this Scripture, or that for relief, still that Sentence would be sounding in me, *For ye know* (*GA*, §145).

And much later,

> It would not be so little as an hundred times that he that did labour to break my peace. O the combats and conflicts that I did then meet with as I strove to hold by this word, that Esau would flie in my face, like to lightening: I should be up and down twenty times in an hour (*GA*, §191).

During Bunyan's protracted conversion period, the Word of God becomes, to use an image from *The Life and Death of Mr. Badman*, 'a Nose of Wax' (*MB*, p.127) to be twisted according to his own tortured preoccupations. All of Scripture must be weighed in the balance against 'that of *Esau* ' (*GA*, §205), even as Bunyan's sin of 'selling Christ' must be weighed against the sins of all his Biblical predecessors. Bunyan counterbalances, *credits*, all of Scripture, according to its agreement with that 'Sentence' in Hebrews, '*For ye know, how that afterward* [...]'. (*GA*, §148). The structure of the Scripture, as of the legacy of sin and salvation, becomes concentric, circling around the central image of Esau which articulates Bunyan's experience of himself. The one constant which rings in Bunyan's ears like the drums of Diabolus is Esau's transgression: 'hearing always the sound of *Esau*'s fall in mine ears, and of the dreadful consequences thereof' (*GA*, §158). Bunyan becomes the passive observer of his fate. 'Wherefore still my life hung in doubt before me, *not knowing which way I should tip*' (*GA*, §175). The image of the scales submerged in this passage becomes explicit later in the text as Bunyan snaps off and weighs each 'piece' of Scripture: 'for this about the sufficiency of grace, and that of *Esau*'s parting with his Birthright, would be like a pair of scales within my mind, sometimes one end would be uppermost, and sometimes again the other' (*GA*, §205).

The man whose chief sins in his youth were dancing, bell-ringing and mesmerizing blasphemy, thus mirrors in his discourse what Terrence Hawkes has recently described as the 'non-discursive power of repetition'. Hawkes writes:

> Perceptible only out of the corner of our cultural eye, repetition's inherent capacity for sudden unnerving derailment shares a covert, 'unofficial' status with matters such as gesture or 'tone of voice', those inevitable concomitant of speech which, although necessary, nevertheless embody a scandalous potential for undermining – or ironicising – the overt 'meaning' of any utterance.

Hawkes goes on to explain that there is a covert 'difference' at the heart of every repetition which enables it to tap into an 'uncanny' cache of energy, 'capable of projecting it into a realm of implication beyond the reach of words'.[10] Repetition conjures the physical and within itself stores an energy that lies beyond articulation. In Bunyan's case we see this played out first in his youthful circling around the bell tower and steeple of the Elstow church, prefiguring, it seems to me, the compulsive idiolect of his coming tribulation over Esau and the 'selling of Christ'. As Sharrock describes it, Bunyan's youthful episodes each partake of his 'obsession with violent physical activity, especially pushing and pulling' (*GA*, p. 138 n53), and this obsession predominates in his later experience with the Scriptures. Emile Marcault, another early critic of Bunyan, has shown how Bunyan preferred metaphors of the physical over the intellectual or emotional to capture his spiritual impressions:

> Il apparait que l'experience religieuse de Bunyan se traduit spontanement, comme si l'imagination, cherchant dans la vie psychique normale des symboles adequats a l'impression ineffable, se trouvait conduite par un pente naturelle, vers l'experience sensorielle, a l'exclusion de l'experience emotionelle ou intellectuelle.

---

10   Terrence Hawkes, review of Hillel Schwartz *The Culture of the Copy*, in *The London Review of Books*, 19 (31 July 1997), 16.

Marcault's early analysis of the sensory nature of Bunyan's writing is one of the few studies which attempts to articulate the intensely physical nature of Bunyan's language and his spirituality. Bunyan was temperamentally sensorial: following his conversion he surrendered the lusts of the flesh for spiritual passion, but Marcault argues, 'Son temperament n'a pas varie: il y a eu en lui transposition non transformation'.[11] He substitutes the spiritual for the physical in conversion but his apprehension remains sensorial. His elaborate resistance to bell-ringing becomes, in this sense, homologous to his reeling from the Esau verses. A close look at Bunyan's struggle at the Elstow bell tower will help interpret the central action of the autobiography, tangling as it does around those verses which 'lay like planks' in his mind. The bell tower episode marks a transition between the world of action and the world of thought in *Grace Abounding*. While Bunyan attempts to honour the Sabbath and to give up bell-ringing, he cannot stop the fantasy:

> I thought such a practice was but vain, and therefore forced my self to leave it; yet my mind hanckered, wherefore I should go to the Steeple house, and look on: though I durst not ring. But I thought this did not become Religion neither, yet I forced my self and would look on still; but quickly after I began to think, How, if one of the Bells should fall (*GA*, §33).

The coy flavour of this passage reminds one of the daredevil Bunyan who plays at the mouths of adders, testing Providence (*GA*, §12). The *thought* of what might happen if the steeple door should fall 'shakes' his mind.

> So after this, I would yet go to see them ring, but would not go farther than the Steeple door; but then it came into my head, how, if the Steeple door it self should fall, and this thought [...] would [...] continually so shake my mind, that I durst not stand at the Steeple door any longer, but was forced to fly, for fear it should fall upon my head (*GA*, §34).

His phobia enacts in miniature his struggle to let go of physical pleasures on the one hand and to embrace the anxious, inward-looking

---

11 Emile Marcault, 'Le 'Cas Bunyan' et le Temperament psychologique', *Melanges litteraires et philosophies* (Clermont-Ferrand, 1910), pp. 217–19.

doctrine of Puritan circumspection on the other. In the conflict between impulse and restraint, Bunyan relinquishes activity. His body becomes so subject to motor inhibition that he feels stricken even when he takes 'a pin or a stick, though but so big as a straw; for my conscience now was sore, and would smart at every touch' (*GA*, §82).

The intensity of Bunyan's conflict around bell-ringing has inspired in many of his readers a bafflement, bordering on contempt, similar to that which his obsession with the Hebrews verse has generated. Harrison, for instance, remarks, that his pleasures, the 'normal fancies of any young man', need not have been invested with so much neurotic guilt.[12] John Brown, Bunyan's Victorian biographer, drily observes, 'Bunyan has hitherto taken pleasure in the somewhat laborious diversion of ringing the bells in the tower of Elstow church. He began to think this was wrong, one does not quite see why'.[13] The obsessional aspects of his narrative have tended to distance readers who recoil from his 'neurotic guilt'. I argue however that these early conflicts help interpret Bunyan's conversion tribulations as well as his eventual freedom.

Psychoanalyst Sandor Ferenczi observed in a clinical context that the connection between the repression of obscene images and words and the eventual repression of 'all kinds of conscious fancying' leads to what he calls the 'dread of the imagination'. Like the Puritan divine, William Ames, who likens the use of fancies and metaphor itself to fornication, the psychoanalyst also notes the relationship between mental imaging and physical activity: 'even the imaginative representation of quite indifferent objects' is instinctively avoided in an attempt to control forbidden lusts. In terms quite relevant to Bunyan's narrative, Ferenczi describes how the attempt to suppress all forbidden thought may provoke a 'phobia of movement', a 'reaction-

---

12   Harrison, *John Bunyan*, p. 17.
13   John Brown, *John Bunyan: his life, times and work*, rev. Frank Mott Harrison (London, 1928), p. 62. On the level of culture, of course, it is the association of this Sabbath violation with calling the townspeople to the games which fuels Bunyan's repudiation of these pleasures: see George Offor (ed.), *The Complete Works of John Bunyan*, 3 vols. (London, 1860–62), 1: xii; and Jack Lindsay, *John Bunyan: maker of myths* (New York, 1969), pp. 79, 232 for an early Marxist reading of the meaning of the tolling bells in the marketplace.

formation against a strong but suppressed, motor tendency to aggression'.[14] Bunyan's attempt to control his fancies and restrain his body is dramatized in *Grace Abounding*. He becomes, in an awkward, literal embodiment of the doctrine of election, the theatre for God's active Word. In the drama around 'that of *Esau*', Bunyan's actual assent to his haunting desire to sell Christ is interior and, for all of his fierce resistance, utterly passive.[15] If his previous resistance to evil suggestion had mobilized even his body to push and thrust away intrusion, here, as he lies vulnerable in his bed, he is overcome. The will seems to be as prostrate as the body in this central scene of his crime of selling Christ.

> one morning, as I did lie in my Bed, I was, as at other times, most fiercely assaulted with this temptation, *to sell and part with Christ*; the wicked suggestion still running in my mind, *Sell him, sell him, sell him, sell him*, as fast as a man could speak; no, not for thousands, thousands, thousands, at least twenty times together, but at last, after much striving, even until I was almost out of breath, I felt this thought pass through my heart, *Let him go if he will!* and I thought I felt my heart freely consent thereto (*GA*, §139).

As the language of this passage suggests, Bunyan has indeed been assaulted by an unholy suggestion and finally consents in a 'disclaiming locution'.[16] He is at once agent and observer, deflecting his inner assent 'I felt this thought pass'; 'I thought also I felt my heart freely consent'. He is more enervated than ever – now by inner guilt instead of external assault: 'thus getting out of my Bed, I went moping into the field' (*GA*, §140). For two years he feels utterly bound as if he, like Judas, had bartered Christ openly in the market of his

---

14 Larzar Ziff, *Puritanism in America* (New York, 1973), p. 14; Sandor Ferenczi, 'On Obscene Words', in *Sex in Psychoanalysis* (New York, 1960), p.148.
15 Bunyan's text describes in the extreme the loss of sensory/motor skills in the 'place of action' typical of the normal child whose attention to the development of his performance on a verbal/conceptual plane 'demands some temporary loss of co-ordination in his accommodation to the physical and practical universe' (Jean Piaget, *The Construction of the Reality of the Child* (New York, 1954), p. 361).
16 See Peter J. Carlton, 'Bunyan: Language, Convention, Authority', *English Literary History*, 51 (1984), 17–32.

murderers. Bunyan's submission to this sin was inevitable; he possesses what Richard Baxter calls the unsound soul's 'vehement urgency' to commit the very sin they most abhor – 'as if something within them urged them to speak such or such a blasphemous or foolish word and they can have no rest unless they yield'.[17]

Freud describes a similar pattern in one of his cases of a blasphemer. The syntactical arrangements which emerge from the patterning of conscious and unconscious thoughts is reminiscent of Bunyan's war of words. Freud writes,

> The words he wanted to use in his prayer were, 'May God protect her', but a hostile 'not' suddenly darted out of his unconscious and inserted itself into the sentence; and he understood that this was an attempt at a curse... If the 'not' had remained mute, he would have found himself in a state of uncertainty and would have kept on prolonging his prayers indefinitely. But since it became articulate he eventually gave up praying. Before doing so, however... he tried every kind of method for preventing the opposite feeling from insinuating itself.[18]

As Bunyan's Satan has mocked, 'cease striving'. Sin is inevitable, the flesh irresistible. Only after Bunyan does, like a bird shot from a tree, succumb to temptation does 'withal' the crucial Sripture passage seize him to articulate his mercenary transaction. Many Sriptural precedents will be invoked here, but the passage from Hebrews xii.16, 17 in which Esau is condemned for selling his birthright for 'a mess of pottage' will reiterate Bunyan's sense that he, likewise, has bartered away his place in Christ's family.

Bunyan stresses that his sin was 'point blank' against the saviour: his sin was not, as in the Old Testament, merely a sin against the 'Law'. It was against an intimate and in this sense is a violation of a covenant bond: a rupture in a relationship not a violation of a code. 'This thought I, is my very condition; once I loved him, feared him, served him; but now I am a rebel; I have sold him, I have said, Let him go if he will' (*GA*, §166). Bunyan links this selling with murder (*GA*, §§154, 155). He compares his sin to Joseph's being sold and

---

17   Cited by Roger Sharrock, *John Bunyan* (London, 1968), p. 175.
18   Sigmund Freud, *Collected Papers*, 5 vols., trans. Alix and James Strachey (New York, 1959), 3: 377.

with the very murder of Christ: 'I was convinced that I was the slayer; and that the avenger of blood pursued me, that I felt with great terrour' (*GA*, §218). This, however, does not settle things: Bunyan ties this crime to 'that of Esau' as a final curse since it is Esau whose cry of repentance will come too late and not be heard. If Bunyan has earlier bemoaned that he could 'scarce shed a tear' (*GA*, §105) now he is certain that his supplications are not heard even if he floods heaven's gate. The verse from Hebrews has a special authority. 'Still that saying about *Esau* would be set at my heart, even like a flaming sword, to keep the way of the tree of Life, lest I should take thereof, and live' (*GA*, §178).

In context, chapter xi of Hebrews is, in fact, a glowing testimony to the faithful witnesses from the Old Testament. This chapter intends to show the members of Christ's New Jerusalem that the Old Testament stories of the faithful and the condemned can be appropriated by the elect of Christ. Yet Bunyan fastens onto verses from the *following* chapter, in which the Lord's discipline, judgement and condemnation of the unfaithful are lifted as threats and promises. Bunyan is convinced that he, like Esau, is among the faithless. Esau in this typology becomes the type of the disenfranchised son, doomed to struggle from the womb. The Genesis narrative of Jacob and Esau tells of Jacob's deception of his brother. Writes one commentator of Isaac's blessing: 'To some extent the words are independent of the speaker [... Isaac] did not mean to bless Jacob; but once the fateful syllables have been pronounced, he is helpless'. Further, 'the story is told without a hint of disapproval, and, as in the birthright story, there may even be a suppressed delight in the cunning of the ancestor of the nation'.[19] The parental favouritism is not then for Jacob but on the contrary for Esau. The Christian interpretative tradition surrounding this narrative – culminating in key passages from Romans as well as Hebrews – tells us about the seemingly arbitrary exclusion of Esau from his natural legacy. In Christian typology, this narrative is without exception understood as a model of God's prophetic and predestined choice of his people. The writer of Hebrews in this sense changes the

---

19 Frederick Carl Eiselen, Edwin Lewis, David G. Downey (ed.), *The Abingdon Bible Commentary* (Nashville NY, 1929), p. 236.

emotional tenor of the Genesis account. In Hebrews, Esau reckons the worth of his birthright cheaper than 'one morsel of meat' and afterwards when he 'would have inherited the blessing', he was rejected. The Hebrews account claims that Esau's second loss of his blessing is consequent on the first violation. Esau who was the first born and the favourite son of his father, lost his sacred right because of his appetites and lost his blessing because of the father's rejection; whereas, in the Genesis account, Esau's loss of Isaac's blessing is due to the disguise and deception of Jacob, spurred on by his mother. Isaac, then, is as trapped as his first born son by this scheme. For the Puritan reader, what comes through in these passages is brought out explicitly in Romans and Hebrews: the mind of God is arbitrary and incomprehensible. This God defies human desire and even human will. Esau's story carries the weight of the paradox of predestination and free will. Jacob was destined to usurp his brother's destiny and sustain the line of Israel: at the same time, Esau is condemned for his choice. For Bunyan the threat is clear. He is as helpless as Esau. Like Esau he has been driven by appetite but determined by divine will. He responds to the pathos of the psychological rivalry, so affectively portrayed, but even more dramatically for his own narrative, Bunyan's responds to the doctrine of uncompromising predestination of Romans. He positively stalls at the threat of the 'unforgivable sin' portrayed in Hebrews. Bunyan fastens onto the Scriptures which shows the human effect of this arbitrary decree (as it is written, 'Jacob I have loved, but Esau I have hated' (Rom. ix.13)). It shows the appetite but also the remorse of Esau's experience of God's will. The portrayal of Hebrews is in fact so dramatic in its depiction of both abjection and desire that Luther, whose credo is constructed on the proclamations of Romans, wished the book out of the Bible rather than confront the picture of a remorseful yet abandoned believer.

In her critique of the 'violent legacy of monotheism', Regina Schwartz has provocatively coined the 'Noah complex', whereby the sons compete for the father and in guilty rage turn in rivalry and murderously on one another. She claims this complex is more influential and more fundamental than Freud's Oedipus complex. Though one might wonder why the father/son drama must take precedence over Freud's primal horde competition for the mother, Schwartz's reading of the key Biblical narratives of Cain and Abel, Jacob and Esau, in the light of this Noah complex does yield insight into the power these narratives have over Bunyan. These eponymous Biblical narratives are placed squarely within a dominant Biblical premise of scarcity and exclusion. Because Jacob has only one blessing the brothers must compete; they ultimately confound one another's destiny. Schwartz stresses the affective impact of this story: 'In a narrative that is otherwise terse [...] the writer suddenly evinces pathos dramatically [...] Overcome Esau virtually stutters his pain [...] When Esau heard his father's words, he burst out with a loud and bitter cry and said to this father, 'Bless me – me too, my father'.[20] In the Genesis account Esau loses both birthright and blessing; these incidents are related as it were prospectively in the prophesy of the Lord to Rebecca and Isaac regarding Jacob's usurping his brother's place but they are related retrospectively in the Christian Scriptures as the writer of Hebrews relates these incidents causally. In Hebrews the motivation for Esau's loss is not prophesy but in his own profanity. The shift is crucial and in its inward motion, tying this historical narrative to an inward state of sin, profanity and fornication, ultimately, of human desire.

It is the burden of desire which motivates Bunyan's obsession with this verse. Profoundly identified with Esau, Bunyan too virtually stutters through the Hebrews account of this narrative. The actual rivalry is of less importance for Bunyan than the role of Esau as the son who is driven, indeed predestined by a 'profane' impulse to sacrifice his birthright (Genesis xxx). For the writer of Hebrews, Esau's impulsive surrender to Jacob's cunning becomes a type of contaminating 'root of bitterness' in the fledgling church. For Bunyan, the admonition of this passage takes on a resonance whose power initially derives from its Scriptural admonishment, but chiefly it clusters around Bunyan's own rewriting of Esau's significance. Bunyan's text will begin to participate in a kind of private typology. If the formula which ran 'sell him, sell him', chased Bunyan into sinful consent, the Scripture from Hebrews similarly takes on an animated, tormenting

---

20 Regina M. Schwartz, *The Curse of Cain: the violent legacy of monotheism* (Chicago, 1997), pp. 80, 81.

stature in his mind, virtually taking over, for a time, Satan's role as antagonist in this narrative:

> And withal, that Scripture did seize upon my Soul, *Or profane person, as Esau, who for one morsel of meat sold his Birth-right; for you know how that afterwards when he would have inherited the blessing, he was rejected, for he found no place of repentance, though he sought it carefully with tears*, Heb. 12:16,17 [...]
> These words were to my Soul like fetters of Brass to my Legs, in the continual sound of which I went for several months together (GA, §§141, 143).

The language of conversion is thus riddled with the rhetoric of torture:

> I should be as tortured on a Rack for whole dayes together (*GA*, §136).
> how I would rather have been torn in pieces, than found a consenter thereto (*GA*, §150).
> Now again should I be as if racked upon the Wheel; when I considered, that [...] I should be *so* bewitched (*GA*, §152).
> my torment would flame out [...] yea, it would grind me as it were to powder (*GA*, §155).

Such examples could be, as Bunyan would say, multiplied twenty times. His language evidences what Michael Foucault has called a 'proliferation of meaning' at the end of the Gothic world whereby the forms of human perception of reality as well as the orthodox images which provided spiritual interpretation of that reality become so overburdened with 'attributes, signs, allusions that they finally lose their own form'. 'Meaning is no longer read in an immediate perception, the figure no longer speaks for itself; between the knowledge which animates it and the form into which it is so transposed, a gap widens. It is free for the dream.' In terms very helpful to understanding Bunyan's uses of the Esau verses, Foucault contends that the collapse of familiar Patristic correspondence between Old Testament prophecy and New Testament fulfilment instances in the post-Gothic world no prophecy but 'equivalence of imagery' which releases the individual's or the culture's fantasy of participation:

> The passion of Christ is not prefigured only by the sacrifice of Abraham; it is surrounded by all the glories of torture and its innumerable dreams; [...] forming beyond all the lessons of the sacrifice, the fantastic tableau of savagery,

of tormented bodies, and of suffering. Thus the image is burdened with supplementary meanings and forced to express them. And dreams, madness, the unreasonable can also slip into this excess of meaning.[21]

Bunyan's own fantasy of participation in the Biblical narrative of Esau's condemnation itself takes an 'unreasonable' turn in his curious yet compulsive omission of one word from his countless citations of the Hebrews xii.16, 17 verse. Bunyan avoids providing, in his myriad citations of the Esau verse, a full reference to the entire Hebrews xii.16, 17 verse which actually reads, as we have seen, 'Lest there be any fornicator, or profane person, as Esau, who for one morsel of meat sold his birthright'. Bunyan fills in every phrase of this verse, citing portions of it, adjusting words and syntax slightly at times, but he unwaveringly avoids quoting the one word 'fornicator' in his otherwise vast descent into the constructed, obsessive fantasy of this passage. Not even when he is 'over' the torment of these verses at the end of his narrative, does he include this offending word in his text. Such a concentrated omission of a word from a sentence otherwise interminably present to his mind must be significant.

Freud's discussion of the language patterns of his notable cases provide interesting parallels to Bunyan's curious involvement with this Scripture and may help interpret this omission. The mode of defence whereby the content of memory is kept from the patient's consciousness, says Freud, is a 'distortion by omission or ellipisis'. Through the choice of 'indefinite or ambiguous wording' the content of a verbal idea can become utterly distorted or misunderstood, only to take on, in the mind of the user, a separately developed identity based on the obsessional distortions:

> After being misunderstood, the wording may find its way into the patient's 'delirium', and whatever further processes of development or substitution his obsession undergoes will then be based upon the misunderstanding and not upon the proper sense of the text. Observation will show however that the delirium constantly tends to form new connections with that part of the matter and wording of the obsession which is not present in consciousness.[22]

21 Michel Foucault, *Madness and Civilization: a history of insanity in the age of reason* (New York, 1965), p. 18.
22 Freud, *Collected Papers*, 3: 362, 381.

The shorthand 'that of *Esau*' conjures a private realm of associations which divorce the verse from its meaning; yet, the content and context of the verse will continue to provoke Bunyan's associations.

It is of course tempting at this juncture to raise the familiar question of Bunyan's youthful improprieties about which he is so guilty and yet so obscure. 'Fornication' of course looms large in this world turned upside down populated by Ranters and other radicals who used their religion as an occasion for the flesh and, as Bunyan reminds us, during his conversion years, 'his flesh was in its prime'. Further, Bunyan did not need to indulge in any sinful acts to be tormented by guilt in this world. 'Those that were never guilty of fornication are oft cast into long and lamentable troubles by letting Satan once into their fantasies, from whence till objects are utterly distant, he is hardly got out; especially when they are guilty of voluntary self-pollution.'[23] Bunyan's omission of this word shows his dread of the flesh and his imagined if not actual guilt for sexual urges. It is in this sense a textual trace to interpret the intensity of his fixation on Esau and offer a framework for our appreciation of his eventual freedom from this verse.[24]

Hebrews xii.16, 17, 'that of *Esau*', assumes the status of what Freud calls, in his famous 'rat-man' case, a 'complex-stimulus word' whereby 'fate' hands the patient the grotesque story of the rat and he, as if in an 'association' test reacts to it with his obsessional ideas and makes it his own.[25] Bunyan's own homely emblem book metaphors describe how 'men's delusive notions' can distort the Scriptures. 'To this [...] mens Notions do compare,/ Who seem to breathe in none but Scripture Air./ They suck it in, but breathe it out again,/ So putrified, that it doth scarce retain/ Anything of its native Excellence./ It only serves to fix the Pestilence/ Of their delusive Notions' (*MW*, 6: 255). Such passages show us the physical traces, the legacy of the body, as it were, in the highly redundant 'debate' of Scripture within Bunyan at the height of his conversion. It is mistaken, it seems to me, to be so attentive to the 'theology' of Bunyan's battle with Scripture passages

---

23 Jack Lindsay, *John Bunyan: maker of myths* (New York, 1969), p. 15.
24 See Camden, 'The Place of Luther's "Commentary"'.
25 Freud, *Collected Papers*, 3: 353.

that one loses sight of their affective and bodily impact – on Bunyan the writer and reader. In this sense Bunyan's transposing of the physical into the spiritual through language becomes virtually a bodily rite. Language itself takes on a materiality in much the same way as metaphor operates in the language of schizophrenia; words take the place of things. Freud's psychotic patients treat 'concrete things as though they were abstract'.[26] Bunyan's anxiety forces him into a kind of madness when he must search the world of objects for signs of his spiritual fate; when, for instance, the very tiles of the roof conspire for his condemnation, when the Scriptures themselves become animated in their status as objects on the page (*GA*, §§187, 207).

Hillel Schwartz's recent work on the 'culture of the copy' provides insight into the relationship of the body to discourse and serves well to introduce a fuller discussion of the covert, healing gestures contained within repetitious passages in *Grace Abounding* which have confused if not irritated his readers over the years. Linking swearing to repetition, Schwartz writes,

> We have been drawn/repulsed by echolalia and coprolalia because these are the boldest symptoms of aping and parroting, disorders of repetitions to which we fear we are most susceptible. At railway stations in the Netherlands in 1990 were large colored posters of a parrot [... giving] bold advice: 'don't be a parrot. Don't swear.' If swearing makes us parrots, becoming parrots damns us to the animality – or humanity – of imitation or repetition. Our linguists and information theorists tell us that redundancy is crucial, *crucial*, to communication. Historians recount the liberating effects of profanity as personal protest and social subversion, from Martin Luther to Lenny Bruce.[27]

Hillel Schwartz here identifies the obsessionality which is provoked in a work like *Grace Abounding* – conjuring as it does the primitive 'tom-tom' of dull reiteration – but he also reminds us of the function of reiteration in all human communication. Both aspects – the physical, tic-like quality of the curse as well as the liberating, incantatory power of the blessing – are at play in Bunyan's repetition of the

---

26 Freud, 'The Unconscious', *Collected Papers*, 4: 136.
27 Hillel Schwartz, *The Culture of the Copy: striking likenesses, unreasonable facsmiles* (New York, 1996), p. 303.

Esau verse. Both aspects are rooted in what Schwartz calls imitation and redundancy.

Contemporary psychoanalyst Arnold Modell recognizes how the past, though often unknowable or unavailable to the patient, is rooted in 'eradicable affective experiences that, through metaphor, are brought to the present time'. Such metaphors do often – and here we see Bunyan's rootedness in 'that of Esau' – become 'frozen' or 'foreclosed', that is, repetitive. 'Repetition compulsion [...] is thus to be seen [...] as a kind of memory disorder and inability to recontextualize experience'.[28] In this sense it is significant that Bunyan's obsession with the story of Esau reaches a climax when it is marshalled alongside companion verses from Hebrews each of which corroborates for him the certainty of judgement against him. In the following passages he supplements the offending passage from Hebrews xii.16, 17 with other passages which are thrilling in their despair:

> but now were brought those sayings to my minde, *For it is impossible for those who were once enlightned and have tasted of the heavenly gift, and were made partakers of the holy Ghost, and have tasted the good Word of God, and the Powers of the World to come; if they shall fall away, to renew them again unto repentance* Heb. 6 (4–6). *For if we sin wilfully after that we have received the knowledge of the truth, there remaineth no more sacrifice for sin, but a certain fearful looking for of Judgement and fiery Indignation, which shall devour the adversaries*, Heb.10. (26–7). Even as Esau, who for one morsel of meat sold his Birthright; for ye know how that afterwards, when he would have inherited the Blessing, he was rejected; for he found no place of repentance, though he sought it carefully with tears, Heb. 12. (16–17) (*GA*, §196).

The verses which he groups all reiterate the doom of the backslider; yet this bleak cross-section from Hebrews does show Bunyan beginning to open up his single minded fixation on the one verse from chapter xii to Scriptural context. His own haunting refrain is put into something of a textual centre, something of a framework within the entire book of Hebrews. His gesture toward context is particularly notable as he has prior to this point avoided any suggestion of the thrust of chapter xii which is, again, in fact a record of the faithful –

---

28 Arnold Modell, 'Reflections on Metaphor and Affect', *The Annual of Psychoanalysis*, 25 (1997), 223.

with Esau as the one only condemned. Even more to the point, however, Bunyan is propelled by this moment of context into a strange set of heretical fancies. Since he despairs of regaining the favour of Jesus whom he has sold, he reasons that 'there was now but one way; and that was, to pray that God the Father would be the Mediator betwixt his Son and me, that we might be reconciled again' (*GA*, §181); but, his line of thought continues, it would be easier for God to make a new world or write a new Bible than thus to reverse the order of the Godhead. And in his despair he puts himself back in the centre of the triangle: he has parted with his Saviour and yet does not share with the rest of humankind in his persecutions of Christ: for 'my sin was not of the nature of them for whom he bled and died'. For Bunyan, alone, Christ must come and die anew (*GA*, §184). Passive abnegation of all personal worth coupled with an ecstatic grandeur about one's evil thus creates an ingenious and nearly impenetrable avoidance of salvation.

> Time and again the Puritan preachers, practiced physicians of the soul thought they were, had to admit defeat in the face of this wilful obstinacy. The victim completely abandons himself to all his morbid fears and takes a perverse delight in resisting all attempts to save him in his uniqueness as the one soul whom not even God himself can save.[29]

Such ecstatic refusal begins to feel very much like Freud's notion of Thanatos. 'These thoughts would so confound me, and imprison me, and tie me up from Faith, that I knew not what to do: but Oh thought I, that he would come down again' (*GA*, §185). In an ironic echo of Christ's promise that heaven and earth will pass way before his Word will, Bunyan laments, 'I knew assuredly, that it was more easie for Heaven and Earth to pass way than for me to have Eternal Life' (*GA*, §184).

In *Beyond the Pleasure Principle*, Freud formulates that the repetition compulsion is a component, a sign, really, of the death instinct. In his account we can recognize the contours of Bunyan's experience: 'Such a compulsion sometimes completely dominates a person's life, giving the appearance of some daemonic force at

---

29   Owen Watkins, *The Puritan Experience* (London, 1972), p. 42.

work.'[30] It is the libido which saves us from the death instinct. However, as J. Preston Cole points out in his critique of Freud's late work, Freud cannot account for the triumph of the libido, lacking as he does any principle of transcendence. 'For Freud it is a matter of returning to an original organic state, namely death, and thus repetition compulsion is about the death instinct which is beyond the pleasure principle.'[31] Indeed, Bunyan's increasing movement toward such recontextualizing of the haunting Scripture passages eventually brings him out of the death grip exerted by the offending Hebrews passages. However, in order to understand this recontextualization of his experience of the Scriptures, it seems to me we must introduce another understanding of repetition not available – or even acceptable – to Freud in his notion of repetition compulsion as heralding the death drive. It is this understanding which is offered in Søren Kierkegaard's allegory *Repetition*.

For Kierkegaard, repetition is a return to a primitive state, but, as he shows in the character of Constantius from his allegory, that return is a confession of perpetual pilgrimage and an invocation of history which provides a way of transcending the self. Kierkegaard makes it clear that for him repetition is entirely a matter of the individual's internal experience – it is not outward, it is not a matter of external movement: 'Since it is within the individual it must be found, and hence the young man [Constantius...] keeps perfectly still'.[32] Like the stricken Bunyan, Constantius 'keeps perfectly still' externally so that internally he is able to 'move' religiously. Religious movement, then, is made possible through repetition, which is a return to origins, an ideal of creation and of the divine. Kierkegaard's repetition is a return to a *status pristimus* before original sin; it is existential in the sense of being present to the self ('I am myself again'). It is teleological: a return rooted in a vision of the future. Though Constantius does not

30   James Strachey (ed.), *The Standard Edition of the Complete Psychological Works of Sigmund Freud*, 24 vols. (London, 1953–66), 18: 65, 34 (hereafter cited as *SE*); J. Preston Cole, *The Problematic Self in Kierkegaard and Freud* (New Haven, 1971), pp. 39, 277.
31   Preston Cole, *The Problematic Self*, p. 277.
32   Søren Kierkegaard, *Repetition: an essay in experimental psychology*, trans. Walter Lowrie (New York, 1964), pp. 14, 382.

make a clear religious movement in the text, its prospect is what gives this text meaning. As such it provides a counterpoint to Freud's vision. For if Freud helps us to understand the neurotic core of Bunyan's obsessionality, if his hermeneutic tools offer us a means to understand the highly charged yet bewildering content of this maze of Biblical association and private typology, then Kierkegaard's allegory offers the libidinal vision which finally accounts for Bunyan's escape from the death instinct which according to Freud drives repetition compulsion. 'Perhaps the keenest insight of all Freud's discoveries about the dynamics of the human mind is his conclusion that the compulsion to repeat is the patient's way of remembering [...] The repetition becomes a kind of existential recollection and since recollection is essential to a successful therapy, the repetition can be used as a therapeutic tool'.[33] It seems obvious that Bunyan's cycles of repetition carry this therapeutic function: the repeating of his sense of sin and condemnation is his way of remembering and ultimately becomes his way of 'working through'. Contemporary psychoanalyst Odilon De Mello Franco recognizes the libidinal, indeed, transcendental urge which may be contained in repetition. He remarks, in terms helpful to understanding Bunyan, that

> the [religious] objects of the internal world and the unconscious fantasies whereby they are represented and assigned meaning are subject to a drive-related dynamic that is not only repetitive but tends to transform. Such a conception is possible if the unconscious is seen as a matrix that constantly generates meanings. Furthermore, this is the quality that makes possible the phenomena we call working through in analysis.[34]

While it is impossible and hopelessly anachronistic to imagine precisely how Scripture substitutes for memory for Bunyan, how this or that verse becomes for him a substitute term for unconscious or repressed trauma, it is possible to work with the textual traces he has left us and to follow the patterns of his narrative obsessions as well as

---

33 Preston Cole, *The Problematic Self*, p. 193.
34 Odilon De Mello Franco, 'Religious Experience and Psychoanalysis: From Man-As-God to Man-With-God', *International Journal of Psychoanalysis*, 79 (1998), 129.

his testimony of recovery. In so doing we take Bunyan at his word, understanding his suffering and it origins in a distracted state which, 'ridiculous' as they seem to others or indeed are 'in themselves', were yet, at the time, inescapable, 'tormenting cogitations' (*GA*, §184) until the very repetition which was like a prison becomes, creative 'return' within the Word.

Bunyan is delivered from his obsession with 'that of *Esau*' when he permits himself to become the site of a kind of 'Holy War' of the soul between the word of the law – that of Esau – and the word of grace – that of Christ. Bunyan makes plain that he wants the Scriptures to collide within him: 'to come together upon me' settling the matter once and for all, permitting him to move forward. As he reaches this climax the verses which volley in him become objects, large in their physical capacity to meet the body of the Hebrews verses: 'but me thought this word *able*, was spoke so loud to me; it showed such a *great* word, it seemed to be writ in *great* letters' (*GA*, §203). This '*great* word' banished his fears in a way he never had felt before. The Esau verse, however, still lingers in the back of his mind: no sooner does comfort pass than 'that other about *Esau* returned upon me as before', turning his soul into 'a pair of Scales again, sometimes up, and sometimes down, now in peace and anon in terror' (*GA*, §207). Reaching a crescendo within himself and his narrative, Bunyan experiences the pull of contrary sets of scriptures which lay claim to his soul. And in direct contradiction, indeed, in battle with 'that of *Esau*' there is raised up within him a counter verse from 2 Corinthians xii.19 which tells him 'My grace is sufficient'. Again, this 'piece of Scripture' achieves a kind of materiality which allows Bunyan to animate these words and propels him into a battle of words. The key words become more 'plastic', more material as other words of hope struggle within him in a tug-of-war for his soul: 'one morning [...] that piece of a sentence darted in upon me. *My grace is sufficient.*' Bunyan is always the passive theatre of this struggle: he waits for God to apply the 'whole sentence' to his soul. The ritual of waiting becomes predictably elaborate was Bunyan counts and measures the size and scope of the various words which visit him:

> that he gave, I gathered; but farther I could not go [...] *My grace is sufficient for thee, my grace is sufficient for thee, my grace is sufficient for thee*; three times together; and O, me-thought that every word was a mighty word unto me; as *my*, and *grace*, and *sufficient*, and *for thee*; they were then and sometimes are still, far bigger than the others be (*GA*, §206).

In the height of his crisis he attempts to break the offending Hebrews verses, those sentences alone which 'keep me out of heaven'. He wishes to reduce these words to their status as signifiers, condense three or four verses to three or four words and, in so doing, undo their infinite signification. Like Luther, he wishes them 'out of the Book'.

> I should also think this with myself, why, How many Scriptures are there against me? There is but three or four, and cannot God miss them, and save me for all of them? Sometimes again I should think, O if it were not for these three or four words, now how might I be comforted! And I could hardly forbear at some times, but to wish them out of the Book (*GA*, §208).

God's great words are as threatening and as thrilling to him as the bell-tower. He encircles them with 'sweet' glances and waits for their lightening bolts upon him. Freud writes extensively about how displacement allows patients to duplicate through repetition the same compulsive attitude toward otherwise unrelated objects, people or activities.[35] The point to emphasize here in connection with Bunyan's elliptical prose is that his appropriation of the Scriptures falls into a line with both his lifelong urge to blaspheme and his youthful appetite for profane pleasures. Language is inextricably linked to the body. The passive language Bunyan uses to describe the war of words within him mirrors his description of his passively selling Christ:

> And I remember one day, as I was in diverse frames of Spirit, and considering that these frames were still according to the nature of the several Scriptures that came in upon my mind; if this of Grace, then I was quiet; but if that of *Esau*, then tormented; Lord thought I, if both these Scriptures would meet in my heart at once, I wonder which of them would get the better of me?

Bunyan gets his wish:

---

35   Freud, 'Dostoevsky and Parricide', *Collected Papers*, 5: 241.

> Well, about two or three dayes after, so they did indeed; they boulted both upon me at a time, and did work and struggle strangely in me for a time; at last that about *Esaus* birthright began to wax weak, and withdraw, and vanish; and this about the sufficiency of Grace prevailed, with peace and joy (*GA*, §212).

Bunyan describes this internal struggle as a tug of war with Satan 'he at one end and I at the other. Oh, what work did we make! [...] we did so tug and strive: he pull'd and I pull'd' (*GA*, §215). Hillel Schwartz records the lament of the 'ticquer' in terms which feel much like Bunyan's striving: 'my mind and body are constantly going at it [...] Both are incredibly strong like two bulls with locked horns, and if one gets the upper hand, I tic. If the other gets the upper hand I go crazy with these thoughts and urges'.[36]

Notwithstanding the victory of the words of grace in this tug of war, 'that of *Esau*' still haunts Bunyan: 'I could not quite be rid thereof, 'twould everyday be with me.' He is, however, at a turning point here and it is worth our deliberation to consider how he works through the barrier of this verse. 'Wherefore' he says, 'now I went another way to work' (*GA*, §216). What is this other way?

The Scriptures which speak to Bunyan's striving to put away his guilt emerge from Joshua xx, which describe the 'slayer' who finds refuge from his avenger because his crime was committed 'unwittingly':

> I was convinced that I was the slayer; and that the avenger of blood pursued me, that I felt with great terrour; only now it remained that I enquire whether I have the right to enter the City of Refuge [...] I thought verily I was the man that must enter, for because I had smitten my Neighboor *unwittingly and hated him not afore-time* [...] and against this wicked Temptation I had strove for a twelve-moneth before; yea, and also when it did pass thorow my heart, it did so in spite of my teeth (*GA*, §§218–19).

Bunyan's guilt over his selling Christ has encompassed no less than his conviction that he is the slayer of the Saviour. What the passage from Joshua seems to do for Bunyan at this juncture is to draw together in one explicit focus the narrative's underlying concern with blood sacrifice and to bring it into conjunction with Bunyan's private

---

36 Schwartz, *Culture of the Copy*, p. 304.

guilt. Bunyan's guilt is linked to a fantasy of harm enacted on the body of Christ and then suffered on his own body:

> Yet I saw my sin most barbarous, and a filthy crime, and could not but conclude [...] that I had horribly abused the holy *Son* of *God*: [which ...] did work at this time such a strong and hot desire of revengement upon my self for the abuse I had done unto him, that, to speak as then I thought, had I a thousand gallons of blood within my veins, I could freely then have spilt it al at the command and feet of this my Lord and Saviour (*GA*, §192).

Bunyan's experience of the pain so central to the Christian myth reminds us of Freud's chart of the economics of masochism whereby the fantasied violence against the father is performed upon the son:

> In the Christian myth man's original sin is undoubtedly an offence against God the Father, and if Christ redeems mankind from the weight of original sin by sacrificing his own life, he forces us to the conclusion that this sin was murder. According to the law of retaliation which in deeply rooted in human feeling, a murder can be atoned only my the sacrifice of another life; the self-sacrifice points to a blood-guilt.[37]

Bunyan's avenger of blood is God: but he may take revenge upon himself and so preserve the love of the Father. In an earlier fantasy, Bunyan had participated in Judas' fate, diving headlong into *Aceldamon*, the field of blood, bowels bursting, breastbone splitting wide (GA, §164). The super-ego, explains Freud, takes over the punitive attributes of the father and the ego becomes passive in relation to its demands. 'The superego becomes sadistic, and the ego becomes masochistic, that is to say, at bottom passive [...] A great need for punishment develops in the ego, which in part offers itself as a victim to fate, and in part finds satisfaction in ill-treatment by the superego (that is, in the sense of guilt)'.[38] The thousand gallons of blood Bunyan would spill recompense the blood he exacted in selling the Saviour. His remorse is felt by Bunyan in the body: 'The glory of the Holiness of God did at this time break me to pieces, and the Bowels and compassion of Christ did break me as on the Wheel; for I could not

---

[37] Freud, *Totem and Taboo*, *SE*, vol. 13: 198.
[38] Freud, 'Dostoevsky', *Collected Papers*, 5: 232.

consider him but as a lost and rejected Christ, the remembrance of which was as the continual breaking of my bones' (*GA*, §244).

Bunyan's fears of selling, slaying, blood guilt and sacrifice lead us to understand the power of the Joshua verse over Bunyan. This verse allows him the chance to at once acknowledge his crime but also to find forgiveness on the basis of his striving against the crime. In effect Bunyan finds refuge in the passivity which had defined his encounter with God since the days of his legalism in which he imagined himself trampled by priests and prelates. He defends himself as he had described himself: disclaiming and unwitting. His reading of the Joshua passage, following as it does the crisis of the Scriptures' confrontation within him, provides him with a way of forgiving his crime. Bunyan takes the words of his blasphemous thought of selling Christ 'at their largest and give them their own natural force and scope, even every word therein' (*GA*, §216). In this parsing of the particulars of his thought he finds protection in his phrasing 'Let him go if he will'. Bunyan explains that he left it up to the Lord's 'free choice' and takes comfort in the promise from Hebrews viii.5 that '*I will never leave thee nor forsake thee*' (*GA*, §216). And this new way to work on the words of his thought 'works' for Bunyan. Within the space of five paragraphs he reasons himself out of his conviction that he has sold his Saviour. His reasons are as follows: 1) his sin was not premeditated but committed 'unwittingly': 'against this wicked Temptation I had strove a for a twelve-moneth before; yea, and also when it did pass thorow my heart it did it in spite of my teeth' (*GA*, §219). 2) His sin could not have been the infamous 'unpardonable sin' because, unlike those hardened sinners, he had received comfort from God through the Scriptures subsequent to his crime. Bunyan explains that he recognized the comforts of God after much 'deliberation' (*GA*, §222): crucially, he does not record that deliberation. He does not need to. He hastens to his conclusion of the Esau episode. Thus the this holy war is won when Bunyan finally forces himself to face the context of the Scriptures surrounding that of Esau, to 'weigh their scope and tendence' (*GA*, §222) and to understand by such a grasp of scriptural context – its historical scope and its allegorical tendency – that his sin has not, finally, the unforgivable sin alluded to by the writer of Hebrews:

> I durst not venture to come nigh unto those most fearful and terrible Scriptures, with which all this while I had been so greatly affrighted and on which indeed before I durst scarce cast my eye, (yea, had much ado an hundred times to forbear wishing of them out of the Bible; for I thought they would destroy me) but now, I say, I began to take some measure of encouragement to come close to them, to read them, and consider them, and to weigh their scope and tendence.
> The which, when I began to do, I found their visage changed [...]
> When I had thus considered these Scriptures, and found that thus to understand them was not against but according to other Scriptures; this added to my encouragement and comfort (*GA*, §§222–3, 228).

He takes an unprecedented active stance in his narrative and sets to searching 'in the Word of God, if I could in any place espy a word of Promise'. The Esau verses upon which he had before been scarcely able to cast his eye are now approached rationally: 'I found their visage changed; for they looked not so grimly on me as before I thought they did' (*GA*, §223). Within the space of merely five paragraphs (§§224–8), Bunyan describes how he resolves and interprets his new understanding of the critical passages from Hebrews and does so by placing them in the context of other Scriptures from Hebrews and also, crucially, from other Biblical passages. The language which he uses to describe this experience of resolution is important, signalling as it does, Bunyan's sense that the battle of words within him has ceased now that he is able to see and to feel that the Scriptures 'agree' within him. He is able to weight one Scripture according to another and to experience their agreement. 'When this I has considered these Scriptures, and found that thus to understand them was not against, but according to other Scriptures; this [...] gave a great blow to that objection, to wit, *That the Scriptures could not agree in the salvation of my Soul*' (*GA*, §228). He moves through this section with rare efficiency; indeed, he progresses. The verses which had 'kill'd me and stood like a spear against me' are now considered in the context of Esau's sins and distinguished from his own. In fact, the whole thrust of these few paragraphs is to separate himself from the identification with Esau. For the first time in his entire experience of the offending verses he refers to the Genesis account of the story of Isaac, Jacob and Esau as figures from Biblical history. And then he comes 'again' to the Apostle 'to see what might be the mind of God in a New-Testament stile and sence concerning *Esau*'s sin'. When Bunyan does repeat the verse itself, he includes an explication of the entire chapter (*GA*, §226). Each of these gestures serves to reverse the incantatory power of the verses in his imagination and prepares the way for his final embrace of the doctrine of Christ's imputed righteousness which may be identified as the true climax of *Grace Abounding* and which follows directly upon his making peace with 'that of *Esau*'.[39] He tells us that the worst of it is over; he is ready to move on as he does exactly in the next paragraph. 'And now remained only the hinder part of the Tempest, for the thunder was gone beyond me' (*GA*, §228).

The moment of his resolution, of his movement from guilt to relief is, rather like the death of Bunyan's Mr. Badman, oddly anti-climactic after such an ordeal. It is surprising how few critics consider this breakthrough in Bunyan's relation to the Scriptures. It falls rather flat in the roller-coaster of his narration but that is, perhaps, its power. He does not claim miraculous reversals, voices from heaven. His depiction is settled, optimistic but quiet. Neil Keeble remarked to me in conversation that the resolution of this obsession is not fully registered and perhaps cannot be fully explained; it simply happens. This is because the work of resolution has, I contend, already occurred in the tedious reiterations which have, precisely, eddied out into the whole of his narrative. As psychoanalyst Franco points out, repetition allows for the 'process of assignment and reassignment of meaning. The transformations of psychic representations, through repetition and association, turns psychic representation into a permanently open process'. The associative processes of language create representations which, once established, invite other representations to become 'superimposed upon them'. Old meanings create new meanings. On the 'transcendence' of this inherently symbolic dynamic, he continues, 'The symbol not only refers us to the symbolic elements within one and the same structure but also opens up for us a practically inexhaustible symbolic prospect. There is no end to the process of assigning meaning'.[40] Thus, if in *Grace Abounding* Bunyan seeks, in

---

39 See Camden, 'The Place of Luther's "Commentary"'.
40 Franco, 'Religious Experience and Psychoanalysis', pp. 128, 129.

Roger Sharrock's apt phrase, utterly to 'abolish literature' so as to render absolute the experience of God's Word in his life, to find himself in the Word, then his spiritual autobiography nakedly and unadornedly renders his soul's transformation under the weight of that Word. This is what Bunyan himself calls his 'plain style':

> *I could also have stepped into a stile much higher then this in which I have here discoursed, and could have adorned all things more then here I have seemed to do: but I dare not:* God *did not play in convincing of me; the* Devil *did not play in tempting of me; neither did I play when I sunk as into a bottomless pit* [...] *wherefore I may not play in my relating of them, but be plain and simple and lay down the thing as it was* (*GA*, pp. 3–4).

The text must be inscribed, 'read onto' the heart and mind of the believer in every particular and its operations are often anguished and repetitive indeed. Yet the Bible verses which coil around Bunyan's tentative formulations of his experience in the narrative have during the period of his affliction the same feeling of magical authority which had so addicted him to blasphemy in his youth. If in his youth John Bunyan had, as he tells us, set hardened sinners a-trembling by his grievous swearing and cursing, so portions of Scripture will set him a-trembling. If 'stuffing' his speech with profanity had given him illusive power in his youth, so stuffing his discourse with Scripture will make him a centre of authority terrifying even to himself.

Bible verses become like talismans to Bunyan, wrenched from any coherent theology and transported from place to place in his text. Yet this agonized dependence will eventually deliver the key to his imaginative flourishing and his genius as both writer and preacher. In *Grace Abounding* Bunyan moves from *eisegesis* to *exegesis*: from an obsessive reduplication of himself in the 'wax' of the Scriptures to an imaginative and intellectual experience of grace-unbounded. Blasphemy is built on belief, just as repetition compulsion has at its core a fantasy of difference, a covert 'self-healing' attempt at mastery in its most apparently mindless repetitions. The chronicle of Bunyan's growing *rapprochement* with the Scriptures constitutes his 'turning again' in *Grace Abounding*. In the Scriptures he discovers a language whose demanding diversity and plentitude finally enables and educates his literary production as well as his extensive theological treatises.

7

NANCY ROSENFELD
'So counterfeit holy would this Divel be':[1] Debate and Disinformation as Satanic Strategies in Milton and Bunyan

Grace Abounding to the Chief of Sinners was first published in 1666; the first edition of *Paradise Lost* appeared in 1667. Although it is doubtful that Milton read *Grace Abounding* while writing *Paradise Lost*, the ideas which shaped both works were pervasive. Christopher Hill notes that Milton 'knew of the discussions and speculations which went on in London congregations and taverns'[2] during the Interregnum, and would quite possibly have participated in them. Both Milton and Bunyan, as Hill points out, had shared a sense of an impending millennium. The breakdown of censorship and ecclesiastical controls characterizing the period of the Civil War exposed them to the possibilities of open expression of ideas, both political and religious; this newfound freedom may in itself have seemed millennial to the young preacher[3] as well as to the older poet-publicist.[4] By the same token, the reinstitution of censorship and the widespread persecution of nonconformists accompanying the Restoration would have been one cause of the profound disappointment felt by both writers on being forced to come to terms with the fact that the millennium had

1 *GA*, §138.
2 Christopher Hill, *Milton and the English Revolution* (London, 1977), p. 109.
3 Maxine Hancock has noted that 'Bunyan was initiated by sermon-hearing and intense discussion into the Calvinistic community of nonconforming English Puritanism as his interpretive community': 'Bunyan as Reader: The Record of *Grace Abounding*', *Bunyan Studies*, 5 (1994), 74.
4 Christopher Hill, *A Turbulent, Seditious, and Factious People: John Bunyan and his church* (Oxford, 1989), p. 9.

not arrived.[5] This deep sense of loss may be one reason why each writer produced a work built around a forceful, dominating Satanic character at this particular time.

The existence of Satan as a concrete being was not generally questioned in the mid-seventeenth century. News accounts of the period contain descriptions of Satanic apparitions said to have been witnessed by respected citizens: on 22 March 1658 the Devil appeared to one Lydia Rogers in a man's shape and made a contract with her in return for money which she needed; Mrs. Rogers had been questioned on the matter by Mr. Johnston, the minister of Wapping.[6] *The Just Devil of Woodstock, or a True Narrative of the Special Apparitions, the Frights and Punishments, inflicted upon the Rumpish Commissioners sent thither to Survey the Mannors and Houses belonging to His Magestie* includes a list of respected citizens who witnessed the said apparitions.[7] 12 February 1661 saw an account of *A Wonder in Staffordshire... Of a strange and horrible apparition of the Divell* which had appeared to James Fisher, a 'phrenatic', in the shape of one of his church brethren.[8] Although 'The details of the War in Heaven were the despair of nearly every expositor in Milton's age', according to C. A. Patrides,[9] for Bunyan and Milton the Satan who had led the rebellion was the palpable source of evil in the universe.[10]

---

5 For this shared experience see N. H. Keeble, '"Till one greater man/ Restore us": Restoration Images in Milton and Bunyan, in David Gay, James G. Randall and Arlette Zinck (ed.), *Awakening Words: Bunyan and the language of community* (Newark DE, 2000), pp. 27–50; but see also Thomas Corns' reply in chapter 1 of the present volume.

6 *The Snare of the Devil Discovered*, printed by Edward Thomas on 1 April 1658.

7 Published in London on 10 January 1660.

8 Printed and sold by Francis Coles of London, pp. 1, 5.

9 C. A. Patrides, *Milton and the Christian Tradition* (Hamden CT, 1979), p. 94.

10 Although in *The Pilgrim's Progress* there is no Satan character of the stature and presence of the Satan of *Paradise Lost* or the Tempter of *Grace Abounding*, Apollyon does partake of the heroic: 'the Monster was hidious to behold, he was cloathed with scales like a Fish (and they are his pride) he had Wings like a Dragon, feet like a Bear, and out of his belly came Fire and Smoak, and his mouth was the mouth of a Lion. [...] In this Combat no man can imagine, unless he had seen and heard as I did, what yelling, and hideous roaring *Apollyon* made all the time of the fight, he spoke like a Dragon' (*PP*, pp. 56, 60);

Supporters of the Restoration quite naturally looked back on the Interregnum as a period of intolerable chaos, during which familiar hierarchies – both political and religious – had been overturned. Yet the very rejoicing which accompanied Charles II's return to the throne was widely perceived, even by those who rejoiced, as wild, even chaotic: according to one contemporary account, when the King entered London on 29 May 1660, 'the World of England was perfectly mad. They were freed from the chaines of darkness and confusion which the Presbyterians and phanaticks had brought upon them'.[11] How much more threatening would this sense of confusion have been for Milton when his ears were assaulted by the 'barbarous dissonance', the 'savage clamour' of the 'wild rout' of Restoration revelry which he heard at night.[12]

For Milton, however, the perceived political and religious confusion of the time was not exclusively evil. In his discussion of Milton's approach to chaos as multifaceted, John P. Rumrich notes that if anyone in *Paradise Lost* desires 'the lasting suppression of chaos it is Satan. Suiting their fixed opposition to God, their lock on despair, Milton's fallen angels could never champion indeterminacy but incline instead to rigidity and parodic orderliness'.[13] For those who rued the Restoration, Satan could thus serve as a useful figure for the victorious political and religious leaders of the 1660s who rejoiced at the return, not only of the King, but of a familiar political and religious order.

To what extent can Milton's Satan be compared with the Tempter who is so central a figure in *Grace Abounding*? On the face of it, there are vast differences between the two genres: the spiritual autobiography which Bunyan set out to write and the epic theodicy which

---

    moreover the fiend's duel with Christian (pp. 56–61) is arguably one of the latter's most memorable encounters with an evil principle.

11   Andrew Clark (ed.), *The Life and Times of Anthony a Wood* (Oxford, 1891), p. 317, cited in Vivian de Sola Pinto, *Enthusiast in Wit* (London, 1962), p. 7.

12   *Paradise Lost*, 7: 32–37, in Alastair Fowler (ed.), *Paradise Lost*, 2nd edn. (London, 1998). Subsequent references to *PL* are to book and line/s in this edition.

13   John P. Rumrich, *Milton Unbound: controversy and reinterpretation* (Cambridge, 1996), p. 126.

Milton was in the process of composing at the same time. The spiritual autobiography had a well-established Puritan tradition behind it; as Anne Hawkins points out, *Grace Abounding* 'derives its thematic properties and structural unity from Bunyan's personal experience of conversion – an experience which is itself derivative of existing models in the theology and cultural milieu of seventeenth-century England'.[14] Yet there is a parallel between Bunyan's description of an internal dialogue between his soul and Satan, and Milton's original plan to tell the story of 'man's first disobedience' by means of dialogue, that is, as a tragical drama (*Adam Unparadized*). Alastair Fowler argues that *Paradise Lost* might be considered 'in part tragical rather than purely heroic';[15] indeed, much of the narrative of *Paradise Lost* is couched in dialogue. It would therefore not be farfetched to claim that both Bunyan's Tempter and Milton's Satan are first and foremost debaters: Bunyan's Tempter can be said to engage in debate with the narrator himself, while Milton's Satan maintains an ongoing dialogue with his mates, with Sin and Death, with the occasional angel, as well as with Eve.

The middle decades of the twentieth century saw lively debate on the nature of Milton's Satan, in the course of which several scholars suggested that in the early books of *Paradise Lost* Milton created a heroic, even admirable Satan character. A. J. A. Waldock finds great differences between the Satan of the early books and the later character: 'The changes [in Satan] do not generate themselves from within: they are imposed from without. Satan, in short, does not degenerate: *he is degraded*'.[16] C. S. Lewis, on the other hand, defends Milton

---

14   Anne Hawkins, 'The Double-Conversion in Bunyan's *Grace Abounding*,' *Philological Quarterly*, 61 (1982), 259.
15   Alastair Fowler, introduction, *PL*, p. 3.
16   A. J. A. Waldock, 'Satan and the Technique of Degradation', in Louis L. Martz (ed.), *Milton: a collection of critical essays* (Englewood Cliffs NJ, 1966), p. 89. R. J. Z. Werblowsky speaks of 'Milton's habit of first ennobling his Satan and then calling him names [...] Milton is somehow aware of the threat his own Satan is becoming to his purpose. He therefore supplies his poem with a running commentary. Now whenever Satan makes one of his spirited and impressive appearances, [...] Milton tries to take him down a peg by quickly

against persistent accusations of making the Satan of the early books more sympathetic than he had intended. Satan, according to Lewis, is absurd: 'he has become more a Lie than a Liar, a personified self-contradiction'.[17] Arnold Stein, however, adopts a more moderate stance, not denying the fiend's essential evil, but noting that Satan's 'evil is not pure'.[18]

Readers throughout the centuries have indeed been attracted to the Satan character of the early books of *Paradise Lost* by the breadth of the fiend's courage and self-awareness. While noting Satan's 'Implacable hate, patient cunning, and a sleepless refinement of device to inflict the extremest anguish on an enemy,' Shelley took up the cudgels for the fiend: 'Nothing can exceed the energy and magnificence of the character of Satan as expressed in *Paradise Lost*. It is a mistake to suppose that he could ever have been intended for the popular personification of evil'.[19] John Carey argues that the 'images of dynamism and magnitude heaped upon Satan carry far more conviction than those applied to any other character'.[20] For Carey:

> Satan's superiority in depth as well as stature is a matter of better writing. Where else are we allowed to see a character in such varied light as when he talks to himself on Niphates (4.32–113)? [...] What other character reacts to anything as complexly as Satan to Eve (9.455–93)? [...] The theory that Satan 'degenerates' or is 'degraded' works out only on a superficial level, because the writing of his part goes on being irresistible. [...] Satan can be reckoned on for poetry and drama right to the end.[21]

The Satan of the early books regrets his own loss of goodness and aches for his intended victims. His pity for his followers is made clear from the epic's outset. Half enclosed round 'With all his peers'

adding a nasty remark': *Lucifer and Prometheus: a study of Milton's Satan* (London, 1952), p. 9.
17   C. S. Lewis, *A Preface to 'Paradise Lost'* (London, 1963), p. 97
18   Arnold Stein, *Answerable Style: essays on 'Paradise Lost'* (Minneapolis, 1953), p. 3
19   Percy Bysshe Shelley, 'A Defense of Poetry', in Donald H. Reiman and Sharon B. Powers (ed.), *Shelley's Poetry and Prose* (New York, 1977), p. 498.
20   John Carey, *Milton* (London, 1969), p. 90.
21   Carey, *Milton*, pp. 90–1.

(*PL*, 1: 617–8), Satan attempts to speak; his voice is choked by 'Tears such as angels weep' (*PL*, 1: 620). Prior to his first attempt on the virtue of Eve by means of entrance into her dream, Satan is stopped by the angel Zephon. Moved by the angel's 'youthful beauty', Satan 'saw/ Virtue in her shape how lovely, saw, and pined/ His loss' (*PL*, 4: 847–9). It is in Satan's soliloquy at the start of Book 4, however, that we feel the acuteness of his inner struggle against what are so like pangs of conscience that no other word will really do:

> now conscience wakes despair
> That slumbered, wakes the bitter memory
> Of what he was, what is, and what must be
> Worse (*PL*, 4: 23–6).

At this point Satan displays understanding, even sympathetic acceptance of the punishment received at the hands of his Father: 'He deserved no such return/ From me, whom he created what I was/ In that bright eminence, and with his good/ Upbraided none' (*PL*, 4: 42–5). With a perhaps unexpected sense of fairness the fiend analyzes his disobedience to God and concludes that he had had 'the same free will and power to stand' as those denizens of Heaven who had not fallen, and then poses to himself the rhetorical question 'whom hast thou then or what to accuse,/ But heaven's free love dealt equally to all' (*PL*, 4: 66–8).

Stein's formulation – Satan's evil is not pure – may also be applied to Bunyan's Tempter. Perhaps one of the most memorable, as well as long-lasting ('for the space of a year' (*GA*, §133)) of the temptation episodes in *Grace Abounding* is that in which Bunyan is urged to sell Christ: '*Sell Christ for this, or sell Christ for that; sell him, sell him*' (*GA*, §135). In much the same way as the Miltonic narrator describes the pain and regret which accompany Satan's awareness of his wrongdoing, Bunyan himself senses the Tempter's shame as he contemplates his victim's sufferings. On being suddenly released from sorrow and guilt by the sentence which 'bolted in upon me': '*The blood of Christ remits all guilt*' (*GA*, §143), Bunyan adds that: 'Now I began to conceive peace in my Soul, and methought I saw as if the Tempter did lear and steal away from me, as being ashamed of what he had done' (*GA*, §144).

The Satan characters of *Paradise Lost* and *Grace Abounding* are not only capable of feeling shame; they can, on occasion, display an ability to tell the truth surprising in one who has traditionally been called the Prince of Lies. The Tempter tells the truth when he makes a prediction as to the progress of Bunyan's conversion; he came upon Bunyan:

> Then hath the Tempter come upon me also with such discouragements as these: [...] continual rocking will lull a crying Child to sleep: I will ply it close, but I will have my end accomplished: though you be burning hot at present, yet, if I can pull you from this fire, I shall have you cold before it be long (*GA*, §110).

Grace Abounding purports to describe a conversion process which was finite; that is, Bunyan details what went on in his soul up to the time at which 'Now was my heart full of comfort' (*GA*, §339). Yet the Christian soul would have continued to be a prime target for those forces of evil embodied in Satan. Or, as Felicity A. Nussbaum notes, *Grace Abounding* is the account more 'of a soul constantly endangered in this world than of a soul saved; it is the account of a self in process rather than a static identity, a self which insists on its power and pride but which acknowledges nagging temptation'.[22] At any given point in time the Devil might be expected to encourage the soul to believe that its struggles are at an end; this would serve to increase the soul's despair when it becomes clear that the struggle for redemption must continue, and will only cease with death. Thus when he warns Bunyan that he will have his end accomplished, the Tempter is giving his victim important information: the powers which he represents have time at their command, and will not give up their struggle for the soul. Bunyan, in other words, is not being misled.[23]

22 Felicity A. Nussbaum, '"By these words I was sustained": Bunyan's *Grace Abounding*', *English Literary History*, 49 (1982), 31.
23 Anne Hawkins explicates Bunyan's conversion as depicted in *Grace Abounding* as an example of *lysis* conversion, in which salvation is perceived 'in the language and metaphor of education, as a gradual process of error and relearning, or fall and recovery, or wrong-doing and punishment whereby the soul matures into a regenerative state': 'Double-Conversion', p. 273

While Adam and Eve are Satan's earliest human targets, the fallen angels, those heavenly creatures who allowed themselves to be (mis)led by the fiend, were the latter's first victims. Indeed, at one of the earliest chronological points in the epic – soon after the Father's exaltation of the Son (*PL*, 5: 577–99) – Satan addressed his companion Beelzebub, who was sleeping and thus especially vulnerable, 'and infused/ Bad influence into the unwary breast/ Of his associate' (*PL*, 5: 694–6). After their defeat and expulsion from heaven, however, Satan does not hide from his followers the difficulties of the path on which they have embarked. In his address to the fallen angels in Book 1 (*PL*, 1: 622–62) Satan lays out clearly the problems inherent in his plans for 'war/ Open or understood' (*PL*, 1: 661–2); nor does he mislead the souls under his influence as to the confusion which had been his own portion when he contemplated the dangers of rebellion:

> what power of mind
> Foreseeing or presaging, from the depth
> Of knowledge past or present, could have feared,
> How such united force of gods, how such
> As stood like these, could ever know repulse? (*PL*, 1: 626–30)

Although Satan's honesty with 'the companions of his fall' seems at times quite direct, even disingenuous, a second parallel between Bunyan's and Milton's visions of Satan is the use each character makes of disinformation in order to convince. If disinformation is defined as incorrect and deliberately misleading information made public, usually by an agency of government, as a means of negating correct information, both Milton and Bunyan would have been aware of its importance as an effective tool in the hands of the politician. As Sharon Achinstein points out: 'In *Paradise Lost*, Milton summons readers to become more keenly aware of their susceptibility to political deception. Milton aimed to promote readerly skills as a means for English citizens to regain the individual freedoms that had slipped through the revolutionary leaders' fingers.'[24]

---

24 Sharon Achinstein, *Milton and the Revolutionary Reader* (Princeton, 1994), p. 202.

Bunyan, too, was aware of the importance of 'readerly skills' for the believer. He speaks to the issue directly in his account of the interrogations attending his arrest and imprisonment: when William Foster of Bedford contended that Bunyan 'understood the Scriptures literally', Bunyan answered that 'those that was to be understood literally we understood them so; but for those that was to be understood otherwise, we endeavoured so to understand them'(*GA*, p. 110). In his examination before a team of judges Bunyan calls attention to Justice Keeling's ignorance when the latter claims that 'the Common Prayer-book hath been ever since the apostles' time'. Bunyan answers: 'shew me the place in the epistles, where the Common Prayer-book is written, or one text of Scripture, that commands me to read it, and I will use it' (*GA*, p. 117); the preacher thus not only puts his interrogator in his place, but demonstrates once again the importance of 'readerly skills' in the fight for religious freedom.

Given the nature of his interrogation as well as the length of his imprisonment, Bunyan clearly understood that he was part of a wider struggle as to who had the right to interpret texts. The preacher knew that the judges who questioned him intended to deny his authority as a reader of texts, and Achinstein's explication of Bunyan's aim in composing *The Pilgrim's Progress* is no less valid when applied to *Grace Abounding*:

> Bunyan aimed to educate his everyman Christian in proper habits of reading, and his own readers, of course, would practice these by reading Bunyan's own allegory. *The Pilgrim's Progress* is its own hornbook, inviting any soul to become qualified; Bunyan supplies marginal notes, repetition, and a plain style to insure that all do. Bunyan, through allegory, appealed to an audience of dissenting souls, writing in code that would be understood by them. The book, however, begs for a wide audience to become part of that distinct group; its message is restricted only by interpretive means, not by social, economic, or political allegiances.[25]

The Interregnum had generally been characterized by a blurring of the boundaries between religious and political debate. For many participants in this debate the Bible constituted the sum total of learning and

---

25   Achinstein, *Revolutionary Reader*, p. 179.

served as the chief, or indeed the only object of attempts at interpretation. There might thus be a concomitant muddling of boundaries between acceptance of the Word as literal, revealed truth and the new, individual, possibly controversial insights to be gained by the reader. In the words of Kathleen M. Swaim, 'Reformation Protestantism by definition cast the believer in the role of literary critic, and Puritan experiences of the Word reach beyond literacy and literalness into the arena of the distinctively "literary" just at that point where the Word gives way to interpretation';[26] and Tamsin Spargo argues that *Grace Abounding* 'may be read as ultimately competing with Scriptural authority, as Scriptural texts form a subtext within Bunyan's text'.[27]

Nonconformist interpretation was often unmediated and intensely personal. According to N. H. Keeble, for nonconformists 'the Bible was no lucid handbook of ethics but an inexhaustible storehouse of wonders and revelations'.[28] In his discussion of *Grace Abounding* Brainerd P. Stranahan notes the significance of the 'dramatic appearance of biblical passages in [Bunyan's] mind: the sudden arrivals of these texts are among the most important happenings in the narrative'.[29] The very legitimacy of the act of interpretation, of course, provides such an agent of evil as Satan with unlimited opportunities for mischief; and Bunyan's Tempter is guilty of disinformation when he attempts to convince the Chief of Sinners of the truth of a particular interpretation of a Biblical text.

A major crisis in Bunyan's spiritual struggle as depicted in *Grace Abounding* is initiated by his acceptance of a piece of wrong information: the idea, ingeniously formulated by Satan, that Bunyan had

---

26 Kathleen M. Swaim, *Pilgrim's Progress, Puritan Progress* (Urbana, 1993), p. 77.
27 Tamsin Spargo, *The Writing of John Bunyan* (Aldershot, 1997), p. 57.
28 N. H. Keeble, *The Literary Culture of Nonconformity in Later Seventeenth-Century England* (Leicester, 1987), p. 250. Keeble notes, moreover, that for Bunyan 'a process of spiritual reappraisal and growth through meditation upon the occasion and circumstances of his imprisonment' would culminate in 'a renewed commitment and a public declaration of constancy' (p. 203).
29 Brainerd P. Stranahan, 'Bunyan's Special Talent: Biblical Texts as "Events" in *Grace Abounding* and *The Pilgrim's Progress*', *English Literary Renaissance*, 11 (1981), 329.

committed a sin for which there was no possible forgiveness. Bunyan's soul is 'seized upon' by the Scripture 'He is of one mind, and who can turn him?'; subsequently his soul is rent asunder by another text – Acts iv.12: *'Neither is there salvation in any other, for there is none other Name under heaven, given amongst men, whereby we must be saved'* (*GA*, §182). At this point 'the most free, and full, and gracious words of the Gospel, were the greatest torment to me' (*GA*, §183). Believing that he had cast off Jesus Christ, the sinner was now liable to accept the Tempter's claim that 'Christ, indeed did pity my case, and was sorry for my loss, but forasmuch as I had sinned, and transgressed as I had done, he could by no means help me, nor save me from what I feared; for my sin was not of the nature of theirs, for whom he bled and died'. Lest we miss Satan's role in convincing Bunyan of the uniquely unforgivable nature of his sin, we are told that 'the ground of all these fears of mine did arise from a stedfast belief that I had of the stability of the holy Word of God, and, also, from my being misinformed of the nature of my sin'(*GA*, §184).

Milton's Satan, too, misinforms Eve in his first attempt on her virtue: his entrance into her sleeping mind in Book 5 (*PL*, 5: 28–94), during which he causes her to dream that an angel convinces her to taste the forbidden fruit. The very framework of this dream-sequence is reminiscent of the Tempter's assaults on Bunyan; most of the action in *Grace Abounding*, after all, occurs in the mind of the narrator. In much the same way as, in the words of Stranahan, 'we cannot tell when a new text will ambush the hero and produce either intense joy or despair in the personal narrative of *Grace Abounding*',[30] Eve tells of being unexpectedly attacked by a dream of 'offence and trouble, which [her] mind/ Knew never till this irksome night' (*PL*, 5: 34–5). She then describes her acute sense of disturbance at Satan's suggestion that she taste the fruit in terms of heat and cold: 'me damp horror chilled/ At such bold words' (*PL*, 5: 65–6). This reaction recalls Bunyan's description of Satan's use of heat and cold imagery in his threats to distance the sinner from his God: 'You are very hot for mercy, but I will cool you [...] I will cool you insensibly, by degrees

---

30   Stranahan, 'Special Talent', p. 331.

[…] though you be burning hot at present, yet, if I can pull you from this fire, I shall have you cold before it be long' (*GA*, §110).

In his dream-assault upon Eve Satan is found standing beside the tree of knowledge 'shaped and winged like one of those from heaven/ By us oft seen; his dewy locks distilled/ Ambrosia' (*PL*, 5: 55–7). Eve envisions Satan apostrophizing the tree, addressing it as if it had sacred properties:

> on that tree he also gazed;
> And O fair plant, said he, with fruit surcharged,
> Deigns none to ease thy load and taste thy sweet (*PL*, 5: 57–9).

When describing Satanic encouragement of tree-worship, both the narrator of *Grace Abounding* and Eve report a frightening sense of lack of control: Bunyan tells of the Devil's attempts to 'turn away my mind, by presenting to my heart and fancy the form of a Bush, a Bull, a Besom, or the like, as if I should pray to those; to these he would also at some times (especially) so hold my mind, that I was as if I could think of nothing else, or pray to nothing else but to these, or such as they' (*GA*, §108); or in Eve's words, 'the pleasant savoury smell [of the tree's fruit in her dream]/ So quickened appetite, that I, methought,/ Could not but taste' (*PL*, 5: 84–6).

Central to Satan's assault on Eve is his use of disinformation when he implants in her mind the idea that by eating of the fruit she could become a goddess:

> Taste this, and be henceforth among the gods
> Thy self a goddess, not to earth confined,
> But sometimes in the air, as we, sometimes
> Ascend to heaven, by merit thine (*PL*, 5: 77–80).

Satan, in other words, would have Eve believe, as he sometimes seems to believe about himself, that 'our puissance is our own' (*PL*, 5: 864). It is possible for the dreamer to fly above the clouds, to behold 'the earth outstretched immense', feeling 'high exaltation' (*PL*, 5: 88, 90). Yet for Milton, as Laura Lunger Knoppers points out, 'Joy and love are less external, visible actions than they are internal modes of discipline, and attempts to regain an immediate, sensuous, public joy are misguided, perverse, and even Satanic'.[31] Satan can thus be said to mislead Eve when he enables her to feel an immediate, sensuous exaltation, since her dream trip proves so shortlived and ends with a sudden sense of falling: 'suddenly/ My guide was gone, and I, methought, sunk down,/ And fell asleep' (*PL*, 5: 90–2).

While Milton's readers know that Satan will eventually succeed in his temptation of Eve, the reader of *Grace Abounding* expects the Tempter's attacks on Bunyan to fail. Yet during his preaching Bunyan was 'often tempted to pride and liftings up of heart' (*GA*, §296); and Satan even tried to lead him to use disinformation in his public appearances as a preacher: 'Sometimes again, when I have been preaching, I have been violently assaulted with thoughts of blasphemy, and strongly tempted to speak the words with my mouth before the Congregation' (*GA*, §293). Satan is herein caught in the act of misleading a preacher of the Gospel, in order that the latter might mislead his congregation.

At the centre of both works – *Paradise Lost* and *Grace Abounding* – is a view of sin as a by-product of a process of temptation in which the victim is led by Satan to confuse the idea of sin with sin itself. The end-product of this process, however, is despair: once convinced that by imagining the sinful act, one has in fact committed it, the soul is overwhelmed by a sense of helplessness and hopelessness. Both works, let us recall, were composed at a time of general despair in the political and religious configurations to which their authors belonged. While Hill argues that Bunyan wrote *Grace Abounding* 'with the confident conviction of one whose elect status has been confirmed by martyrdom' – i.e. lengthy imprisonment[32] – Keeble would have us remember that for Bunyan and his comrades:

> Daily life [during the 1660s] presented itself as a series of queries, quandaries and challenges: whether or not to conform, to attend a meeting, to take precautionary measures, to trust a stranger; how to respond to requests for information, to official interrogation, to legal proceedings; and, above all, how to endure material deprivation, destitution and impoverishment.[33]

31 Laura Lunger Knoppers, *Historicizing Milton* (Athens GA, 1994), p. 79.
32 Hill, *Turbulent People*, p. 74.
33 Keeble, *Literary Culture*, p. 50.

Milton, too, as he makes clear in the Invocation which opens Book 7, had 'fallen on evil days,/ On evil days though fallen, and evil tongues;[34]/ In darkness, and with dangers compassed round,/ And solitude' (*PL*, 7: 25–8). There is a sense of ongoing struggle which can only be waged if the believer understands that salvation is a process, and moreover a process which he himself does not initiate and only partially controls. The external political atmosphere of the time, characterized as it was by persecution of religious nonconformists as well as of political opponents, confronted nonconformists with the awareness that the millennium had not, after all, arrived, and was not even on the horizon; the religious and political reality is then reflected in the despair attendant on the soul's personal, internal struggle.

Early in his description of the process of his own conversion, Bunyan notes the sudden sense of sin which overtook him during a game of cat (a seemingly harmless boys' game in which a ball is hit with a stick): 'this kind of despair did so possess my Soul, that I was perswaded I could never attain to other comfort then what I should get in sin; for Heaven was gone already' (*GA*, §24). The narrator then continues:

> And I am very confident, that this temptation of the Devil is more usual amongst poor creatures then many are aware of, even to over-run their spirits with a scurvie and seared frame of heart, and benumming of conscience: which frame, he stilly and slyly supplyeth with such despair, that though not much guilt attendeth the Soul, yet they continually have a secret conclusion within them, that there is no hopes for them (*GA*, §25).

The Tempter, in other words, leads Christians to believe that they have committed an unforgiveable sin even when, in fact, 'not much guilt attendeth' the sin.

In paragraphs 22–25 Bunyan tells of committing an offence – he did, after all, take part in the game of cat – but then he is misled by the Tempter to consider his sin unforgiveable. This attempt is a way-station on the road to an even more serious assault on the soul which

---

34 Bunyan, too, suffered from 'evil tongues'; he avers that Satan had stirred up 'the minds of the ignorant and malicious, to load me with slanders and reproaches' in an unsuccessful attempt to undermine his ministry (*GA*, §306).

is depicted in paragraphs 132–140. 'For the space of a year' Satan encourages the narrator 'to sell and part with this most blessed Christ, to exchange him for the things of this life; for any thing' (*GA*, §133). Bunyan bravely resists these temptations, but 'sometimes also the Tempter would make me believe I had consented to it, then should I be as tortured on a Rack for whole dayes together' (*GA*, §136). Satan, in other words, has led Bunyan to confuse the idea of sin with sin itself; the boundaries between imagining sin and committing it have been erased. Milton's Satan uses the same ploy when, 'Squat like a toad, close at the ear of Eve' (*PL*, 4: 800), he insinuates a dream of sin into her sleeping mind. While it may at first seem that Satan merely intended to plant the idea of disobedience in Eve's consciousness, Eve's reaction to the dream, both while it is taking place and upon awakening, shows that Satan has succeeded in leading Eve and Adam to raise the possibility that the very dream – the idea of the sin – constituted the sin itself.

At the beginning of Book 5 Adam awakens while Eve is still asleep and watches her as she dreams:[35]

> His wonder was to find unwakened Eve
> With tresses discomposed, and glowing cheek,
> As through unquiet rest (*PL*, 5: 9–11).

After waking up and recalling her dream Eve concludes 'O how glad I waked/ To find this but a dream!' (*PL*, 5: 92–3). Adam, too, is described at this point as 'sad' (*PL*, 5: 94); he wrestles with an intuitive sense of sin in the speech beginning 'But know that in the soul/ Are many lesser faculties that serve/ Reason as chief' (*PL*, 5: 100ff.). Since the faculty psychology which Adam here explicates was part of the conventional wisdom of the time,[36] Adam's lecture serves less to

---

35 Lest we miss the importance of Adam's displeasure at Eve's dream, we are told in the Argument preceding Book 5 that the dream is 'troublesome' and that Adam 'likes it not'.
36 See Robert Burton's *Anatomy of Melancholy*, ed. Holbrook Jackson, 3 vols. (London, 1977): 'In time of sleep this faculty [imagination] is free, and many times conceives strange, stupend, absurd shapes [...] it is subject and governed by reason, or at least should be' (I.i.2.vii).

forward the reader's intellectual enlightenment than to defeat a Satanic plot aimed at convincing the struggling soul that by admitting the idea of sin into its mind, it has already sinned:

> Evil into the mind of god or man
> May come and go, so unapproved, and leave
> No spot or blame behind (*PL*, 5: 117–9).

Although this argument is meant to convince Eve that no sin has taken place, it appears that Adam succeeds neither in convincing himself nor his wife. We are told, on the one hand, that Eve was cheered (*PL*, 5: 129); but on the other hand,

> [She] silently a gentle tear let fall
> From either eye, and wiped them with her hair;
> Two other precious drops that ready stood,
> Each in their crystal sluice, he [Adam] ere they fell
> Kissed as the gracious signs of sweet remorse
> And pious awe, that feared to have offended (*PL*, 5:130–6).

The presence of weeping that can with difficulty be controlled,[37] of remorse, as well as the fear of having offended, are clear signals that Satan has indeed left the First Parents with the belief that a sin has already been committed.

Both Bunyan and Milton responded to the challenges of contemporary controversies by creating a Satan character who embodied techniques of debate and disinformation used in the lively, even stirring, yet often bitter and tendentious public discourse of the time. The central role played by the development of moveable type in the

---

37 Margo Swiss has made a case for viewing the Satan character of *Paradise Lost* as representing the quality of obduracy, or inability to experience pity, grief, despair. Swiss posits Satan as a response to the extant tradition of tracts of contrition: popular handbooks which argued that sobbing, even floods of tears, are outward signs of the presence of a sense of sin; one who is incapable of this kind of weeping is all too probably a reprobate ('Satan's Obduracy in *Paradise Lost*', *Milton Quarterly*, 28 (1994), 56–61). Satan is known, of course, to cry 'Tears such as angels weep' (*PL*, 1: 620), but Swiss suggests that Satan's grieving is 'provided as a demonic parody of godly sorrow' such as that displayed by Adam and Eve in *PL*, 10: 1089–93 (p. 58).

Reformation is a commonplace; and, as Keeble notes, 'by the seventeenth century no religious cause could make its way without the public as its patron, the vernacular its medium of expression and print its means of communication'; and members of nonconformist religious configurations in particular depended on publication for their very survival:

> In their various kinds of seclusion, they could in writing come to terms with the events which had, apparently so finally, overthrown them; and through publication they could declare their continuing, and renewed, commitment despite those events, their willing submission to God's Providence. This commitment could use the printed book to refute the government's presentation of them as seditious rebels and episcopalian caricatures of them as hypocritical dissemblers.[38]

Milton chose to come to terms with his cause's defeat by writing about it, and Bunyan was forced by his imprisonment to communicate with his brethren by means of the printed page. Both were sensitive to the blessings of debate and to the dangers of disinformation. Their Satan characters may be taken as their engagement with blessings and dangers alike, as guide and warning: the reader is adjured to beware the assaults of Satan, of a Tempter who has the ability to enter into the believer's mind and by an ingenious mixture of truth and lies, reminiscent of those disinformation techniques often used by contemporary political leaders, convince him that he has sinned, thus leading the soul into despair.

---

38 Keeble, *Literary Culture*, p. 83.

8

ARLETTE ZINCK
From Apocalypse to Prophecy: the Didactic Strategies of The Holy War

At first glance Bunyan's militaristic allegory *The Holy War* appears the logical literary response to the fear and panic that gripped England's nonconformist communities in the height of the political unrest of the late 1670s and early 1680s. A fantasy wherein the persecuted townsfolk are promised deliverance from evil by a glorious, divine Prince might serve as a welcome antidote to the fears of 'cutting of throats, of being burned in our beds, and of seeing our children dashed to pieces before our faces' that gripped Bunyan and his church-fellows in the 'days of trouble' that followed the discovery of the Popish Plot (*MW*, 12: 21). A closer look at *The Holy War*, however, belies this easy conclusion. The allegory echoes the themes of Biblical prophecy that are explored in Bunyan's contemporaneous prose tracts. Bunyan's approach to Biblical prophecy is, however, at significant odds with the practices of many of his contemporaries. He eschews the predictive tendencies so popular among his peers and refrains from reading contemporary political events as allegorical equivalents for key passages within Revelation. In *The Holy War*, Bunyan's narrator assumes the voice of the prophet: he gestures toward the apocalyptic theme of final consolation in the framework of the allegory, but suspends the glorious and ultimate victory that might provide quick relief to anxious souls offering instead a tale of sin and repentance that rests in the prophetic call to righteousness.

When Bunyan wrote *The Holy War* there was a resurgence of interest in the style of apocalyptic prophecies that had enjoyed such a wide and enthusiastic audience during the earlier part of the century. Recent events like the Popish Plot and Exclusion Crisis served to renew hopes among the dissenting communities for the institution of a divine monarchy. The old habit of calculating the time and place of the impending overthrow of the Antichrist once again fuelled the imagination of many writers who began producing specific dates for the fulfilment of Biblical promises of relief and for the establishment of divine reign on earth. Many dissenting ministers had already set out to provide consolation to their beleaguered readerships by interpreting contemporary events in terms of Biblical promises: the allegorical symbolism of the apocalypse was particularly attractive to these authors. Specific calculations of the date and time of the Antichrist's fall and of the faithful's release from suffering were offered in numerous expositions of Revelation.

In order to appreciate Bunyan's different approach to Biblical prophecy and apocalyptic themes, the depth and breadth of the predictive impulse among both his predecessors and his contemporaries must be appreciated. The desire to calculate the future dominated both secular and religious concerns alike: almanacs that predicted everything from the outcome of wars to the weather were consumed in great numbers. According to a seventeenth-century printer's bill, for example, William Lilly's almanac *Merlinus Anglicus* sold 18,500 copies in 1649.[1] Astrology was a widely practiced art throughout this period, and both the King and commoners maintained an interest in prophecies that predicted both natural disasters and the political fates of nations.[2]

Early in the seventeenth century, King James himself had sanctioned the public's interest in apocalyptic themes when he produced his own commentary on Revelation. Protestants of all varieties developed a near insatiable appetite for documents that provided an allegorical reading of contemporary history by way of the interpretative keys provided in Revelation. The Protestant community's

---

[1] B. S. Capp reports this fact in his study *The Fifth Monarchy Men: a study in seventeenth-century English millenarianism* (London, 1972). For the bill itself, see H. R. Plomer, 'A Printer's Bill in the 17th Century', *The Library*, new ser. 7 (1906), 42. For more information about the popularity of these predictive documents, see H. Rusche, 'Astrology and Propaganda from 1644 to 1651', *English Historical Review*, 80 (1965), 322–33.

[2] See Capp, *Fifth Monarchy Men*, p. 17.

serious interest in these apocalyptic predictions had already been enhanced by a campaign on the part of Jesuit counter-reformers to destabilize the assumptions of the chronological apocalyptic vision that was already well entrenched. Protestant writers responded with an abundance of end-times meditations that develop and then refine complex formulae for calculating the dates and times of the Apocalypse itself.[3] Among the many who contributed to this outpouring was Arthur Dent whose earlier work *The Plaine Man's Pathway to Heaven* was so influential for Bunyan. Dent's *The Ruine of Rome or an Exposition Upon the Whole Revelation* was published in London in 1603.

During the Civil War period and the early years of the Cromwellian regime, interests in apocalyptic prophecies began to divide along new lines. For many nonconformists, and, as Richard Greaves suggests, perhaps for Bunyan himself, the preoccupation with apocalyptic predictions evolved into a specifically millenarian expectation for the 'fifth monarchy' (the everlasting era of divine rule predicted in the Old Testament book of Daniel).[4] For Thomas Venner and the more radical members of the Fifth Monarchist movement, the expectation of King Jesus' reign was coupled with a commitment to 'violent political action and sweeping social changes'[5] that culminated in the rebellion of 1661 and resulted in the renewed oppression of the nonconformist groups. Bunyan's sympathies with the Fifth Monarchist cause appear to have been limited even at the height of the movement; in any case, by 1658, evidence of whatever enthusiasm he may have had for the movement disappears.[6] Bunyan's clear and repeated repudiation of violent resistance against the state and his refusal to engage in predictions of specific dates set him well outside of the more radical factions of the millenarian community. His insistence that legitimate

---

3 This observation is made by Paul Christianson in his comprehensive discussion of early seventeenth-century treatises in *Reformers of Babylon: English apocalyptic visions from the reformation to the end of the Civil War* (Toronto, 1978), pp. 93–4. See also Crawford Gribben's study entitled *The Puritan Millennium: literature and theology, 1550–1682* (Dublin, 2000).
4 Richard Greaves, 'John Bunyan and the Fifth Monarchists', *Albion*, 13 (1981), 83–95.
5 Capp, *Fifth Monarchy Men*, p. 20.
6 Greaves, 'John Bunyan and the Fifth Monarchists', p. 86.

prophecy occurs in Scripture alone separates him from both the Quakers and Ranters who assume the voice of prophecy for themselves, and from the secular fortune-tellers who retain a large measure of popular interest.

The popular recourse to apocalyptic doctrine and apocalyptic prophecies that was made by the persecuted nonconformist communities at this time was logical. The promise of release from the otherwise relentlessly repetitive wheel of fortune that is offered in apocalyptic doctrines is one of the defining characteristics of the Judaeo-Christian faith. For a culture in which the predominant view of history was cyclic, the doctrine of end-times offered an important hope for resolution.[7] The danger in emphasizing this doctrine, however, was made clear in the mid-century when the spiritualizing of militaristic imagery that emanated from many British pulpits helped to mobilize a battle-weary British populace into full-scale Civil War.[8] It was a short step that took the persecuted churchgoer from the recognition that the Antichrist and his supporters would be defeated, to the decision to help bring about that eventuality with military action.

The prose treatises that Bunyan wrote between 1679 and 1683 demonstrate clearly that he was aware of the dangers that lie on both sides of the end-times theology.[9] By ignoring or denying Biblical promises of release and restitution, he risked despair; by looking to these same doctrines for resolution in contemporary history, he risked rebellion. As these treatises indicate, Bunyan, like his fellow preachers, had apocalypse in mind, but he deviated significantly from his peers by renouncing their predictive tendencies. The reasons for Bunyan's restraint seem to be centred in his belief in the respon-

---

[7] Achsah Guibbory attributes the dominance of the cyclic view of historiography in part to the relatively recent rediscovery of Classical texts. See *The Map of Time: seventeenth-century English literature and ideas of pattern in history* (Urbana, 1986), p. 8.

[8] See J. R. Hale, 'Incitement to Violence? English Divines on the Theme of War 1578–1631', in J. G. Rowe and W. H. Stockdale (ed.), *Florilegium Historiale* (Toronto, 1971), pp. 368–99.

[9] In my suppositions about what Bunyan was likely to have written, as opposed to published, during these years I defer to Richard Greaves and W. R. Owens; see their introductions to *MW*, vols. 12 and 13.

sibilities of the reformed churches for leadership and example to the worldly, and in his understanding of what constitutes a right reading of Biblical prophecy. His views on both issues are made clear in the tract *Of Antichrist and his Ruine*.

> It is to be bewailed the forwardness of some in this matter, who have predicted concerning the time of the Downfall of Antichrist, to the shame of them and their Brethren: Nor will the wrong that such by their boldness have done to the Church of God, be ever repaired by them nor their Works (MW, 10: 457).

Bunyan links his condemnation of the pervasive societal obsession with predictions and calculation of the dates for end times specifically to the church's responsibility for evangelism. In 'missing the mark' those who have been 'so hasty, or presumed too much upon their own abilities' have 'hardened the Heart of the Enemy, stumbled the weak, and shamed them that loved them' (*MW*, 10: 458).

Bunyan points out that the business of assigning dates and times to divine promises has been folly since Moses first prophesied about the land of Canaan. The mistake is then repeated when the Israelites encounter Jeremiah and the other prophets. The problem, he avers, is not with the prophets but in 'the Peoples mistaking the times' (*MW*, 10: 457). Bunyan knew, however, that the habit of reading contemporary events through Biblical texts was already well ingrained in the nonconformist readership. Just how one was to understand prophetic and apocalyptic Scripture and gain consolation for this particularly turbulent period of unrest is his concern throughout the tracts contemporary with *The Holy War*, and in *The Holy War* itself.

Both *A Treatise of the Fear of God* (1679) and *Of Antichrist and his Ruine* deal with the Revelation text directly. The first is a careful exposition of the seventh verse of the fourteenth chapter. Rather than exploit the obvious opportunity to console his readership with promises of divine relief from persecution, Bunyan instead takes up the theme of personal reformation. He does not seek to quell any fears resident in the reader, but rather to refocus them on a more worthy subject: God himself. The fear that is discussed in this treatise is of the sanctifying variety, and it is therefore something to be nurtured. If used rightly, this fear will result in personal reform. Thus, 'The Word to the Hypocrites' that closes the treatise serves, not to soothe, but rather to provoke fear in the reader.[10] The assurance that God will eventually condemn the unrighteous is as close as Bunyan comes to a retributive fantasy.

Of Antichrist and his Ruine also deals specifically with end-times theology. Once again, Bunyan concentrates on personal reformation. St. John's Christian prophecy is not presented as a tantalizing promise of impending release from persecution. On the contrary, Bunyan warns his readership against any assumptions about how God will manage the closing chapters of history. 'For it doth not follow, because God hath begun to deliver his People, that therefore their Deliverance must be completed without stop or let' (*MW*, 10: 426). He makes the implications of his statements apparent by linking them to recent events in France where Protestants had suffered forcible conversions and other grave oppression under the direction of the Roman Catholic Church in the years leading up to the revocation of the Edict of Nantes in 1685. Once again the rhetoric of this tract moves toward a recommitment to personal sanctity and away from any immediate expectation of release:

> I conclude then, first with a word of Counsel, and then with a word of Caution. *First*, Let us mend our paces in the way of Reformation, that is the way to hasten the downfall of *Antichrist*. Ministers need reforming, particular Congregations need reforming; there are but few Church-Members but need reforming (*MW*, 10: 427).

As the Church Book from the Bedford Congregation attests, Bunyan's comments here apply not only as universal statements about

---

10 *A Case of Conscience Resolved* (1682?) marks a minor departure from the general theme of return to personal and communal sanctity. The exception is easily justified by the fact that in this treatise Bunyan is reacting to a particular issue, in fact to the particular tract by Mr. K. Bunyan's preoccupation with renewal and reform in his particular congregation may in part explain the hard line that he takes with the women of Bedford on the issue of separate worship (*MW*, 4: 293–330).

the church, but also as a particular critique of his own community.[11] Bunyan sees the need for a true prophetic message in the heat of persecution, a message that, in keeping with the Old Testament tradition, calls the people back to godliness. Biblical scholarship has demonstrated that this issue of salvation versus judgment separated Isaiah, Jeremiah and the other Biblical prophets from their contemporary, institutional counterparts.[12] In his concentration on the theme of judgment and reform, Bunyan aligns himself with the Biblical prophets and sets himself against all other forms of prophecy that privilege messages of escape and salvation. In this context the connection between the tracts written around *The Holy War* is clear. *The Greatness of the Soul* (1682) and *A Holy Life* (1683) and *Seasonable Counsel* (1684) pick up the discussion where *Fear of God* (1679) and *Of Antichrist* (early 1680s) leave off. These first tracts establish the need for reform in the context of impending apocalypse; the second group exhort the faithful to reform and instruct in its particularities. He begins *The Greatness of the Soul* with a challenge:

> I have therefore pitch'd upon this Text at this time; to see, if peradventure the Discourse which God shall help me to make upon it, will awaken you, rouse you off of your Beds of ease, security and pleasure, and fetch you down upon your knees before him, to beg of him Grace to be concerned about the Salvation of your Souls (*MW*, 10: 138).

Clarifying his reasons for issuing such a challenge, he quotes Ezekiel iii.18–19: the prophet or preacher who fails to give warning will be charged with the blood of those lost. Throughout this tract Bunyan helps his readers to understand and appreciate the value of their souls by making the intangible aspects of them more concrete. In this case, he employs a series of similes to make the comparisons. The abstract concept of the 'will' is easier to understand if its purpose is likened to a 'foot'. The purpose of a soul 'illuminate by the Holy ghost' (*MW*, 9:

---

11 See H. G. Tibbutt (ed.), *The Minutes of the First Independent Church (now Bunyan Meeting) at Bedford 1656–1766* (Bedford, 1976), pp. 66–72. Cf. also Richard Greaves' discussion in his introduction to *MW*, 9: xvi.

12 See E. W. Heaton, *A Short Introduction to the Old Testament Prophets* (Oxford, 1977), p. 42.

148) is more readily understood when it is compared to the visual function of the eye. Throughout, Bunyan makes the functioning of the soul easier for his readers to understand in order that they may then be able to attend to it more carefully and begin the process of reform. He concludes by underscoring the necessity of such a reformation: eternal damnation awaits those who fail to care for their souls. 'It is a fearful thing,' he says, 'to fall into the hands of the living God' (*MW*, 9: 245). Once again the soothing salvific message is undercut by the clear threat of judgment.

His direction does not change in either *A Holy Life* or in *Seasonable Counsel*. Bunyan underscores the timeliness of his lament for the sinful state in the introduction to *A Holy Life* and calls for a return to holiness: '*Repentance is* rare this *day, and yet without doubt things will grow worse and worse.*' He compares his own time to that of ancient Israel when even though '*the Prophets so bitterly denounced Gods judgements against them*' the people persisted in a wrongheaded belief in their own innocence. The connection between the current deteriorated state of the reformed churches and their ongoing persecutions is addressed directly: sometimes even when reform comes, it is too late. How then can those who hope for salvation from '*temporal judgments, whether they Repent and Reform, or do otherwise*' hope for better treatment? Bunyan confesses that those faithful who persist in the fantasy of exemption from judgment when they themselves have not repented leave him, like the Old Testament prophets before him, '*in a Wilderness*' (*MW*, 9: 257). In *Seasonable Counsel*, this call for a return to God is accompanied with an explicit injunction against revenge and an exhortation to the beleaguered to suffer well (*MW*, 10: 100–1).

Throughout these tracts Bunyan negotiates carefully the difficult ground that links the theology of the principle Christian prophecy – Revelation – with its Old Testament precursors. As Gerhard von Rad asserts in his study of the prophets, there is collision of values between the prophetic assumption of the redemption of an ever-changing history, and the apocalyptic insistence upon the providential course of all things: that all things are worked out as it was planned in the beginning.[13] Bunyan addresses precisely this collision of values during the period of stress and anxiety surrounding the anti-Papist agitation, the constitutional uncertainty and the renewed persecution of the nonconformists concurrent with the Tory backlash of the late 1670s and early 1680s. Throughout the tracts written around *The Holy War*, and especially in *The Holy War* itself, Bunyan assumes the role of the prophet. He calls the faithful to repentance in order that the terrifying promise of apocalyptic justice might indeed mean salvation. His careful mediation of the apocalyptic vision, prophetic judgment, and call to repentance is negotiated throughout the structure and the content of *The Holy War*.

The structure of *The Holy War* is apparent in the opening pages of the allegory. In his epic tale about the town of Mansoul, the narrator establishes both the great span of time accommodating the course of Biblical history, and the expansive scope of the narrative, which accommodates the inhabitants of earth, heaven and hell. The narrator, who represents himself as a historian of Mansoul, begins his account with a synopsis of the town's inception that echoes the themes of Genesis:

> As to the Situation of this Town, it lieth just between the two worlds, and the first founder, and builder of it, so far as by the best, and most Authentick records I can gather, was one *Shaddai*; and he built it for his own delight. He made it the mirrour, and glory of all that he made, even the Top-piece beyond any thing else that he did in the Countrey (*HW*, p. 8).

The events of the allegory move from the temptation and fall of humanity into a relation of Old Testament history. This is followed by a representation of the Christian era that arrives after Emanuel's first liberation of the city. The final segment of the allegory treats a period after Emanuel's second liberation of the city, equated by the Oxford editors to the Protestant Reformation (*HW*, p. xxviii). A note of apocalyptic expectation concludes the allegory as the heavenly Prince exhorts the townspeople to 'hold fast' (*HW*, p. 250) until he returns again.

---

13 See Gerhard von Rad, *The Message of the Prophets* (New York, 1962), p. 272.

Throughout the course of the text's popular and critical reception the expansive framework of *The Holy War* has been cited as one of its weaknesses that, despite the self-conscious artistry implied in its design, has never been as popular as *The Pilgrim's Progress*. As Donald MacKenzie suggests in his discussion of *The Holy War*, the allegory is correctly evaluated in terms of the apocalyptic, but it must also be graded as a failure in these same terms. Mackenzie contends that, 'To succeed as the cosmic allegory to which it aspires, it would have to be apocalyptic: there is no other paradigm of cosmic history available to Bunyan'.[14] He then argues that the cosmic scope required of apocalypse is absent, and that the mundane and folkloric elements, the set-piece style and the repetitions in the structure all serve to diminish any truly apocalyptic sentiment. However, while Mackenzie is correct in his observations about Bunyan's homely application of the grand apocalyptic themes, he is incorrect in his basic assumption that apocalypse is the only genre at play in Bunyan's text. More importantly, he is incorrect in his assumption that apocalypse is the only paradigm of cosmic history available to Bunyan. The prophetic genre offers another paradigm. In fact, as many scholars have pointed out, the most influential Biblical model of the apocalyptic, Revelation, is itself is a mix of both prophetic and apocalyptic genres. As Richard Bauckham argues in his study of Revelation, the concerns of John's apocalypse 'are exclusively prophetic. He uses the apocalyptic genre as a vehicle of prophecy, as not all Jewish apocalyptists did consistently. So it would be best to call John's work a prophetic apocalypse or apocalyptic prophecy'.[15] Substituting the name of John Bunyan for St. John, Bauckham's comments are equally true. It may be that a misunderstanding about the ways in which the prophetic and the apocalyptic are combined in *The Holy War* has impaired both critical and popular appreciation of this allegory.

The prophetic voice is soon apparent in *The Holy War*. In the address 'To the Reader' that begins the book, Bunyan signals an alter-

---

14 Donald Mackenzie 'Rhetoric versus Apocalypse: the Oratory of *The Holy War*', *Bunyan Studies*, 2 (1990), 39.
15 Richard Bauckham, *The Theology of the Book of Revelation* (Cambridge, 1993), p. 6.

ation in his relationship with his audience. Unlike the similar address that prefaces *The Pilgrim's Progress* where the author introduces the work in his own voice, *The Holy War*'s 'To the Reader' is written by a persona, a narrator, who once lived in the town. In the thirty-ninth line of the text the narrator tells about himself and his relation to the subject of his story: '*For my part I (my self) was in the* Town,/ *Both when 'twas up, and when pulling down*' (*HW*, p. 2). Like both the Old Testament prophets and the author of Revelation, this narrator is simultaneously 'in the town', that is a member of the community, and a detached observer who sees from both panoramic and particular perspectives. Like both the prophets and St. John, Bunyan's narrator speaks a symbolic language that encompasses the scope of human history. Most significantly, in the many parts of the text where Emanuel, as risen Christ, speaks to Mansoul, Bunyan's narrator acts as a messenger for God himself. This narrator is also aligned with the Biblical prophets in his solitary stance and in the fact that he offers his tale without its having been requested. Historically, the Old Testament prophets were independent, and they differed from the institutional prophets who worked in guilds and from whom the people often requested optimistic messages of salvation. As E. W. Heaton argues, 'The independent prophets were not specialist consultants, who were paid for their services; characteristically, they take the initiative in proclaiming their messages, without waiting to be asked'.[16] Bunyan's narrator offers the story of Mansoul despite the fact that those who '*do excell /Their Equals in* Historiology,/ *Speak not of* Mansoul's *wars, but let them lye/Dead*'. His purpose is also decidedly didactic: until readers know the story of Mansoul they are 'to themselves unknown' (*HW*, p. 1).

Bunyan's structural repetitions may also be better understood in the context of a prophetic mode. So long as the final apocalyptic resolution of events is understood to be the primary objective of the allegory, the seemingly infinite number of attacks and counter-attacks that go on between the Diabolonians and the residents of Mansoul appear redundant, and the double rescue of Mansoul by Emanuel feels needlessly repetitious. If, however, the prophetic pattern of sin and re-

---

16 See Heaton, *Short Introduction*, p. 42.

demption is understood as the foundation upon which the apocalyptic thrust of the plot is built, then these repetitions are appropriate. Furthermore, if the prophet's call to awareness of sin and repentance is understood to be operative in the allegory, then the variety and number of attacks and counter-attacks is instructive, indeed, necessary. The prefatory address clarifies that the import of this story does not rest in any suspense within the plot: the repetitions in the plot itself are underscored and outlined in some detail in the initial address. Rather, the nuances in the relationship between Mansoul and Emanuel and in the machinations of the Diabolonian forces create the story's significance. The Old Testament prophetic books similarly rely on patterns of relationship rather than on suspense in the plot structure itself. Heaton argues that the prophetic books are read most productively as a record of God's dealings with his people in history, in 'the totality of their historical existence'. The prophetic works are also repetitious in nature because they chronicle the progresses and regresses of Israel: 'It was the prophets, in particular who taught Israel to trust God as he was encountered in everyday human existence, where by definition there can be no certainty and no resting place'.[17]

Contrary to MacKenzie's critique, Christine Sizemore finds sanction for the repetition in the structure of Bunyan's plot in the book of Revelation. In a comparison of texts that brings *The Holy War* together with Revelation by way of Spenser's *The Faerie Queene*, Sizemore argues that, 'the tradition of the Revelation as a tragedy' may be used as an important literary and thematic precedent for the repetitions in Bunyan's own plot.[18] However the repetitions in the structure are justified, the salvific effect is most apparent in the context of the prophetic mode. The very structure of this allegory makes the point that Bunyan has belabored in the tracts he wrote at this time: the work of salvation is not complete upon conversion. Any promise and hope for release from suffering implied in Christ's second coming is entirely dependent upon the continued sanctification of his people.

17   Heaton, *Short Introduction*, pp. 9–10.
18   See Christine Sizemore, 'The Literary Artistry of John Bunyan's *The Holy War*', University of Pennsylvania Ph.D. thesis (Ann Arbor: University Microfilms, 1975), p. 29.

Both Sizemore and MacKenzie acknowledge that the temporal and cosmic scope of Bunyan's allegory links it directly with the apocalyptic tradition. The prophetic works, especially Isaiah, reference the entire scope of Biblical history in their narratives and represent the activities of earth, heaven and hell; however, the linear structure of Biblical history, and especially time's march toward its ultimate ending, is most evident in the apocalyptic texts. Bunyan's allegory begins with a Genesis account and ends with a lengthy speech by Emanuel; more precisely, it ends with a quotation from Revelation that promises the ultimate ending of Christ's final return. All aspects of the allegory have built toward this conclusion, but the promise is not realized in the narrative itself. The completion that is promised by Christ's ultimate return rests suspended over the final page of the allegory: the prophetic impulse of the structure rests short of apocalyptic resolution.

While Bunyan's allegory deliberately evades its apocalyptic theme, it does sustain an epic-style perspective that is appropriate to the genre. Throughout the allegory Bunyan is at some pains to maintain a distanced and analytical perspective. The characters are, for the most part, undeveloped. The cosy identification with a central character that was encouraged in *The Pilgrim's Progress* is actively discouraged here. Where readers are able to identify with Christian from the outset and to learn more about him in the various excursions and digressions characteristic of that work, Mansoul is not readily available for that kind of identification. Rather, Mansoul is only understood as a discreet and unified entity through readers' conscious assemblage of its component parts. As a result, the broad temporal and cosmic perspective outlined explicitly at the outset is maintained throughout the text; the flow of the narrative itself creates meaningful patterns. The narrative structure of the allegory is inherently distancing; the parameters of these patterns are more readily apparent at a remove. Thus, in *The Holy War*, form follows function: the soteriological concerns of the prophet are placed within an echatological framework. This allegory encourages focus on the development of personal righteousness in the midst of life's battles, but, by distancing the action, the structure of the allegory also bolsters resolve for righteousness with the awareness that ultimate and final consolation is immanent.

The text's modulation between the apocalyptic and prophetic genres appears in the details of the plot. A false prophet by the name of Carnal Security who begins Mansoul's second descent into sinfulness. The town is made 'drunk in the doctrine' (*HW*, p. 154) of Mr. Carnal Security as he flatters them into disregard of their Prince Emanuel and of the town's dependence upon him. Not until after Emanuel has left and the town is apprised of its true state by the true prophet, Mr. Godly Fear, is Mr. Carnal Security named for what he really represents:

> And with that, that saying of their Prince came very hot into their minds, which he had bidden them do to such as were false Prophets that should arise to delude the Town of *Mansoul*. So they took Mr. *Carnal Security* (concluding that he must be he) and burned his house upon him with fire, for he also was a Diabolonian by nature (*HW*, p. 157).

The town is then brought from this state of regret and fear toward righteous hope by the Lord Mayor, Lord Understanding, who analyses the Lord Secretary's words and finds consolation in them. Lord Understanding is pronounced 'more than a Prophet' after he gives the apocalyptic promise that, although Mansoul must 'suffer for [its] sins, [...] after a few more sorrows Emanuel will come and be our help' (*HW*, p. 191). By labelling him 'more than a Prophet' the townsfolk acknowledge that he is both a prophet and an apocalyptist. Lord Understanding, like the narrative in which he is featured, places Mansoul's battles for righteousness within the larger context of providential history. In doing so, he ensures that the townsfolk understand the relationship between the ongoing and often repetitious battles for personal and communal righteousness, and the promised final release from their struggles.

With these considerations in mind, the convergence between the contemporary pastoral issues addressed in Bunyan's prose tracts and the issues at play in the allegorical text becomes clear. In writing *The Fear of God*, and *Of Antichrist and his Ruine*, Bunyan himself plays the role of Mr. Godlyfear. He speaks of judgment to a readership that is hungry for consolation but which has, 'This twenty years [...] been degenerating, both as to Principles, and as to Practice; and have grown at last into an amazing likeness to the World, both as to Religion, and civil Demeanor' (*MW*, 13: 427). To the extent that his readership concurred with his judgments, Bunyan, like Mr. Godlyfear, may have been 'look[ed] upon [...] as a Prophet' (*HW*, p. 157). When in *Greatness of the Soul, Seasonable Counsel* and *A Holy Life* Bunyan guides his readership in the particularities of continued sanctification and holds out the promise of forgiveness, he moves beyond the prophetic role to become, like the Lord Mayor, Lord Understanding, something more than a prophet. He becomes an apocalyptic voice that trains believers to hope for salvation while calling them to live a righteous and godly life.

Thus, Bunyan's fiction mirrors in its form and its content the concerns outlined in his non-fictional prose. The plot of *The Holy War* concerns prophecy and apocalyptic prophecy just as the allegory itself is written within both the prophetic and apocalyptic genres. Far from an escapist fantasy of the carnally secure *The Holy War* negotiates apocalyptic and prophetic sentiments in both form and content in order to arrive at a corrected view of apocalyptic hope. End-times doctrine is solace only to those who use it as a challenge to repent.

In the final speech by Emanuel, structure and plot converge to produce a single prophetic and apocalyptic moment. The narrator becomes the divine messenger and the divine message puts the past, present and future of Mansoul into the perspective of providential history. Emanuel begins by explaining the history of the town retold from God's point of view. Mansoul's suffering is assigned purpose and meaning. An end to suffering is projected when Mansoul will be taken down 'stick and stone, to the ground' (*HW*, p. 247) and rebuilt in the Kingdom of the Father. Life there will be 'sweet and new' (*HW*, p. 247), but this vision is followed quickly by an injunction for proper duty and practice. Fulfilment of the promise is dependent upon right action, just as it is throughout the Biblical prophecies, just as it is throughout Bunyan's prose tracts. The careful balancing of hope and responsibility, promise and duty that have been worked out throughout *The Holy War* meet in the final lines of Emanuel's speech and the closing of the allegory. In words taken from Revelation Emanuel commands: 'hold fast till I come' (*HW*, p. 250).

When Bunyan's *The Holy War* is understood in terms of its prophetic impulses, many of the complaints and curiosities of the allegorical text are resolved. The repetitious structure is justified in the prophetic call for repentance, a returning to God. The distanced perspective is required by the apocalyptic structure that seeks to compress past, present and future into one eternal moment where the righteousness of God's people is required above all else. Finally, too, the superiority of the *bellum intestum* theme to Bunyan's literary purpose is more clearly recognizable. The leisure and space required for the journey in *The Pilgrim's Progress* collapse into an epic battle herein the final determination of the soul depends upon its warring in an eternal present, upon its response to prophetic call.

9

ROGER POOLEY
The Life and Death of Mr. Badman and Seventeenth-Century Discourses of Atheism

Was *The Life and Death of Mr. Badman* the planned sequel to *The Pilgrim's Progress*? If so, it was notably less successful – only three editions in Bunyan's lifetime, as opposed to the twelve of the First Part and the immediate reprinting of the subsequent Second Part of *The Pilgrim's Progress*. Why? It may be that Bunyan was too aware of the problems inherent in representing evil imaginatively. '*The man also that writeth Mr.* Badmans *life, had need be fenced with a* Coat of Mail, *and with the Staffe of a Spear*' he writes in '*The Author to the Reader*' (*MB*, p. 5). Bunyan, it appears, set out to create an unseductive villain, an ethically and theologically impressive achievement, but one that only sporadically gains imaginative life. No-one could claim, as Blake and others have for Milton's Satan, that Bunyan has a sneaking regard for his villain.

There have been several attempts to make out a case for *Mr. Badman*. Michael Mullett's recent book argues that it 'achieves considerable success in combining a horror story with an essay in Reformed soteriology'.[1] Paul Salzman, while reprinting only extracts in his anthology of prose fiction of the perod, praises it as 'a remarkable spiritual contribution to an otherwise dramatically secular genre'.[2] More often, though, the critical note has been one of disappointment. Roger Sharrock complains that 'it lacks the emotional heights and

---

1 Michael A. Mullett, *John Bunyan in Context* (Keele, 1996), p. 229.
2 Paul Salzman, ed., *An Anthology of Seventeenth-Century Fiction* (Oxford, 1991), p. xxii.

depths of its predecessor' and 'the seriousness and universality', too.[3] Monica Furlong judges that 'it lacks the psychological credibility needed for a story'.[4] Christopher Hill suggests it 'is less successful because in relating the life of a man predestined to eternal damnation there is no struggle, no conflict, no suspense. Mr. Badman's life is all of a piece, from his horrid childhood to his impenitent death'.[5]

It may be that modern readers find *Mr. Badman* hard to deal with because they misunderstand the genre, or the context in which it might be most fruitfully read. So Stuart Sim has argued that 'the work's apparent "offensiveness" is in fact a carefully calculated exercise in social critique on the author's part'.[6] We are not meant to like *Mr. Badman,* and our dislike is calculated to generate a political awareness of the social, as well as spiritual evils it attacks. However, Sim's more recent book on Bunyan, co-authored with David Walker, is less convinced of *Mr. Badman*'s virtues, and identifies a problem with the authority of Wiseman (and behind him, Bunyan) being no more than authoritarian, a matter of rhetorical assertion.[7] More recently, Ann Dunan has proposed nonconformist writings on youth as an illuminating generic context: 'through the presentation of Badman as the archetype of the young fool, and through the instruction of Attentive, Bunyan is also indebted to books written especially for English youth'.[8] The strength of this argument is that it accounts for two of the major features of the book that other readers have found difficult – Bunyan's conduct of the dialogue form, and the unremitting nature of Badman's badness. The most successful defences of *Mr. Badman*

---

3 Roger Sharrock, *John Bunyan* (London, 1968), pp.106, 117. 'Universality' was a term of praise then.
4 Monica Furlong, *Puritan's Progress* (London, 1975), p. 127.
5 Christopher Hill, *A Turbulent, Seditious and Factious People: John Bunyan and his church 1628–1688* (Oxford, 1988), p. 231.
6 Stuart Sim, 'Isolating the Reprobate: Paradox as a Strategy for Social Critique in *The Life and Death of Mr. Badman, Bunyan Studies,* 1, 2 (1989), 30–41.
7 Stuart Sim and David Walker, *Bunyan and Authority: the rhetoric of dissent and the legitimation crisis in seventeenth-century England* (Bern, 2000), ch. 9.
8 Ann Dunan, '*The Life and Death of Mr. Badman* as a "Compassionate Counsel to all Young Men": John Bunyan and Nonconformist Writings on Youth', *Bunyan Studies,* 9 (1999/2000), 50–68.

have, then, been able to suggest both an appropriate context, or background against which to read the text, along with some literary or generic resiting which will stop us feeling like disappointed novel readers.

In this essay I will propose that the literary successes and shortcomings of *Mr. Badman* become more understandable if we place it in the context of the Restoration concern with atheism. My central thesis is that the discourse of atheism closely matches the procedural doubleness of *Mr. Badman*. On the one hand, the discourse of atheism proposes quite a precise definition of philosophical and behavioural atheism, with an inevitable slide into debauched behaviour and a complete denial of God. On the other hand, it is an umbrella term, almost a scare label, for a whole range of unorthodox positions and shocking behaviour. The problem with *Mr. Badman*, I would argue, is that it sometimes reads like a catalogue, a miscellany of wicked actions and beliefs held by the hero and others, bolstered by a range of reference in contemporary compilations; struggling against that, and often only partly victorious, is the story of an atheist's progress. Like much of the discourse of atheism, it veers between seeing its subject as exceptionally, almost unthinkably evil and wrong-headed, and regarding him as an example of a widespread phenomenon.

I am using the term 'discourse of atheism', because most of the material discussing atheism in the period is anti-atheist. It is very difficult to find a self-confessed atheist in the period, yet there is a body of writing and preaching in the Restoration which suggests that atheism was on the increase, and that debauched behaviour was leading to philosophical atheism (not the other way round, surprisingly). This can be paralleled with Bunyan's address to the moral state of his nation at the opening of *Mr. Badman*: '*O Debauchery, Debauchery, what hast thou done in* England! *Thou hast corrupted our Young men, and hast made our Old men beasts; thou hast deflowered our Virgins, and hast made Matrons bawds*' (*MB*, p. 7).

Alongside the anxiety about atheistical debauchery, we can find a fear of the political consequences of atheism. The continuing reaction to Thomas Hobbes' *Leviathan* (1651) reveals a further twist in the long-running argument that those who discount the existence of hell are unlikely to be reliable citizens and subjects. While Hobbes spent much of his great work on theological matters, the assumption of his contemporaries was that his heresy, his mortalism in particular, was as good as atheism. This reminds us that 'atheism' in the period was not so much about the existence of God as a challenge two key doctrines: the first, that God would conduct a Last Judgement, sending the reprobate to Hell; the second, an interventionist doctrine of Providence: that God did not just create the world, but continues to sustain it, and organise it as a system of rewards and punishments. The spectacular occurrences reported in *Mr. Badman*, some of them derived from contemporary accounts, would be ridiculous without such a belief.

Atheism as a word, if not a concept, is new in the sixteenth century. The first usage cited by the *Oxford English Dictionary* is actually 'atheonism' in Polydore Vergil, who uses it as an alternative to 'impietie'. It would be fair to say that medieval Christianity could get away with impiety, or heresy, or the infidel, as descriptors of those who reject God, or the Christian God. Humanist writers of the mid-sixteenth century needed the new word. It appears in Roger Ascham; and there is a little-noticed appendix to John Lyly's *Euphues and his England* (1580) where a character called Atheos is converted to Christianity by Euphues.

The historiography of atheism in the early modern period is not substantial, but it has attracted some distinguished contributions. The twentieth-century interest picks up in Lucien Febvre's *The Problem of Unbelief in the Sixteenth Century: the religion of Rabelais*, first published in French in 1942. Febvre argues against making the sixteenth century too sceptical or free-thinking – he describes it as a period that wanted to believe. Don Cameron Allen's *Doubt's Boundless Sea* (1964) operates on a wider, international scale and a longer timespan, and, as a result, finds atheists, and the moral panic of the apologists for Christianity, aplenty in European literature of the sixteenth and seventeenth centuries. However, the most significant recent work has been that of Michael Hunter and David Wootton, in a book they co-edited about the problem of unbelief in early modern Europe, and in two key essays, Hunter's 'The Problem of "Atheism" in Early Modern

England' and Wootton's 'Unbelief in Early Modern Europe'.[9] James Turner's book on the origins of unbelief in America makes some important general points about the historical changes needed to make atheism possible; and Michael Buckley argues that modern, scientific atheism is really only, philosophically speaking, posited in the eighteenth century with the French encyclopaedists.[10]

The increased interest in science in the Restoration period is rarely perceived as a pressure on orthodox belief, but it sometimes feeds into a wider debate about the precise role of God as creator and sustainer in nature. 'Nature', suspected some, including Robert Boyle, one of the most distinguished scientists in the Royal Society, was misused as a substitute for God. What might have been a fair term for God's creation, or an intermediary order of things, was developing an independent life. An atheist could use it as, effectively, a code word for the absence of God in his view of the universe: 'many atheists ascribe so much to nature that they think it needless to have recourse to a deity for the giving an account of the phenomena of the universe'.[11] Boyle is also concerned that Christians have turned nature into an 'intelligent overseer' of God's work, and thus marginalised God's wisdom and power. We are, however, more likely to find atheistical figures in the opposition to the Royal Society's project. In the opening scene of Thomas Shadwell's *The Virtuoso* (1676), a comedy satirising the new science, the two witty characters who expose the pretences of the scientific virtuoso Sir Nicholas Gimcrack, Bruce and Longvil, are found quoting Lucretius approvingly, usually a code for atheism. Aphra Behn praises Creech's verse translation of Lucretius in 1683 in these terms:

---

9   Michael Hunter and David Wootton (ed.), *Atheism from the Reformation to the Enlightenment* (Oxford, 1992); Michael Hunter, 'The Problem of "Atheism" in Early Modern England', *Transactions of the Royal Historical Society*, 5th ser. 35 (1985), 135–57; David Wootton, 'Unbelief in Early Modern Europe', *History Workshop*, 20 (1985), 82–100.

10 James Turner, *Without God, Without Creed: the origins of unbelief in America* (Baltimore, 1985); Michael Buckley, *At the Origins of Modern Atheism* (New Haven, 1987).

11 Robert Boyle, *A Free Inquiry into the Vulgarly Received Notion of Nature*, ed. Edward B. Davis and Michael Hunter (Cambridge, 1996), p. 3.

> It pierces, conquers, and compels,
> Beyond poor feeble faith's dull oracles.
> Faith, the despairing soul's content,
> Faith, the last shift of routed argument.[12]

In the Restoration, those who argue against atheism perceive two philosophical roots. The first is Classical, the tradition of Epicurus and Lucretius; the other is political, in which the central figure is now Hobbes, where it might once have been Machiavelli. These may seem a long way from Bunyan's reading and from his characteristic mode of engagement with his contemporaries, but they both contribute to that double sense of atheism that I am arguing for, its almost unthinkable denial of what most people believe hand-in-hand with a fear of its increasing pervasiveness. A moral panic? Certainly, at times when there was panic, during the Exclusion Crisis for example, atheism could be perceived as part of a more general threat of disloyalty. A broadside of 1681 advises its readers:

> Reject with Scorn and Contempt all persons of debaucht Principles, although they should make never so great pretences, and large promises of being faithful to the Interest of the Nation; for assure yourselves, that an Atheist, who hath not Religion to bias him, will be for you no longer than till he can advance himself by being against you.[13]

Atheists are less trustworthy than Papists, then (or Protestants). This adds to the contention that atheists were politically suspect because they did not believe in the judgement of God.

From Walter Charleton's *The Darkness of Atheism Dispelled by the Light of Nature* (1652) to Ralph Cudworth's *The True Intellectual System of the Universe...wherein, All the Reason and Philosophy of Atheism is Confuted; and its Impossibility Demonstrated* (1678), to take two of the most significant examples, the anti-atheists tend to argue from natural rather than supernatural revelation. After all, what atheist would be impressed by a proof-text from the Bible? As a result, though, there is a tendency for the Greek theist philosophers,

---

12   Aphra Behn, *Oroonoko and other writings*, ed. Paul Salzman (Oxford, 1994), pp. 240–1.
13   *Advice to the Freemen of England* (London, 1681).

rather than Jesus Christ, to be the main sources of authority and argument. Opposite the title-page of Cudworth's massive treatise, an engraving puts the atheist Classical philosophers Epicurus, Strato and Anaximander against the theist philosophers Aristotle, Socrates and Pythagoras. Cudworth, for one, is aware that 'meer Speculation, and Dry Mathematical Reason' will not persuade 'Minds unpurified' of the existence of God; 'a Certain Higher and Diviner Power in the Soul, that peculiarly Correspondeth with the Deity' is needed.[14] J. M., in the 1672 tract *The Atheist Silenced*, had argued that 'an undeniable Mathematical Method' could prove the existence of a deity. For all the theological distance between Cudworth and Bunyan, they could agree that an appeal to reason alone would not do the trick. Henry More, in his *An Antidote against Atheisme*, goes a stage further. Although the full title (*An Appeal to the Natural Faculties of the Minde of Man*) and a version of the argument from design are designed to suggest that atheism is the product of fancy rather than reason, More considers arguments from miracles too. He also confronts some of the problems of theodicy, of the good suffering, which is part of Mr. Badman's rationale for not believing in God. Towards the end of the book, More tells us of his convictions about witchcraft changing as a result of visiting some women accused of witchcraft in a Cambridge prison:

> As for my own part, I should have looked upon this whole Narration as a mere idle fancy or sick dream, had it not beene that my beliefe was so much enlarged by that palpable satisfaction I received from what we heard from foure or five *witches* which we lately examined before [...][15]

More's deployment of the evidence from witchcraft is of a piece with other Restoration defences of the existence of a spiritual world, like Joseph Glanvill's *A Blow at Modern Saddicism* (1668) and *Saducismus Triumphatus* (1681), the second particularly concerned with existence of witches as part of the case against atheism, and Richard Baxter's *Certainty of the Worlds of Spirits* (1691). This may also help to explain Bunyan's frequent use of anecdotes from Samuel

---

14 Ralph Cudworth, *The True Intellectual System of the Universe* (London, 1678), 'The Preface to the Reader'.
15 Henry More, *An Antidote against Atheisme* (London, 1653), p.130.

Clarke's compilation of startling judgements on sinners, *A Mirrour or Looking-Glass both for Saints and Sinners* (1671). Bunyan inserts narratives from Clarke almost *verbatim* into his text, many of them far more lurid than the escapades of Mr Badman himself. They could be said to enliven the text, though they may be more troubling to a modern reader. Wiseman has his own advice about such stories of God judging before the last judgement, commenting on the fate of an informer on nonconformist meetings, who died of a gangrenous dog bite:

> There can be no pleasure in the *telling* of such stories, though to hear of them may do us a pleasure: They may put us in mind that there is a God that judgeth in the earth, and that doth not always forget nor deferre to hear the Crye of the destitute; They also carry along with them both Caution and Counsel to those that are the survivers of such (*MB*, pp. 82–3).

Politically and socially, atheists are seen as a danger to society because they do not have any scruples about their actions, because they only fear being punished in this world, not the next. 'Judgements' then perform a double function in the anti-atheist discourse, asserting the judgement of God and the here-and-now existence of a spiritual world beyond natural explanation. Bunyan's extensive use of Clarke demonstrates this double awareness.

There is a more particular question for students of Bunyan which is not to do with the specifically Restoration, or at least later seventeenth-century, concerns about atheism, and that is the position of atheism within Bunyan's version of Calvinism. What everyone knows about Calvinism – predestination or election – is not necessarily its most important feature, but it has a crucial bearing on the expectation that there will be atheism. While in prison, in 1663 or 1664 Bunyan published *A Mapp shewing the Order & Causes of Salvation & Damnation* and while no copy of the original broadsheet survives, it was reprinted in Doe's folio of 1692.[16] Bunyan may have

---

16 See the reproductions in *MW*, 12: 418–23 and W.R.Owens' discussion on pp. xxvi–xxvii; and Gordon Campbell, 'The Source of Bunyan's *Mapp of Salvation*', *Journal of the Warburg and Courtauld Institute*, 44 (1981), 240–1 and plates 38–9, which also reproduces Perkins' map. A more legible version of

got the idea from William Perkins' *A Golden Chaine* (1616), which has a similar layout. It is a visual representation, a popularisation perhaps, of the grand scheme of double predestination. Bunyan's scheme is more detailed, but more accessible than Perkins', deploying Biblical texts as supplements to Perkins' theological abstractions. For students of *The Pilgrim's Progress* one omission is significant. Along the side of those predestined to be damned, Perkins has a little side-track of those who have a temporary and fruitless response to an 'ineffectual calling'. Bunyan's 'false pilgrims', as we might call them, such as Talkative or Pliable, are precisely accounted for in Perkin's scheme. It is possible that in the early 1660s, when the first *Mapp* was produced, Bunyan had not yet developed his interest in this particular problem of practical soteriology. What he has already considered is atheism. The sequence of damnation is conveniently numbered – I put the numbers in square brackets after the text: '*At which Satan renews his possession* Mat 12:45 [9] *who worketh blindnesse of Heart* 2 Cor 4:4 [10] *which begeteth impenitence* Rom 2:5 [11] *which increaseth all manner of iniquity* Rom 2:3 [12] *which strengtheneth Unbeliefe into Atheisme* Acts 13:41 [13]'. The choice of text is interesting. Instead of the more usual Psalm xiv.1, 'The fool hath said in his heart, there is no God', Bunyan goes to Paul's sermon at Antioch for a more comprehensive treatment of the unbeliever and his fate: 'Behold, ye despisers, and wonder, and perish: for I work a work in your days, a work which ye shall in no wise believe, though a man declare it unto you' (Paul is quoting from Habakkuk i.5). Bunyan's atheist, we should conclude, is not just saying there is no God; he is openly refusing to recognise God's work as God's. In that way it is closer to the sin against the Holy Ghost, the unforgivable sin which Bunyan himself feared he had once committed and often wrote about, not just in *Grace Abounding*. As far as the *Mapp* is concerned, atheism is a late step along the road to damnation.

Bunyan's debauchee *becomes* an atheist. It is not a moment of anti-conversion, or of renunciation. However, it is a definable point in the process of his decline and damnation. While he still talks of

the latter is available in *The Works of William Perkins*, ed. I. Breward (Abingdon, 1970).

Justice and Religion when in the company of the honest, he comes to 'perfection' in bad company, railing at religion while drinking, swearing and whoring. At this point in the story Attentive exclaims:

> I think he was an Atheist: For no man but an Atheist can do this. I say, it cannot be, but that the man that is such as this Mr Badman, must be a rank and stinking Atheist; for he that believes there is either God or Devil, Heaven or Hell, or Death, and Judgment after, cannot do as Mr Badman did; I mean, if he could do these things without reluctancy and check of Conscience; yea, if he had not sorrow and remorse for such abominable sins as these (*MB*, p. 84).

The definition is interesting. Part of the anti-atheist case is that conscience is part of the evidence for God. Thomas Good, in the dialogue *Firmanius and Dubitantius* (1674), argues that evil men tormented by conscience shows that a good God exists. Mr. Badman, despite his best efforts, is often afflicted with attacks of conscience, even quite late on. After Badman has broken his leg while drunk and called on God for mercy, Wiseman notes sardonically 'his conscience was choaked, before his legg was healed' (*MB*, p. 135). Earlier on he makes a parallel point:

> An Atheist he was no doubt, if there be such a thing as an Atheist in the world, but for all his brags of perfection and security in his wickedness, I believe that at times God did let down fire from Heaven into his Conscience (*MB*, p.85).

Predestined does not mean abandoned. We must remember that the damned as well as the saved are to bring glory to God; there should be no excuse, and predestination is no excuse either. Wiseman is also betraying a classic response of the believers of this time to atheism – can there really be such a thing without some small sense of God still remaining somewhere? A few lines later he is saying that 'there are many that are endeavouring to attain to the same pitch of wickedness'. Within a sense of salvation bound by the notion of the elect, there is bound to be some suspicion that there are a lot of unbelievers around. Can we say that Calvinism generated an expectation of atheism? I cannot find a contemporary of Bunyan's who would put it that way. The divisions within Christianity are often cited, and not just by Catholics. Anglicans blame nonconformity – Good's dialogue mentioned above has Dubitantius moving from Presbyterian to Independent to Anabaptist to Quaker to Papist (an odd move, but a lot of Anglicans thought they posed a similar threat) through to seeker, sceptic, and finally, atheist. Bacon puts it this way in his 1625 essay 'Of atheism':

> The causes of atheism are: divisions in religion, if they be many; for any one division addeth zeal to both sides; but many divisions introduce atheism. Another is, scandal of priests...A third is, custom of profane scoffing in holy matters; which doth by little and little deface the reverence of religion. And lastly, learned times, specially with peace and prosperity; for troubles and adversities do more bow men's minds to religion.[17]

Bunyan would certainly agree with the last two, if *Mr. Badman* is any guide.

Mr. Badman is not Bunyan's first essay on atheism. In Part I of *The Pilgrim's Progress*, Christian and Hopeful meet a man coming 'softly and alone' in the opposite direction, 'with his back to *Sion*' as Christian notes (*PP*, p. 134). Atheist is a scoffer – he laughs at the pilgrims' ignorance, as he terms it. But, although he now *'takes up his content in this World'* as the margin puts it, he has been seeking and not finding for some time: 'When I was at home in mine own Countrey, I heard as you now affirm, and from that hearing went out to see, and have been seeking this City this twenty years; But find no more of it, than I did the first day I set out' (*PP*, p. 135). While he is presented as a temptation like the Flatterers as far as the pilgrims are concerned, there is a residual poignancy about his story of the seeker who found nothing. It is a note that is sounded only occasionally in *Mr. Badman*, though it is there in the account of his first wife's death, and in his own. There is, however, no romance in unbelief; it is too dangerous a challenge, still on the edge of thinkability nearly a century after Marlowe's death.

It is clear that there are some points of contact between *Mr. Badman* and some of the seventeenth-century discourses of atheism. Some of the features of the text that trouble readers, the supernatural scare stories, and in particular the way that a single-minded narrative starts

---

17   Brian Vickers (ed.), *The Oxford Authors: Francis Bacon* (Oxford, 1996), p. 372.

to take on the features of a catalogue, might be explained by this affinity. Sometimes the anti-atheist literature sees atheism as part of a process, sometimes as a range of attitudes. I do not pretend that atheism is the key to unlocking the critical problems of *Mr. Badman*; but it does provide an important and neglected context, both theological and generic.

10

David Hawkes
Master of His Ways? Determinism and the Market in The Life and Death of Mr. Badman

> To prevent possible misunderstanding, let me say this. I do not by any means depict the capitalist and the landowner in rosy colours. But individuals are dealt with here only in so far as they are the personifications of economic categories, the bearers of particular class-relations and interests. My standpoint, from which the development of the economic formation of society is viewed as a process of natural history, can less than any other make the individual responsible for relations whose creature he remains, socially speaking, however much he may subjectively raise himself above them.
>
> (Karl Marx, preface to the first edition of *Capital*)[1]

I

Bunyan goes to considerable lengths to emphasize that *The Life and Death of Mr. Badman* is a topical work. In its preface he claims that '*England* shakes and totters already, by reason of the burden that *Mr. Badman* and his friends have wickedly laid upon it' (*MB*, p. 2), and he explains his decision to publish on the grounds that 'wickedness like a flood is like to drown our English world' (*MB*, p. 7). When the interrogative figure Mr. Attentive enters he is bewailing 'the badness of the times', and in response the surrogate narrator Wiseman predicts that 'bad they will be, until men are better: for they are bad men that make bad times; if men therefore would mend, so would the times' (*MB*,

---

1 Karl Marx, *Capital: a critique of political economy*, trans. Ben Fowkes (London, 1976), p. 92.

p. 13)[2] At first glance, this stress on the immediate historical circumstances to which the text addresses itself might seem to sit awkwardly with the formal demands of its allegorical technique.[3] Bunyan is insistent that Badman is not a realistic individual but an allegorical abstraction, whose actions we might therefore presume to be determined by the abstract quality of which he is a personification, rather than by the particular historical circumstances in which he is located. The reader is never allowed to forget the absolutely determining power of

[2] Stuart Sim goes so far as to claim that Badman 'is designed to symbolize the Restoration society Bunyan so despised' ('"Safe for those for whom it is to be Safe": Salvation and Damnation in Bunyan's Fiction', in Anne Laurence, W. R. Owens and Stuart Sim (ed.), *John Bunyan and his England, 1628–88* (London and Ronceverte WV, 1990), p. 154).

[3] On the generic status of Bunyan's work in general, see Ian P. Watt, *The Rise of the Novel: studies in Defoe, Richardson and Fielding* (London, 1957), p. 80. It is generally agreed that Bunyan's figural mode represents a decisive departure from the established, Spenserian allegorical tradition. Joan Webber argues that Bunyan's innovation emerges from his decision to distinguish the local and material incidents described in *Grace Abounding* sharply from the abstract and ideal phenomena of *The Pilgrim's Progress*: 'Bunyan separates general from particular completely, concentrating first on the particular, in autobiography, then on the general, in allegory'(*The Eloquent 'I': style and self in seventeenth-century prose* (Madison, 1968), p. 37). Rosemund Tuve connects this development to the decline of the Renaissance world-picture, with its intricate correspondences between the levels of creation, finding 'a belief in a principle of analogy, under Spenser's presentation of allegory (quite vanished by Bunyan's time)' (*Allegorical Imagery: some Medieval books and their posterity* (Princeton, 1966), p. 86). Michael Murrin has argued that allegory was 'rapidly dying' as early as the late sixteenth century (*The Veil of Allegory: some notes towards a theory of allegorical rhetoric in the English Renaissance* (Chicago, 1969), p. 196), while Michael McKeon sees Bunyan as 'straining' towards the novel form through the compelling nature of his plot, which threatens to subsume its allegorical significance (*The Origins of the English Novel: 1600–1740* (Baltimore, 1987), p. 297). McKeon builds on the argument of Stanley Fish in *Self-Consuming Artifacts: the experience of seventeenth-century literature* (Berkeley, Los Angeles and London, 1972). See also Michael Murrin, *The Allegorical Epic: essays in its rise and decline* (Chicago, 1980); Maureen Quilligan, *The Language of Allegory* (Ithaca, 1979), 129; E. Beatrice Batson, *John Bunyan: allegory and imagination* (London, 1984), and Michael Mullett's comments on *Mr. Badman* in *John Bunyan in Context* (Keele, 1996), p. 211.

Badman's figural status. At one stage Wiseman asks, 'But what need I thus talk of the particular actions, or rather prodigious sins of Mr. *Badman*, when his whole Life and all his actions, went as it were to the making up one massie body of sin? (*MB*, pp. 126–7). It often seems that we are to take 'Mr. Badman' as a theologically precise personification of the Calvinist concept of predestined reprobation. Wiseman stresses that despite the good influence of his parents, Badman's earliest behaviour 'manifested him to be notoriously infected by original corruption' (*MB*, p. 17). The reader is constantly told that Badman's badness is intrinsic, that it is his essence, and that his actions are completely predetermined by the definitive quality of badness, so that his behaviour is merely the outward manifestation of this allegorical figure: 'they be not bad deeds that make a bad man, but he is already a bad man that doth bad deeds' (*MB*, p. 89).

Much of the book's humour springs from the fact that Bunyan expresses this predestined evil at the level of allegorical form through the exact correspondence between vehicle and tenor. Mr. Badman acts badly because he personifies the abstract quality of badness. Thus a marginal comment notes that 'Badman had all advantages to be good, but continued Badman still' (*MB*, p. 40), and later, in the text, that '*This beginning was bad; but what shall I say? 'twas like Mr.* Badman *himself* (*MB*, p. 69), and that, while he had the resources to settle honestly with his creditors, 'had he done so, he had not done like himself, like Mr. *Badman*; had he, I say, dealt like an honest man, he had then gone out of Mr. *Badman's* road' (*MB*, p. 89–90). Badman's will, in fact, is in a double bondage: at the theological level he acts badly because he is predestined to reprobation, and on the generic level he acts badly because he is an allegorical personification of badness.[4] There is thus a certain tension between Badman's unwavering ad-

---

4 The rhetorical device whereby allegory makes manifest an abstract quality in a concrete personage whose precise correspondence to his allegorical significance is the source of irony, humour or instruction was known to the Classical world as *prosopopeia*. See Phillip Rinson, *Classical Theories of Allegory and Christian Culture* (Pittsburgh, 1981), p. 160, and Valentine Cunningham, 'Glossing and Glozing: Bunyan and Allegory' in N. H. Keeble (ed.), *John Bunyan: Conventicle and Parnassus – tercentenary essays* (Oxford, 1988), p. 221.

herence to his predestined allegorical role and the fact that the actual manifestations of his 'badness' are historically specific to late seventeenth-century England. In what follows, I will argue that this tension is alleviated once we recognize that the figure of Mr. Badman represents the literary debut of Hobbesian man. *The Life and Death of Mr. Badman* is certainly a detailed anatomy of unregenerate human nature, and a dissection of the reprobate character in general, but this analysis is carried out within the very specific and clearly defined context of the Restoration economy. While Mr. Badman is undoubtedly a figure for unregenerate human nature, he is also an embodiment of *homo economicus*, who is driven along his path of sin and reprobation by his relentless pursuit of material self-interest.[5]

The assumption that the pursuit of self-interest is a natural, and thus an ineradicable, element of the human character is central to the Hobbesian view of the world, and especially to the science of political economy to which that world-view gave rise in Restoration England. Hobbes's belief in universal selfishness, his opinion that 'of all Voluntary Acts, the Object is to every man his own Good'[6] leads him to conclude that the free market is the most natural means of determining value. He scorns those traditionalist commentators who argue

---

[5] The connection between allegorical personification and the commodity-form was first explored by Walter Benjamin in *The Origin of German Tragic Drama*, trans. John Osborne (London, 1977). Terry Eagleton has extrapolated from Benjamin's ideas in *Walter Benjamin, or Towards a Revolutionary Criticism* (London, 1981). See also Frederic Jameson's comment that 'allegory is precisely the dominant mode of expression of a world in which things have been for whatever reason utterly sundered from meanings, from spirit, from genuine human existence' (*Marxism and Form: twentieth-century dialectical theories of literature* (Princeton, 1971), p. 71), and Ellen Cantarow, 'A Wilderness of Opinions Confounded: Allegory and Ideology', *College English*, 34 (1972), 215–55. It is interesting to recall in this context that the literal meaning of 'allegory' is 'other-speaking for the market-place'. See Angus Fletcher, *Allegory: the theory of a symbolic mode* (Ithaca, 1964), p. 2n1. More recently, connections between the burgeoning market and the development of literary form have been noted by James Thompson in *Models of Value: eighteenth-century political economy and the novel* (Durham, 1996) and by Sandra Sherman in *Finance and Fictionality in the Early Eighteenth Century* (Cambridge, 1996).

[6] Thomas Hobbes, *Leviathan* (London, 1985), p. 209.

As if it were Injustice to sell dearer than we buy; or to give more to a man than he merits. The value of all things contracted for, is measured by the Appetite of the Contractors: and therefore the just value, is that which they be contented to give.[7]

For Hobbes, the 'just price' is the market price, whereas for traditional, scholastic ethics it is a value inherent in the object itself, so that any attempt to sell or buy for other than an object's intrinsic worth is 'extortion'. If this is so, a Hobbesian would retort, then all men are extortioners by nature. In fact, the inevitability of market participants' pursuit of self-interest provided the early political economists with the single constant factor they needed in order to construct a rational science out of the apparently random fluctuations of large-scale trading economies.

In the retailer, self-interest takes the form of attempting to maximize profit; in the consumer it takes the form of attempting to satisfy desires at the lowest possible cost. Early rationalizations of the market assumed that people will not repress or attempt to quell their self-interest, but that they will always pursue it to the best of their abilities. Joyce Oldham Appleby has shown how this embryonic political economy retained the influence of the Calvinist doctrine of total depravity, being founded on the assumption that, in the marketplace, people will always and inevitably behave in a selfish manner:

> As a social activity, economics offered only once source of predictability: a consistent pattern of human behavior [...] if, in certain areas, observers found a behavior so consistent as to be predictable, that social area would lend itself to scientific investigation. Thus, the conception of human nature embedded in discussions of economic behavior became crucial to the adoption of the scientific mode of analysis. All the theorizing about economic life that imputed lawfulness to market relations rested upon the inevitable desire of the market participants to seek their profit while reaching a bargain.[8]

---

7 Hobbes, *Leviathan*, p. 208.
8 Joyce Oldham Appleby, *Economic Thought and Ideology in Seventeenth-Century England* (Princeton, 1978), p. 247. See also Albert O. Hirschmann, *The Passions and the Interests: political arguments for capitalism before its triumph* (Princeton, 1977).

In order to become the object of a rational science, human activity must be abstracted – individual actions must be quantified in statistical form. When William Petty, the founder of bourgeois economics, began to develop the science he called 'political arithmatick', he announced 'the most important Consideration in Political Oeconomies, viz. How to make a Par and Equation between Lands and Labor, so as to express the Value of any thing by either alone'.[9] The theoretical gap which Petty seeks to fill is the ability to consider human activity in the *abstract*, and he attempts to find ways in which 'an Equation may be made between drudging Labour, and Favour, Acquaintance, Interest, Friends, Eloquence, Reputation, Power, Authority, &c.'.[10] These qualitative attributes of human behaviour must, in Petty's view, be translated into quantifiable terms. This technique of abstraction is an indispensable prerequisite for political economy, which seeks to conjure out of the millions of particular, individual exchanges an abstract 'market' defined by regularities which can then become the object of scientific investigation.[11] Since the 'market' is actually made up of many local instances of human activity, it can only come into conceptual existence through a deliberate mental act of abstraction. And since each of these individual acts of exchange is supposed to share the common characteristic that in them each participant is seeking their own advantage, this presupposition of universal selfishness be-

9 William Petty, *The Political Anatomy of Ireland* (1691), in Charles Henry Hull (ed.), *The Economic Writings of Sir William Petty*, 2 vols. (Cambridge, 1899), 1: 181.
10 Petty, *Economic Writings*, 1: 182.
11 Petty sums up his methodological principle in a letter of 1687: '[Algebra] came out of Arabia by the Moores into Spaine and from thence hither, and W[illiam] P[etty] hath applied it to other than purely mathematical matters, viz: to policy by the name of *Political Arithmetick* by reducing many termes of matter to termes of number, weight, and measure, in order to be handled Mathematically' (cited in Alessandro Roncaglia, *Petty: the origins of political economy*, trans. Isabella Cherubini (Armonck, 1985), pp. 19–20). See also Richard Olson's summary of Petty's technique of abstraction from human behavior, on the assumption that 'There are quantifiable regularities in aggregate behaviors (we now call these statistical laws) which can be empirically discovered even if we cannot know precisely how each individual event is caused' (*The Emergence of the Social Sciences, 1642–1792* (New York, 1993), p. 62).

came the very foundation of political economy. The abstract figure of total depravity which is Bunyan's 'Mr. Badman' represents a grotesque, parodic rendering of precisely this objectified and abstracted conception of human nature.

The emerging science of political economy thus assumed that what Christian ethics called sin and depravity was the natural condition of properly functioning economic man. In the works of the earliest political economists, which are roughly contemporary with *Mr. Badman*, we find impulses and lusts which must be condemned as sinful from a Christian viewpoint celebrated for their economic benefits. As Nicholas Barbon remarks in *A Discourse of Trade* (1690):

> The Wants of the Mind are infinite, Man naturally Aspires, and as his Mind is elevated, his Senses grow more refined, and more capable of Delight; his Desires are inlarged, and his Wants increase with his Wishes, which is for every thing that is rare, can gratifie his Senses, adorn his Body, and promote the Ease, Pleasure, and Pomp of Life.[12]

In his *Discourses Upon Trade* (1691), Sir Dudley North makes a more explicit connection between sinful behaviour and material prosperity:

> The main spur to Trade, or rather to Industry and Ingenuity, is the exorbitant Appetites of Men [...] The Glutton works hard to purchase Delicacies, wherewith to gorge himself; the Gamester, for Money to venture at Play; the Miser, to hoard; and so others. Now in their pursuit of those Appetites, other Men less exorbitant are benefitted.[13]

It is not only that the market exploits mankind's sinful nature: North also argues that, to the extent that they participate in the market, human beings will inevitably pursue their private interest at the expense of others. Indeed, he practically identifies the free market with the untrammelled pursuit of self-interest:

> For whenever Men consult for the Publick Good, as for the advancement of Trade, wherein all are concerned, they usually esteem the immediate Interest of their own to be the common Measure of Good and Evil. And there are many, who to gain a little in their own Trades, care not how much others suffer; and

---

12 Nicholas Barbon, *A Discourse of Trade* (Baltimore, 1905), p. 14.
13 Sir Dudley North, *Discourses Upon Trade* (Baltimore, 1907), p. 27.

each Man strives, that all others must be forc'd, in their dealings, to act subserviently for his Profit, but under the covert of the Publick.[14]

If we look forward thirty years, we can see how the ethical questions raised by Petty, Barbon and North reach fruition in the happy assertion of Bernard Mandeville that private vices are public benefits. In *The Fable of the Bees* (1723), Mandeville takes mischievous pleasure in pointing out the hypocrisy of participants in the market who claim to be acting out of altruism:

> the merchant that sends corn or cloth into foreign parts to purchase wines and brandies encourages the growth or manufacture of his own country. He is a benefactor to navigation, increases the customs, and is in many ways beneficial to the public. Yet it is not to be denied but that his greatest dependence is lavishness and drunkenness [...] The same may be said not only of card and dicemakers, that are the immediate ministers to a legion of vices, but of mercers, upholsterers, tailors, and many others, that would be starved in half a year's time if pride and luxury were at once to be banished from the nation.[15]

Envy, avarice, gluttony, pride, lust – all these, according to Mandeville, are absolutely necessary for the prosperous flourishing of a market economy. Moreover, it is both inevitable and natural that, in such an economy, human beings will act in a selfish manner and pursue their own self-interest at the expense of others. The concept of the intrinsic, 'just price' is therefore simply inconsistent with human nature:

> To pass by the innumerable artifices, by which buyers and sellers outwit one another that are daily allowed of and practiced among the fairest of dealers; shew me the tradesman that has always discovered the defects of his goods to those that cheapened them; nay, where will you find one that has not at one time or other industriously concealed them to the detriment of the buyer?

---

14 North, *Discourses*, p. 12.
15 Bernard Mandeville, *The Fable of the Bees and Other Writings*; ed. E. J. Hundert (Indianapolis, 1997), p. 56. Unless otherwise stated, subsequent references to Mandeville are to this edition.

> Where is the merchant that has never against his conscience extolled his wares beyond their worth, to make them go off the better?[16]

Mandeville gleefully follows the Calvinist notion of total depravity to its logical conclusion. If 'it is impossible that man, mere fallen man, should act with any other view but to please himself',[17] then the moralistic strictures of the clergy against avarice and ambition must be futile and hypocritical. In fact, declares Mandeville, the rise of the market economy, by confirming the inevitably self-seeking condition of human nature, has made necessary a new, relativistic moral order. As he notes:

> It may be said that virtue is made friends with vice when industrious good people, who maintain their families and bring up their children handsomely, pay taxes, and are several ways good members of the society, get a livelihood by something that chiefly depends on, or is very much influenced by the vices of others.[18]

As a result, Mandeville concludes that moral virtue is not intrinsic, but relational: 'things are only good and evil in reference to something else, and according to the light and position they are placed in'.[19] This declaration represents the death knell of the moral economy, and of Aristotle's ontological privileging of use-value over exchange-value. It is at root a transference to the sphere of personal morality of the economic contention, expressed in such works as John Asgill's *Several Assertions Proved.*

16 Bernard Mandeville, *The Fable of the Bees* (1723), pp. 46–7. I have modernized spelling and punctuation for the sake of consistency with the quotations from Hundert's abridgement.
17 Mandeville, *Fable of the Bees*, p. 137.
18 Mandeville, *Fable of the Bees*, pp. 55–6.
19 Mandeville, *Fable of the Bees*, p. 146.

II

These views are heartily endorsed by Mr. Badman. He earns his living as an unspecified, and thus generic, kind of shopkeeper, whose occupation Bunyan summarizes as 'making the Shekel great'. Fully a third of the book is devoted to cataloguing Badman's nefarious business practices, which include not only overt deceit, such as fraudulent bankruptcy or the use of false weights and measures, but also aspects of market behaviour which were becoming acceptable even in Bunyan's time. Mr. Badman is repeatedly said to practise 'extortion', which is here defined in terms which, from the Hobbesian perspective, represent an ethically neutral, canny exploitation of market forces. Wiseman remarks that:

> Mr. *Badman* also had *this art*; could he get a man at advantage, that is, if his chapman durst not go from him, or if the comodity he wanted could not for the present be conveniently had elsewhere; Then let him look to himself, he would surely make his purse-strings crack; he would exact upon him without any pity or conscience (*MB*, p. 108).

This, the characters agree, is 'extortion', which 'is most commonly committed by men of Trade, who without all conscience, when they have the advantage, will make a prey of their neighbour' (*MB*, p. 108). A long discussion follows noting the contemporary prevalence of this sin. Those guilty of it are

> above all, your *Hucksters*, that buy up the poor mans Victuals by whole-sale, and sell it to him again for unreasonable gains, by retale, and as we call it, by piece-meal; they are got into a way, after a stingeing rate, to play their game upon such by Extortion: I mean such who buy up Butter, Cheese, Eggs, Bacon, &c. by whole sale, and sell it again (as they call it) by penny worths, two penny worths, a half penny worth, or the like, to the poor, all the week after the market is past (*MB*, p. 109).

Mr. Badman is, in fact, a polemical intervention in the contemporary debate about economic morality. In that debate, the traditional standards of the moral economy derived from Aristotle's *Politics* and from Deuteronomy[20] were being incrementally displaced by rationalizations of large-scale trade and capital investment. Bunyan takes up a firmly conservative stance, defending the scholastic standard of the 'just price', and of the 'good conscience' which enables traders to adhere to it. These concepts depend upon the Aristotelian claims that the worth of objects is essential, and that it is a violation of natural morality to manipulate the value of things in order to exploit the market. Attentive points out to Wiseman that 'you seem to import that it is not lawful for a man to make the best of his own'. His mentor gladly concedes the point:

> If by making the best, you mean to sell for as much as by *hook* or by *crook* he can get for his comodity; then I say *it is not lawful*. And if I should say the contrary, I should justifie Mr. *Badman* and all the rest of that Gang; but that I shall never doe, for the Word of God condemns them (*MB*, p. 110).

It is immoral to replace inherent value with the market price. To attempt to maximize one's profit in exchange is to take advantage either of a neighbour's 'ignorance', 'necessity' or 'fondness' for one's commodity. It is precisely this tendency of market participants to seek their own advantage that is represented in the figure of Mr. Badman:

> Wise. [...] a man [...] should not always sell too dear, nor buy as cheap as he can: but should use good Conscience to God, and Charity to his Neighbour in both.
> Attent. But were some men here, to hear you, I believe they would laugh you to scorn.
> Wise. I question that not at all, for so Mr. *Badman* used to doe, when any man told him of his faults (*MB*, p. 114).

---

20 The relevant primary passages are Aristotle's *Politics*, bk. I, chap. ix, 1257a1–1258a1, and Deuteronomy xxiii.20. On the influence of Aristotle, see especially John T. Noonan, *The Scholastic Analysis of Usury* (Cambridge MA, 1957), and Odd Langholm, *The Aristotelian Analysis of Usury* (Oslo, 1984). On the influence of Deuteronomy, see especially Benjamin Nelson, *The Idea of Usury: from tribal brotherhood to universal otherhood* (Princeton, 1949), and Norman Jones, *God and the Money-lenders: usury and law in early modern England* (Oxford, 1989).

The pursuit of self-interest in exchange transactions is both unacceptably selfish in itself ('He that sells his commodity as dear, or for as much money as he can, seeks himself and himself only' (*MB*, p. 112)), and also inevitably involves the trader in many other sins:

> If it be lawful for me to sell my commodity [...] as dear as I can, then there can be no sin in my Trading, how unreasonably soever I manage my calling, whether by Lying, Swearing, Cursing, Cheating; for all this is but to sell my commodity as dear as I can: but that there is sin in these is evident, therefore I may not sell my commodity always as dear as I can (*MB*, p. 113).

Bunyan in fact is careful to connect even those of Badman's sins which are not obviously economic in nature to his status as a trader. The earliest of his vices to manifest itself, we are told, was lying. Attentive wonders why people tell lies, and the first motive given by both Wiseman and the marginal note is economic: 'you shall have some that will lye it over and over, and that for a peny profit' (*MB*, p. 19). Similarly, the motive for swearing is 'frequently to get gain thereby' (*MB*, p. 29), and Wiseman advises that 'no buyer should lay out one farthing with him that is a common Swearer in his Calling' (*MB*, p. 29). Furthermore, this mode of economic malpractice is highly contagious, so that 'If the Master be unconscionable in his Dealing, and trades with lying words; or if bad Commodities be avouched to be good, or if he seeks after unreasonable gain, or the like; his servant sees it, and it is enough to undo him' (*MB*, p. 40).

Bunyan's Aristotelian-scholastic view of economic morality had been hammered into the minds of ordinary Englishmen by generations of preachers and pamphleteers. The most obvious formal model for *Mr. Badman* is Arthur Dent's *The Plaine Man's Pathway to Heaven* (1601), a copy of which Bunyan received as part of his wife's dowry. In that work, the wise Theologus remarks that

> It is too true, that lying and dissembling are most rife, and over-common amongst all sorts of men; but especially it both overflows and superabounds in shopkeepers and [their] servants. For both these make a trade and occupation of it. *They can do no other but lie.* It cleaveth to them as the nail to the boot.[21]

---

21 Arthur Dent, *The Plaine Mans Pathway to Heaven* (1601), pp. 154–5.

Dent's 'honest man' Philargus concurs, demanding 'what is their life (if customers come in apace) but swearing, lying, dissembling and deceiving. They will lie as fast, as a Dog will trot'. The market economy, with its inducements to pride, luxury, avarice and venality, is identified in Dent, as in Bunyan, as an important cause of sin, and sin becomes second nature to those involved in economic exchange.

So it seems that we are being offered another, more historically specific, explanation for Badman's badness than his status as the embodiment of unregenerate human nature: he is also the personification of market forces. Perhaps the best way to describe him is as a symbol of the action of unregenerate human nature when left exposed to the free play of the market, undefended by Biblical or Classical strictures concerning fairness in trade. '*What think you of Mr. Badman now?*' asks Wiseman, after detailing the antihero's relentless pursuit of 'his own advantage'. '*Think!*' replies Attentive, '*Why I can think no other but that he was a man left to himself*' (*MB*, p. 100). Unconfined by traditional morality, egocentric and individualistic, ruthlessly competitive in the pursuit of his self-interest, Mr. Badman stands simultaneously for the sinful nature of the human race as a whole, and for that nature as it appears when it is allowed to express itself without restraint, as in the burgeoning market economy of Restoration England.

The Life and Death of Mr. Badman is at once a satirical protest against this emergent capitalist morality and a minute analysis of its psychological effects. Bunyan uses the determining power of the abstract quality of badness over the individual who personifies it as a way of reflecting on the contention that the relentless pursuit of self-interest is part of human nature. Badman must always act badly because he is a predestined reprobate, but Bunyan's emphasis falls on the historically specific practices in which his reprobation manifests itself, and in particular on his automatic impulse 'to make the best of his own'. The great irony is that Badman himself is utterly committed to the emergent, relativistic understanding of value and morality. He remains blissfully ignorant as to the true nature of his own condition. In fact, he experiences himself as entirely autonomous and self-determining. He considers himself a mercurial, transgressive, amorphous character who is able to exchange one identity for another according to the dictates of circumstance:

> And to pursue his ends the better, he began now to study to please all men, and to suit himself to any company; he could now *be* as they, *say* as they, that is, if he listed; and then he *would* list, when he perceived that by so doing, he might either make them his Customers or Creditors for his Commodities [...] He would often-times please himself with the thought of what he could do in this matter, saying within himself, I can be religious and irreligious, I can be any thing or nothing; I can swear, and speak against swearing; I can lye, and speak against lying; I can drink, wench, be unclean, and defraud, and not be troubled for it: Now I enjoy my self, and am Master of my own wayes, and not they of me (*MB*, pp. 83–5).

Of course, the joke lies in the fact that the reader has already been shown how completely Badman's 'ways' are predetermined by his intrinsic identity. Allegory places the reader in a position of epistemological superiority to its characters: we can see that Badman acts as he does because he is an allegorical personification of badness, but Badman himself cannot. His illusions of chimerical independence are thus revealed to the reader as ideological obfuscations. Badman believes that his identity is defined by the opinion in which he is held by others, and Bunyan repeatedly informs us that the community at large views Badman benignly. The reader, however, knows him to be determined, at both the allegorical and the naturalistic levels, by the essential quality of badness, and we are thus able to recognize his fantasies of autonomy as false consciousness. Bunyan shows us, in other words, that Badman's appearance systematically contradicts his essence, just as the exchange-value of a commodity overrides the inherent qualities of its use-value.

III

Bunyan, however, was well aware that the value of things was henceforth to be fixed by the market, and he recognized the profound implications of this fact for traditional ethics. With the collapse of the idea that an object's worth is inherent, the entire edifice of Aristotelian essentialism begins to totter and the commodity-form displaces *telos*. Hobbes's dictum, quoted above, that 'of all Voluntary Acts, the Object is to every man his own Good' is a materialist, quantified version of Aristotelian teleology. In Aristotle, of course, the *telos* of man is the Good, considered as an ideal essence. For Hobbes, the goal of any man's free actions is 'his own Good' in the narrowly economic, quantifiable, sense. Thus were the foundations laid of the anti-essentialist conception of the subject which has finally triumphed along with market capitalism in the postmodern era. With capitalist social mobility, human identity becomes fluid and relational; with the rise of usury and credit, the opinion of others comes to define personal worth; with the growth of mercantile wealth and power, disguise, theatricality and shape-shifting become predominant themes in literature. With the birth of Mr. Badman, Western society embarks on its long journey towards the postmodern 'hyper-real'.

The development of the market economy obscured the essential qualities of things, replacing natural use-value with customary exchange-value, and spreading a cloak of symbolic representation over bare reality. *Mr. Badman* is Bunyan's comment upon this process. Wiseman addresses the issue in his rules for honest trading:

> 1. If thou sellest, do not commend; if thou buyest, do not dispraise, any otherwise, but to give the thing that thou hast to do with, its just value and worth [...]
> 2. Art thou a seller, and do things grow dear? set not thy hand to help, or hold them up higher; this cannot be done without wickedness neither, *for this is a making of the sheckle great* (*MB*, p. 116).

The shekel, however, was already great by the time Bunyan wrote *Mr. Badman*, and it was becoming visibly greater. The rise of the market and the commodification of the world necessarily changed people's perceptions of reality. Aristotelian essentialism was elbowed aside by the symbolic, shifting, chimerical identities produced by exchange value. In the following exchange Attentive points this out to Wiseman with uncharacteristic acuity:

> *Wise.* [...] He that useth not good conscience to God, and charity to his neighbour, in buying and selling, dwells next door to an Infidel, and is near of kin to Mr. *Badman.*
> *Atten.* Well, but what will you say to this question? (you know that there is no settled price set by God upon any Commodity that is bought and sold under the Sun; but all things that we buy and sell, do ebbe and flow, as to price, like the Tide:) How (then) shall a man of tender conscience doe, neither to wrong the seller, buyer, nor himself, in buying and selling of commodities?
> *Wise.*: This Question is thought to be frivolous by all that are of Mr. *Badmans* way; 'tis also difficult in it self: yet I will endeavour to shape you an Answer (*MB*, p. 115).

As it turns out, Wiseman can only fall back upon the scholastic 'good conscience' and recommend 'much moderation in dealing'. The inadequacy of his response pays reluctant testimony to the degree to which the market's dominance had already made it impractical and unrealistic to insist on a traditional essentialist ethics in economic practice.

Bunyan's figural technique in *Mr. Badman* parallels the abstraction from the particular to the general which characterizes the process of commodification, by means of which essential differences are displaced by the levelling equivalence of exchange-value. As Barbon noted in 1696, 'one sort of Wares are as good as another, if the Values be equal. An hundred pounds worth of Lead or Iron, is as good as an hundred pounds worth of Silver or Gold'.[22] Once again, it was left to the cynical forthrightness of Mandeville to reveal the ethical implications of this economic doctrine. In his *Enquiry into the Origin of Honour* (1732), Mandeville announces the transfiguration of the classical notion of 'virtue' – a quality which is intrinsic to an individual – into the modern concept of 'honour' – an attribute bestowed by public opinion. The desire for honour springs from 'self-liking', by which Mandeville intends the pride which he assumes everyone feels

---

22 Barbon, *Discourse Concerning Coining*, p. 53.

when contemplating their own character. The suggestion, not advanced without a certain satisfaction, is 'that we are Idols to our Selves, and that Honour is diametrically opposite to Christianity'.[23]

Mandeville's phrasing may contain a deliberate allusion to Christian's claim in Vanity Fair 'That Christianity and the Customs of our Town of Vanity were Diametrically opposite, and could not be reconciled' (*PP*, p. 93). As Christopher Hill has remarked, Vanity Fair represents simultaneously the market and the idolatrous consciousness associated with such an economy.[24] Cerainly in speeches like the one quoted above, Mr. Badman makes an idol of his 'self', and in Bunyan's address to the reader he compares his portrait of Badman to the 'images' of the deceased which are sometimes displayed at funerals. In *The Holy War*, Lucifer also connect the market with the dissembling manipulation of images:

> *you know* Mansoul *is a Market-Town; and a Town that delights in commerce, what therefore if some of our* Diabolonians *shall feign themselves far-country men, and shall go out and bring to the Market of* Mansoul *some of our wares to sell* (*HW*, p. 216).

The implication is that the social mobility and theatrical shifts in identity which a market economy facilitates are in reality masks, fantasies which disguise the deeper predetermination of the character of market participants. That character is certainly predestined to reprobation after the Calvinist fashion, but it is also defined by its single constant feature, which is the automatic pursuit of self-interest.

In the figure of Mr. Badman, then, Bunyan has constructed an remarkably acute parody of capitalist psychology. Badman's loud insistence and unquestioning belief that he acts as a free agent converges neatly with his role as a proto-realistic character. Unlike the figures of allegory, the actions of a character in a realistic novel are not openly predetermined by their figural status. Realistic fiction attempts to give the impression that its characters are acting autono-

---

23 Bernard Mandeville, *An Enquiry into the Origin of Honour and the Usefulness of Christianity in War* (London, 1971), p. 89
24 Christopher Hill, *A Turbulent, Seditious and Factious People: John Bunyan and his church, 1620–1688* (Oxford, 1988), p. 225

mously. And in fact it is this realistic individuality of his characters, the fact that they seem to break free from the determining power of their allegorical referents, which has attracted generations of readers trained in the conventions of realistic fiction to Bunyan. Coleridge sums up this appeal concisely in his comments on:

> that admirable allegory, the first part of the Pilgrim's Progress, which delights everyone, the interest is so great that spite of all the writer's attempts to force the allegoric purpose on the Reader's mind by his strange names – Old Stupidity of the Tower of honesty, &c., &c., – his piety was baffled by his Genius, the Bunyan of Parnassus had the better of Bunyan of the Conventicle – and [...] we go on with his characters as real persons, who had been nicknamed by their neighbours.[25]

Coleridge, however, does not notice that his belief that Bunyan's figures are freely-acting individuals chimes with the self-image of several distinctly dubious characters – including, as we have seen, Mr. Badman. In *The Pilgrim's Progress*, the avaricious By-Ends protests, upon being correctly identified by Christian, that 'This is not my name, but indeed it is a nickname that is given to me by some that cannot abide me' (*PP*, pp. 99–100). In reply, Christian insists that By-Ends' allegorical title is definitive of his essential nature: 'I fear this name belongs to you more properly than you are willing we should think it doth' (*PP*, p. 100). This exchange is one of several in which the 'bad' characters assert their autonomous individuality, only to be corrected by a virtuous figure, who equates them with an allegorical abstraction. As in the case of Badman, the irony here arises from the fact that By-Ends's illusions about his own identity are themselves evidence of his absolute predetermination by his allegorical essence. As he puts it:

> The worst that ever I did to give them occasion to give me this name, was, that I had always the luck to jump in my Judgement with the present way of the times, whatever it was, and my chance was to get thereby (*PP*, p. 100).

---

25   Samuel Taylor Coleridge, *Collected Works*, ed. Kathleen Coburn (Princeton, 1987), 7: 103.

In the context of Restoration England, this indicates that By-Ends is a Latitudinarian, who feels that it is legitimate to adapt his religious practice to the demands of the secular government. He assuages his conscience with the pretence that his trimming springs from spontaneous changes in his free 'Judgement', but Christian knows that his opinions are actually predetermined by his pursuit of self-interest. Thus, when the pilgrims pass by the Silver Mine at Lucre Hill, Christian accurately predicts that By-Ends will fall into it, 'for his principles lead him that way' (*PP*, p. 107).

This exchange is one of several in which the bad characters assert their autonomous individuality, only to be corrected by a virtuous figure, who equates them with an allegorical abstraction. Bunyan again deploys this device to comic effect in *The Holy War*. In one of that work's trial scenes, a character who has been 'indicted by the name of False-Peace' responds:

> I acknowledg that my name is Mr. *Peace*, but that my name is *False-peace* I utterly deny [...] my name is not *False-peace* but *Peace*. Wherefore I cannot plead to this Indictment, for as much as my name is not inserted therein (*HW*, p. 125).[26]

It is, of course, allegorically entirely predictable that a character named 'Falsepeace' should falsely claim to be called Peace. Like By-Ends and Badman, Falsepeace unwittingly reveals his allegorical status in the very act of denying it. Such characters operate under the delusion that they are free and autonomous agents, and the joke in every case springs from the reader's recognition that this delusion is itself evidence of these characters' absolutely predestined behaviour. Nor should it seem strange that Bunyan employs scholastic essentialism in order to criticize the psychology of the market. It is worth recalling here R. H. Tawney's famous remark that 'the last of the

---

26 Thomas Luxon provides the theological rationale behind this technique in *Literal Figures: Puritan allegory and the Reformation crisis in representation* (Chicago, 1995), p. 32: 'Life in "this world" is unavoidably reinstated as an allegory of true life, so Bunyan's much-celebrated "realism" literally *is* allegory. Thus, the only escape from this "carnal", and therefore utterly allegorical, existence is to be newly born into that other world, the one that is never quite present, always yet to come'.

schoolmen was Karl Marx'.[27] Marx based his indictment of capital on Aristotle's distinction between inherent, essential use-value, and arbitrary, symbolic exchange-value. The philosophy of our own, market-dominated era frequently takes a dim view of essentialism, just as the postmodern economics of Hayek and Baudrillard dispute the very existence of use-value. It may be salutary, however, to remind ourselves that, from the perspective of early commentators on the market such as Bunyan, an exchange-based economy does not produce the liberated, ludic, transgressive self of postmodern utopians, but rather the sensual and depraved figure of Mr. Badman. Perhaps this figure, whose actions are completely predetermined by economic forces beyond his control, but who consoles himself for his lack of autonomy through vainglorious assertions of his liberation from the outmoded constrictions of *logos* and *telos*, may not strike postmodern readers as entirely unfamiliar.

---

27 R. H. Tawney, *Religion and the Rise of Capitalism* (Gloucester MA, 1962), p. 36.

11

Peter Marbais
The Tormented Body in The Life and Death of Mr. Badman

In *The Life and Death of Mr. Badman* John Bunyan admonishes the reader through a dialogue between two upright Christians that employs familiarity, a facet of realism that the writer uses to situate the reader in the local world of seventeenth-century England through particular details of everyday life and concerns. Bunyan's use of realism and familiarity in his cautionary tales throughout *Mr. Badman* constructs a picture of his England, but it is the construction of the body in vivid, often gruesome detail that is the most striking aspect of this familiarity which he establishes with the reader. Most scholarship has neglected the discourse of the body in *Mr. Badman*, yet this realistic, often gruesomely brutal construction of the body reveals Bunyan's concerns about the dichotomy of the spiritual and physical world.

The body as it is depicted in *Mr. Badman* helps defeat simple notions of the body/spirit dichotomy popular in Bunyan's day and reveals the significance of suffering, both internal and external. Bunyan's depiction of the body in *Mr. Badman* allows the reader to experience the local world at its most intimate; more importantly, it allows the reader to understand why such a wicked person as Badman suffered little during his lifetime and died a quiet death. The body itself, the connection of body and spirit, and the sufferer's explanations of how her/his body feels pain are often misunderstood, so Bunyan constructs *Mr. Badman* to explain his understanding of spirituality and physicality. To explain how suffering operates in the text, especially in regards to Badman's death, I draw upon Elaine Scarry's analysis of the body and its suffering in *The Body in Pain: the making and unmaking of the world*.

Scarry's study of how pain is expressed reveals the fact that pain has no referential object as do other emotional, perceptual, and somatic states; this lack of a referential object makes it nearly impossible for anyone not experiencing the pain to be wholly cognizant of the fact that a person is suffering. There is more to pain than intensity, and since the person who is not in pain cannot actually feel the sufferer's pain, the observer doubts the extent of the sufferer's pain.[1] Scarry reveals how the body has been misconstructed by society in relation to its actual physical composition, providing insight into Bunyan's complicated and often grotesque depictions of the body in pain. Scarry's work on the tormented body sheds light on why Bunyan depicts devils tearing at flesh and fevered persons eviscerating themselves in the familiar, local world of *Mr. Badman*. These depictions of the body reveal Bunyan's perception of how the conscience is tormented by the spirit. Bunyan insists throughout the text that the spirit makes the conscience suffer; in order to make the reader aware of the extent of this torment, he depicts suffering in the most tangible and easily accessible vehicle any reader can relate to: the physical body. Bunyan also removes the body from the main narrative about Badman in order to prove that physical suffering does not always equal spiritual suffering. My analysis will first focus on the suffering of the physical body in the inset stories of Badman, and then upon the body's absence from the main narrative.

Bunyan defies seventeenth-century folk wisdom which dwells on the notion that the physical state of a person is an absolute representation of that person's spiritual state by explicating the dichotomy of body and soul. He establishes this dichotomy by writing about the body through the low realism of *Mr. Badman* and about the soul through the more complex, arguably loftier conventions of allegory found in *The Holy War* and in both parts of *The Pilgrim's Progress*. According to seventeenth-century popular culture, Monica Furlong writes, some works contemporary to *Mr. Badman* are

---

[1] Elaine Scarry, *The Body in Pain: the making and unmaking of the world* (New York, 1985), p. 7.

bent on assuring us that the wicked get their just deserts, and not only in the world to come but this one too. The drunken fall off their horses on the way home from the inn, the promiscuous get the pox, those who are continually calling to the Devil to take them (as the custom was in seventeenth-century cursing) disappear or die in terrifying circumstances. There is a solid folk wisdom behind this kind of morality.[2]

I employ Furlong's notion of folk wisdom to explain this morality that Bunyan attacks with his more complex system of punishment for wickedness. The physical suffering in his text implies that although there is a greater inward suffering delivered by the spirit, many sinners ignore this suffering and so their physical well being is not a direct reflection of their spiritual well being.

In Bunyan, the body and soul are not reflections of one another, as seventeenth-century folk wisdom implies; the suffering the body undergoes by the spirit may make the sinner realize that even greater suffering awaits after death. Since Badman is so blind to the torments of his conscience, Wiseman and Attentive construct many inset stories to detail how the physical bodies of sinners endure many torments before the final silencing of death arrives, thereby insinuating that the torments of the body are much like the torments of the soul. Bunyan attacks folk wisdom when he writes that 'the common people' conclude a man is not wicked if he has a quiet death (*MB*, p. 161). Furlong notes how Bunyan treats the simplistic folk wisdom that demands sinners get their just deserts both in this world and the next: 'Bunyan was too intelligent and experienced to believe that the wicked always got their deserts in this world [...] So that we must recognise the note of patronage, the patronage perhaps of a pastor having to deal with simple-minded people, and using rather crude methods for their own good.'[3] Folk wisdom demands sinners suffer both in the material world and in the eternal, yet Christopher Hill also notes 'Bunyan was anxious to controvert the "frivolous and vain" opinion "among the ignorant" that a quiet death means a safe passage

---

2 Monica Furlong, *Puritan's Progress* (New York, 1975), p. 128.
3 Furlong, *Puritan's Progress*, p. 128.

to heaven'.[4] Bunyan constructs Badman's story to refute such a belief, but he also constructs several inset stories to show that sometimes this folk wisdom may be true.

Many critics note the inset stories of the narrative as Bunyan's best examples of the low realism which was to be a feature of the novel, and of, as Sharrock has aptly put it, language that is 'naked, strong, and popular'.[5] The depictions are usually those of everyday people, painting wonderfully accurate pictures of the times in which they are situated. These inset stories are often borrowed from earlier texts, most frequently Arthur Dent's *The Plaine Mans Path-Way to Heaven* (1601) and Samuel Clarke's *A Mirrour or Looking-Glass both for Saints and Sinners* (1671).[6] Bunyan's realism, praised by his editors (*MB*, p. xxiii), is far more colourful than the texts from which he borrows most of his cautionary tales. I wish to discuss these examples and their representation of the relationship between the body and the soul.

Throughout *Mr. Badman*, Bunyan insists that suffering leads to salvation only if the sufferer repents and accepts the free grace offered through Christ. Wiseman explains that suffering does not lead to damnation; ignorance of God leads to damnation. The inset stories Wiseman and Attentive discuss employ the body as an agency for instruction about suffering. Here, the body is displayed in the most graphic terms when various characters are snatched from the earth and their bodies tortured to foretell what their souls will suffer. Dorothy Mately's swearing that she did not steal two pence from a certain lad leads to the ground swallowing her up. Dorothy's cries are cut off when a great stone falls upon her head, silencing her cursing and swearing forever (*MB*, p. 33). Attentive's discussion of what happens to cursers is one of the most extreme versions of the body's possession by the Devil:

---

[4] Christopher Hill, *A Turbulent, Factious and Seditious People: John Bunyan and his church, 1620–1688* (Oxford, 1988), p. 239.

[5] Roger Sharrock, '*The Life and Death of Mr. Badman*: Facts and Problems', *Modern Language Review*, 82 (1987), 15–29 (p. 18).

[6] Noted by James F. Forrest and Roger Sharrock in the introduction to *MB*, p. xxv, and by Hill, *Turbulent People*, p. 231.

> *Well, so it came to pass, through the righteous Judgement of God, that* Neds *Wishes and Curses were in a little time fulfilled upon his Father; for not many months passed between them after this manner, but the* Devil *did indeed take him, possess him, and also in a few days carried him out of this world by death* (*MB*, p. 35).

The body of Ned's father suffers as his soul will, just as folk wisdom would determine. The curses that come from Ned's mouth lead to an affliction that at first stifles, then ultimately destroys his father's voice when the Devil fetches him. Not even the smoke from a pan of coals can chase away the Devil, as Attentive further relates, so the old man is bound for Hell just as is Dorothy Mately.

Silencing the voice is a means of making torture mimetic of death, so it is no surprise that speech is often affected before the wicked meet their wicked ends. Scarry elaborates upon why silencing the voice or limiting language to simple cries signifies death:

> The goal of the torturer is to make the one, the body, emphatically and crushingly *present* by destroying it, and to make the other, the voice, absent by destroying it. It is in part this combination that makes torture, like any experience of great physical pain, mimetic of death; for in death the body is emphatically present while the most elusive part represented by the voice is so alarmingly absent that the heavens are created to explain its whereabouts.[7]

Just as the torturer silences the tortured subject in order to reinforce the immediacy of death with the pain inflicted during torture, so do the wicked feel the immediacy of death when they find themselves raving, crying, or incapable of any sound at all. Speech is taken from them; they do not have the ability to make their thoughts known to others as Badman's saintly first wife does when on her death bed. Wiseman tells of an N.P. at Wimbleton in Surrey who, 'after a horrible fit of Swearing and Cursing of some persons that did not please him, suddenly fell sick, and in a little time died raving, cursing, and swearing' (*MB*, p. 32). An informer Wiseman knew, a certain W.S., faces a similar fate after cursing the dissenters whom he has been sent to spy upon. Wiseman describes how God strikes W.S. by noting the gradual process of silencing, until 'his speech went quite away, and he

---

[7] Furlong, *Puritan's Progress*, p. 131.

could speak no more than a Swine or Bear' (*MB*, p. 81). W.S. is eventually struck down by God after living for a half year unable to speak. In each instance cited above, the sinner can no longer speak before he or she actually dies. This destruction of the voice foretells the ultimate annihilation of the voice that comes with death itself.

One of the most controversial inset stories is the cautionary tale of John Cox, told by Wiseman in order to enforce the notion that the wicked will go to Hell even if their last moments before dying do not foreshadow this fate. The story is lengthy, quite graphic, and enforces the justice meted out in stories which reflect folk wisdom: the wicked must suffer in both the afterlife and this life. This passage may reflect Bunyan's own masochistic fantasies found in *Grace Abounding*, or it may simply be him at his best when using low realism to make a point. Attentive tells Wiseman that '*I did once know a man, a Barber, that took his own Raisor, and cut his own* Throat, *and then put his head out of his Chamber-window, to shew the neighbours what he had done, and after a little while died*' (*MB*, p. 158). Wiseman is not to be outdone by Attentive, so he tells a more graphic story to further the point. He tells how John Cox grew desperate while fearing for his family's welfare since he could not participate in the harvest due to an illness. Here the body is subjected to horrors in vivid, visceral realism:

> he fell into deep despair about the world [...] he desired his wife to depart the room [...] quickly took his *Raisor*, and therewith cut up a great hole in his side, out of which he pulled, and cut off some of his guts, and threw them, with the blood, up and down the Chamber. But this not speeding of him so soon as he desired, he took the same Raisor and therewith cut his own throat [...] and so after a few gasps died desperately. When he had turned him of his back, to the wall, the blood ran out of his belly as out of a boul, and soaked quite through the bed to the boards, and through the chinks of the boards it ran pouring down to the ground (*MB*, p. 159).

Tormented by his inability to feed his family during the next hay-time, John Cox kills himself to end the suffering this life has given him. The horrifying vividness of the story shocks the reader and makes the reader aware of the reality and physicality of the body.

The familiarity of the passage not only implies that Wiseman knows of the suicide, it makes the immediacy of the body grossly apparent to the reader. If one has forgotten the physicality of Badman's body, Wiseman tells a story that makes the image of the body present in the reader's mind. The story is a warning that taking one's life, no matter how attractive the opportunity may seem, leads to damnation. It is told in vivid detail so that the reader may relate to the sufferings of the physical body, yet Furlong objects to Bunyan's dwelling on suicide as a mere cautionary tale:

> Bunyan goes on to protest rather thinly that he relates this horrible tale 'as a warning'; against what, it is hard to imagine. Not many of his flock can have felt a temptation to follow poor John Cox's example. Its real significance is that it recalls Bunyan's own suicidal tendencies; in its psychotic destructiveness he lives again his temptations to self-injury.[8]

Bunyan displays the maimed body in this story to emphasize the severity of physical pain, to make his audience imagine the pain that afflicts the sinner who denies the grace of God and desires to take his own life.

Although critics and scholars cite such inset stories as the greatest strength of the text, Forrest and Sharrock also stress that these stories may back the folk wisdom notion that evil sinners get their just deserts in life and the afterlife; however,

> What is impressive about the construction of the book is that such fearful punishments are totally absent from the main story; diabolic bloodshed and disemboweling threaten from the edge of the narrative, but Badman's history is recounted realistically and without undue sensationalism (*MB*, p. xxv).

The inset stories may appeal to the simple-minded, but they are not the core of the text. Bunyan includes them to describe the physical body in pain, thereby placing torment in the simplest terms possible so others may realize they should learn that suffering is sent by the grace of God in order to make the sinner convert, accept the grace of God, and so avoid the even greater torment that awaits sinners in the afterlife.

The main narrative complicates the relationship between the body and soul, for the irony of Badman's quiet death after a relatively

---

8   Furlong, *Puritan's Progress*, p. 131.

enjoyable life has no place within the simplistic worldview of folk wisdom. Wiseman discountenances this world-view when, discussing the manner of Badman's death, he asserts to Attentive:

> he dyed very stilly and quietly; upon which you made observation, that the common people conclude, that if a man dyes quietly; and as they call it, like a Lamb, he is certainly gone to Heaven: when alas, if a wicked man dyes quietly, if a man that has all his dayes lived in nortorious sin, dyeth quietyly; his quiet dying is so far off from being a sign of his being saved, that it is an uncontrollable proof of his damnation (*MB*, p. 161).

Here, the state of the body does not give an indication of the state of the soul. The message of *Mr. Badman* is straightforward: it defies folk wisdom in order to emphasize that a good death does not mean a good afterlife.

The portrayal of the body in *Mr. Badman* is problematic; the detailed physical descriptions in the many inset stories told by both Attentive and Wiseman contrast greatly with the absence of Badman's body. Badman's voice is completely absent from the story, and his body is not present while Attentive and Wiseman discuss his life and death. Furlong suggests that this absence of voice may be due to Badman's being Bunyan's alter ego; the greatest argument for this interpretation parallels Badman's childhood sins to those of Bunyan in *Grace Abounding*. By silencing Badman first and then having two others discuss his sins, Bunyan amputates this part of his own identity and then dissects its wickedness.[9] Bunyan does not depict an active, present Badman because Badman is a part of himself that he wishes dead.

Perhaps the strongest reason for the absence of Badman's voice is that he does not learn anything from suffering as Bunyan does in *Grace Abounding*. Such a sinner is so wicked that he could have nothing worthwhile to say, so his story must be related through two morally upright Christians. Badman's physical absence is also a statement about how suffering is mimetic of death. As Elaine Scarry explains, both suffering and death

---

9 Furlong, *Puritan's Progress*, p. 132.

are radical and absolute, found only at the boundaries they themselves create. That pain is so frequently used as a symbolic substitute for death in the initiation rites of many tribes is surely attributable to an intuitive human recognition that pain is the equivalent in felt-experience of what is unfeelable in death. Each only happens because of the body. In each, the contents of consciousness are destroyed. The two are the most intense forms of negation, the purest expressions of the anti-human, of annihilation, of total aversiveness, though one is an absence and the other a felt presence, one occurring in the cessation of sentience, the other expressing itself in grotesque overload. Regardless, then, of the context in which it occurs, physical pain always mimes death and the infliction of physical pain is always a mock execution.[10]

The death of youth in an adolescent's rite of passage or the death of the sinner in a seventeenth-century convert's conversion narrative are symbolic deaths that may be reinforced by painful ceremonies. Conversion narratives of the seventeenth century depict the convert's struggles to receive free grace. Bunyan's own struggles are often internal, as when he struggles with despair: 'Now began my heart to again to ake, and fear I might meet with disappointment at the last' (*GA*, §196). In her spiritual autobiography, Hannah Allen's painful conversion process is often manifested in the body as well as the mind: 'Here I practiced many devices to make away my self [commit suicide], sometimes by Spiders (as before) sometimes endeavoring to let my self blood with a pair of sharp sizers.'[11] Sarah Wight and other converts tell similar stories of suicide and other forms of physical and mental suffering in their spiritual autobiographies. Often, the conversion process is a painful ordeal which results in the defeat of the person's former sinful self, though not a true death. In *Grace Abounding*, Bunyan assures the reader that there are still trials ahead, for the Devil forever preys upon the good Christian.

Pain and death control the body by making the person who experiences them realize how immediate, how real they are, whether it is through the cessation of life itself which death brings, or the painful amplification of sensation which pain delivers. The person in pain fears more pain and the possibility of dying, thus becoming more

---

10 Scarry, *Body in Pain*, p. 31.
11 Hannah Allen, *Satan his Methods and Malice Baffled. A narrative of God's gracious dealings with that choice Christian Mrs. Hannah Allen* (1683), p. 44.

aware of the body itself, and less conscious of anything else, as if the entire world outside the body has been completely negated. Bunyan does not allow Badman to narrate his own story as he does himself in *Grace Abounding* because of Badman's blindness to the fire sent by God to torment his own conscience. Badman does not fear what may come to him after death, so others must narrate what will become of this composite reprobate who is thief, liar, curser, swearer, fornicator, and extortionist.

By having others narrate Badman's story, Bunyan makes him present for the reader while destroying Badman's voice. The stinking body at the funeral cannot speak for itself or defend its misdeeds. Badman has rarely ever suffered, so Bunyan has his two Christians discuss the sufferings of many sinners to make up for the suffering often seen in conversion tales. Scarry notes how the torturer makes the person tortured aware of how the body is present by inflicting pain, but also makes the voice absent, thus severing the person's voice from the body, by making the tortured person aware that they have no voice while the body still exists, as is the case with death: 'for in death the body is emphatically present while that more elusive part represented by the voice is so alarmingly absent that heavens are created to explain its whereabouts'.[12] The voice may be taken by the torturer or by the oppressor, but in any case it is a reminder of death. Without a voice one does not truly live, no matter how aware one is of the body itself. Once the spirit has departed, the voice is gone, leaving only the physical body. Badman never worries about the heavens which his spirit, his voice, may aspire to reach, just as he never fears to what hells his bodiless self will plummet. The near absence of suffering in his life has not made him fear the loss of voice that comes with death. Badman is a strange creature whose voice must be silenced and who must be discussed in concrete, realistic terms so others such as Attentive can understand how such a sinner can die a quiet natural death.

The spirit torments the sinner to lead a godly, just life, for eternal life or eternal death awaits everyone. Wiseman knows that the sinner is tormented by the spirit, for he cites both Scripture and Christian experience: 'He that knows himself to be a sinner, is molested, espe-

---

12   Scarry, *Body in Pain*, p. 49.

cially if that knowledge comes not to him untill he is cast upon his death-bed; molested, I say, before he can dye quietly. Yea, he is molested, dejected and cast down, he is also made to cry out, to hunger and thirst after mercy by Christ' (*MB*, pp. 161–2). Bunyan writes of such torments he experiences himself in *Grace Abounding*, as in paragraph 56: 'This resemblance abode upon my spirit many dayes, all which time I saw myself in a forlorn and sad condition, but yet was provoked to a vehement hunger, and desire to be one of that number that did sit in this Sun-Shine [of God's merciful face]' (*GA*, §56). Contrary to Bunyan, Badman ignores such molestation and so passes from natural death to eternal death. Badman does not have the capacity to understand inward, spiritual suffering, so once the physical suffering ceases, he is able to forget about the temporary torments and ignore the eternal torments that await him. He only repents his wicked deeds twice, when he is sick or in pain. Pain may bring awareness of death to Badman, but life makes him forget about the eternal, and he always returns to his wicked ways. He so enjoys the pleasures of the physical body and the natural world that he never worries about eternity.

Badman's eternal condition is easy to determine since he never learns from suffering and he is always quick to return to his many wicked ways. Wiseman tells Attentive 'I believe that at times God did let down fire from Heaven into his Conscience. True, I believe he would quickly put it out again' (*MB*, p. 85). This fire sent by God only comes to Badman twice, Wiseman says, 'Once when he broke his legg as he came home drunk from the Ale-house; and another time when he fell sick, and thought he should die' (*MB*, p.131). Badman does call upon God for mercy while he is in pain, but Wiseman notes that Badman also swore and went about with his wickedness as the pain went away. For a brief moment, Badman worries about death and the next world, but it is only while he is in pain. Badman is not one to thank God for good fortune, as though he cannot remember the times he suffers, and that he will one day suffer eternally, as Wiseman insists happens as soon as Badman dies.

The second time Badman shows signs of conscience and repentance is when his body is in danger. While sick, Badman apologizes to his wife and praises her for being godly; he listens to godly ministers and seems about to change, or so his wife and the whole town begins to believe. Yet as soon as the suffering stops, so does his desire to be godly, and Wiseman continues: 'For so soon as ever he had hopes of mending, and found that his strength began to renew, his trouble began to goe off his heart, and he grew as great a stranger to his frights and fears, as if he had never had them' (*MB*, p.138). Badman never learns, for he dismisses the pain as quickly as he can in order to enjoy life as he always has. Wiseman tells Attentive how the physician explained Badman's brief lapse into godliness as distemper:

> *That those fears and Out-cries did arise from the height of his distemper, for that disease was often attended with lightness of the head, by reason the sick party could not sleep, and for that the vapours disturbed the brain: But you see Sir, quoth he, that so soon as you got sleep and betook your self to rest, and your head settled, and so these frenzies left you* (*MB*, p. 138).

This rationalization may sit well with atheists, yet it is a kind of murder which Bunyan addresses in the margins of the text: 'Ignorant physicians kill souls while they cure bodyes' (*MB*, p. 138). This killing of the soul is much like the removal of the voice which a torturer achieves. The body, its presence, is the source of all that is good as far as Badman can reason, just as the body is the source of all pain as far as the tortured person can reason. Scarry's argument that political regimes employ torture in order to force the tortured subjects to identify the regime's insignia as the source of pain and the source of great power sheds much light on the physician's reasoning that religion constructs suffering to achieve certain ends. In the first part of her study, Scarry elaborates how the tortured subject associates pain with weapons, then domestic tools, then the very room of a dwelling, to the core of what one needs to survive: food, shelter, and reproduction. The body itself is seen as the source, and cause of pain, but it is only so because the political regime has the power to turn the entire domestic, social, and physical world against the tortured subject. Unlike the political regime which wields torture to make its subjects compliant, no one gains anything by Badman's damnation; no one except for the Devil who claimed the souls mentioned by Wiseman and Attentive.

Badman's death must disturb those who believe the actual death must indicate the dying person's afterlife. There is no period of slobbering as occurred with the informer W.S., who 'was taken with a drauling, or slabbering at his mouth, which slabber sometime would hang at his mouth well nigh half way down to the ground' (*MB*, p. 81), nor does any Devil fetch him as it did Ned's father. When Wiseman tells of Badman's death, it is in direct opposition to folk wisdom: 'he lived wickedly to the last, and then went quietly out of the world: therefore *Mr. Badman* is gone to Hell' (*MB*, p. 161). Such logic reflects Wiseman's earlier point that the manner of how the body is destroyed is not as important as the state of that person's soul, whether that person has been wicked or good (*MB*, p. 157). Badman's body does create a horrifying stench that the common people must have interpreted as a sign of his damnation, but Wiseman returns to the point that 'this is an heavy judgment of God upon wicked men; (Job xxi. 23) one goes to Hell in peace, another goes to Hell in trouble' (*MB*, p. 168). Bunyan has Wiseman insist that Badman's wickedness, not the stench of his body, is the proof of his damnation. The body suffers physical afflictions and the soul suffers spiritual affliction; as a sexually licentious person's body will stink of syphilis, so will his or her soul stink of the sin of uncleanliness; however, it is the sinner's wickedness, not the syphilis itself, which leads to eternal suffering. Physical suffering is simply a precursor, not a direct reflection of eternal suffering.

The image of the body in *Mr. Badman* is ever present and continually torn and rent in the many inset tales told throughout Wiseman and Attentive's dialogue as an image of what the conscience suffers under the torment of the spirit. This torment differs from the oppression that earthly institutions such as the Restoration government inflicted, for the power which sends fire into Badman's conscience is greater than any earthly institution. Bunyan includes the inset stories and the details about Badman's stinking corpse so that his audience may imagine even greater torments if they continue to lead wicked lives. Physical suffering is a foretaste of eternity; when coupled with godly advice and examples, it should be a strong deterrent to curb wickedness.

12

STUART SIM
'Transworld Depravity' and 'Invariant Assertions': John Bunyan's Possible Worlds

In *Postcultural Theory: critical theory after the Marxist paradigm*, Eve Tavor Bannet sought to establish some new directions for literary theory, on the basis that most of the schools of thought that had held the stage for the last couple of decades or so – poststructuralism, deconstruction, new historicism, second-wave feminism, etc. – had all become rather tired and predictable, and that some new sources of inspiration were required in order to revitalise the art of literary analysis. One of the sources that she suggested might 'take us beyond the boundaries and the limitations of the current paradigm' was 'possible worlds theory'.[1] A somewhat technical branch of philosophical logic dealing with issues of necessity and contingency, this theory had already attracted a certain amount of attention from literary scholars, notably from Thomas Pavel.[2] It has even been argued that a self-conscious attitude towards the construction of possible worlds is a defining characteristic of postmodern literature.[3] In what follows, I will be arguing that possible worlds theory is peculiarly appropriate to the study of the work of John Bunyan. Bunyan's fictional world, after

---

1 Eve Tavor Bannet, *Postcultural Theory: critical theory after the Marxist paradigm* (Basingstoke, 1993), p. xi.
2 See particularly Pavel's *Fictional Worlds* (Cambridge MA, 1986). Other key studies cited by Bannet include Doreen Maitre, *Literature and Possible Worlds* (London, 1983); Floyd Merrell, *Pararealities: the nature of our fictions and how we know them* (Amsterdam, 1988); and Umberto Eco, *The Limits of Interpretation* (Bloomington, 1990).
3 See, for example, the work of Brian McHale, for whom 'the postmodernist condition [is] an anarchic landscape of worlds in the plural' (Brian McHale, *Postmodernist Fiction* (New York and London, 1987), p. 37).

all, is one in which issues of necessity, most particularly in the guise of *predestinarian* necessity, have a critical role to play.

Possible Worlds Theory

Before going any further, it would be helpful to give a short, and hopefully not overly technical, exposition of possible worlds theory. Possible worlds have been defined by the American philosopher Alvin Plantinga, in his fascinating book, *God, Freedom and Evil*, as follows:

> The basic idea is that a possible world is a *way things could have been*; it is a *state of affairs* of some kind [...] What sort of a thing is a state of affairs? The following would be examples:
> Nixon's having won the 1972 election
> 7 + 5's being equal to 12
> All men's being mortal [...]
> A proposition *p corresponds* to a state of affairs *s*, in this sense, if it is impossible that *p* be true and *s* fail to obtain and impossible that *s* obtain and *p* fail to be true [...] Of course not every possible state of affairs is a possible world [...] To be a possible world, a state of affairs must be very large – so large as to be *complete* or *maximal*.[4]

Plantinga's study is one of the more creative excursions into possible worlds theory in the philosophical literature, and I will be referring to it frequently from now onwards.[5] The theory itself is usually traced back to the work of Leibniz, and his famous, or infamous, contention that we live in the best of all possible worlds that God could create.

---

4   Alvin Plantinga, 'God, Possible Worlds and the Problem of Evil', in Ted Honderich and Myles Burnyeat (ed.), *Philosophy As It Is* (Harmondsworth, 1979), pp. 417–46 (pp. 426–7).
5   For more on possible worlds theory see chapters 4–8 of Alvin Plantinga, *The Nature of Necessity* (Oxford, 1974). Other notable studies on the topic are Nicholas Rescher, *A Theory of Possibility* (Oxford, 1975); Saul Kripke, *Naming and Necessity* (Oxford, 1980); and David Lewis, *On the Plurality of Worlds* (Oxford, 1986).

The nature of Leibniz's God has been neatly summarised by Plantinga as follows:

> Before God created anything at all, he was confronted with an enormous range of choices; he could create or bring into actuality any of the myriads of different possible worlds. Being perfectly good, he must have chosen to create the best world he could; being omniscient, he was able to create any possible world he pleased. He must, therefore, have chosen the best of all possible worlds; and hence *this* world, the one he did create, must be the best possible.[6]

Much argument has raged over this belief, from the days of Voltaire onwards, and philosophers nowadays are prone to ask awkward questions such as whether God could create a world in which he did not exist – since that is, after all, a *possible* world. Interesting though this line of questioning undoubtedly is (from both a philosophical and a theological perspective), I do not intend to pursue it here since it goes beyond the bounds of the present enquiry; but in leading us towards paradox it succeeds in putting us in the right framework for the kind of questions I *do* want to consider. Questions such as: how free is God, or the author, if we assume the existence of predestination? (are there worlds that neither God nor Bunyan *could* create?) what is the *degree* of necessity present in predestination? what is the *relationship* between logical and predestinarian necessity? could there be a world in which the saved and the damned changed places with one another?

On that issue of necessity, Plantinga notes that,

> Leibniz pointed out that a proposition p is necessary if it is true in every possible world. We may add that p is possible if it is true in at least one world and impossible if true in none. Furthermore, p *entails* q if there is no possible world in which p is true and q is false; and *p is consistent with q* if there is at least one world in which both p and q are true.[7]

Predestinarian soteriology raises precisely that question as to whether there is a proposition p that is true in every possible world, and we shall be exploring shortly what implications this holds for Bunyan's

---

6   Plantinga, 'God, Possible Worlds', p. 426.
7   Plantinga, 'God, Possible Worlds', p. 429.

narrative practice. Before that, however, let us consider an intriguing concept of Plantinga's entitled 'transworld depravity'. For Plantinga,

> A person P *suffers from transworld depravity* if and only if the following holds: for every world W such that P is significantly free in W and P does only what is right in W, there is an action A and a maximal world segment S' such that
> (1) S' includes A's being morally significant for P
> (2) S' includes P's being free with respect to A
> (3) S' is included in W and includes neither P's performing A nor P's refraining from performing A

and

> (4) If S' were actual, P would go wrong with respect to A.
> (In thinking about this definition, remember that (4) is to be true in fact, in the actual world – not in that world W.)[8]

Now, I suspect this *is* straying into the overly technical dimension that I promised earlier to try to avoid, but Plantinga's subsequent conclusion leaves us in no doubt what is at stake: 'What is important about the idea of transworld depravity', he emphasises, 'is that if a person suffers from it, then it wasn't within God's power to actualize any world in which that person is significantly free but does no wrong – that is, a world in which he produces moral good but no moral evil'.[9] In other words, once depraved, *always* depraved – and *everywhere* depraved. Depravity is an inalterable part of that person's character, which cannot be theorised differently. Cue Ignorance, or Mr. Badman – and cue as well, one would imagine, wholehearted agreement from all predestinarian soteriologists, especially those of the supralapsarian variety, who would be only too happy to embrace any theory which absolved God of responsibility as far as sin and evil were concerned.[10]

---

8   Plantinga, 'God, Possible Worlds', pp. 438–9. In Plantinga's argument, S equals an actual state of affairs, S' a particular example of a possible one; and a 'maximal world segment' is a state of affairs compatible with a particular possible world, which is made up of a collection of such segments.
9   Plantinga, 'God, Possible Worlds', p. 439.
10 Supralapsarians believe that God decreed the spiritual fate of all mankind *prior* to the Fall, thus anticipating the sin on which damnation notionally depends.

To some extent here I am following up an invitation extended by Plantinga: 'I leave as homework the problems of comparing transworld depravity with what Calvinists call "total depravity"'.[11] 'Total' in this case means applying, in some sense, to all mankind. As William J. Bouwsma has pointed out, Calvin believes that 'sin has vitiated every part' of human being, although some ray of hope does shine through this fairly gloomy prognosis. Calvin's position, Bouwsma goes on to argue, is 'not that there is no capacity for good in human beings, but that no human activity is altogether blameless'.[12] Human good does exist, therefore, but in tainted form; in Calvin's own words, it comes 'still always spotted and corrupted with some impurity of the flesh and has, so to speak, some dregs mixed with it'.[13] Given those permanently residual dregs to contend with, the two forms of depravity seem very much comparable.

Transworld depravity is backed up by what Plantinga calls 'world-indexed' properties, that we have, as an essential part of our individual being, across all possible worlds.[14] These offer little comfort for the transworld depraved either, I am afraid. On the basis of an invented transworld depraved character called 'Curley Smith' (Mayor of Boston in a sometime possible world), Plantinga gives us the following formulation:

> So if Curley suffers from transworld depravity, then Curley's essence has this property: God could not have created any world W such that Curleyhood

---

11   Plantinga, 'God, Possible Worlds', p. 438.
12   William J. Bouwsma, *John Calvin: a sixteenth-century portrait* (New York and Oxford, 1988), p. 139.
13   John Calvin, *Institutes of the Christian Religion*, ed. John T. McNeill, trans. Ford Lewis Battles, 2 vols. (Philadelphia and London, 1960), 1: 776 (III.xiv.9 of the original).
14   Plantinga, 'God, Possible Worlds', p. 440. Eco similarly speaks of a 'transworld identity' based on essential properties (Umberto Eco, *The Role of the Reader: explorations in the semiotics of texts* (Bloomington, and London, 1979), p. 229). We can also note Saul Kripke's concept of the 'rigid designator' in this context; proper names, for example, designate 'the same object in all possible worlds' (Saul Kripke, 'Identity and Necessity', in Honderich and Burnyeat, *Philosophy As It Is*, pp. 478–513 (p. 488)).

contains the properties *is significantly free in W* and *always does what is right in W*.[15]

Substitute 'Ignorancehood' or 'Badmanhood' for 'Curleyhood' and the implications of such an argument for Bunyan's fictional worlds begin to declare themselves; the *coup-de-grace* being, in Plantinga's chilling words, that,

> if every essence suffers from transworld depravity, then no matter which essences God instantiates, the resulting persons, if free with respect to morally significant actions, would always perform at least some wrong actions. If every essence suffers from transworld depravity, then it was beyond the power of God himself to create a world containing moral good but no moral evil.[16]

As far as the unfortunate individual goes, therefore, transworld depravity is a nasty, brutish, and anything but short experience.

Narrative and Possible Worlds

That narrative fiction deals in possible worlds is an obvious, even trivial point to make: taking 'possible world' in the non-technical sense of an imagined world. Narrative can be constructed in a variety of ways, but in each case there needs to be some point of contact, or recognition, between the imagined world of the author and the world we actually inhabit – something to nurture our suspension of disbelief; what Brian McHale, commenting on Pavel's theories, has called 'a semipermeable membrane' between narrative world and real world.[17] As Pavel himself has put it, 'Far from being well-defined and sealed off, fictional borders appear to be variously accessible, sometimes easy to trespass, obeying different sorts of constraints in different contexts'.[18] Narrative is also a possible world in the philosophical sense

---

15 Plantinga, 'God, Possible Worlds', p. 442.
16 Plantinga, 'God, Possible Worlds', p. 443.
17 McHale, *Postmodernist Fiction*, p. 34.
18 Thomas Pavel, 'The Borders of Fiction', *Poetics Today*, 4 (1983), 88.

of the term: internally self-consistent ('maximal' in Plantinga's scheme) and bound by certain constraints which dictate what can and cannot *logically* happen within the given narrative space. We might think of fictional narrative as *counterfactual*: if certain aspects of our world had turned out differently from the way they did, then the fiction we are presented with would make perfect sense. In Bannet's words, we are dealing with,

> what could be the case, or could have been the case, or might yet be the case, without ever necessarily being the case. The possible is what might exist, be done, be thought or happen; it is another way things could occur, or another way things could be thought or spoken or done.[19]

Our willing suspension of disbelief hangs to a large extent on the internal logic of the narrative counterfactual. There is no City of Destruction, except in the symbolic sense; but if there were, it would no doubt entail certain sets of circumstances such as the necessity to flee, and to undertake a perilous journey of the nature of Christian's. There is a remorseless logic to that journey that sweeps the reader along within the confines of Bunyan's possible world, from that terse opening injunction of Evangelist to '*Fly from the wrath to come*' (*PP*, p. 10) right through to Christian's triumphal reception into the Celestial City.

It is that internal logic in Bunyan's fiction which constitutes my main object of enquiry here. I will also be taking issue with Bannet's contention that we need to distance ourselves from the technically logical aspect of possible worlds theory in order to make the most of it in a literary context. The theory, she complains,

> is at present still plagued by imports from traditional logic and extant literary theory – imports such as the law of non-contradiction, the correspondence theory of truth, the two-tier model of real infra-structure and fictional superstructures, and the notion that we need fixed typological models and invariant across the worlds assertions – all assumptions which severely and unnecessarily

---

19   Bannet, *Postcultural Theory*, 117–8. For more on fiction as a form of counterfactual, see David Lewis, 'Truth in Fiction', *American Philosophical Review*, 15 (1978), 37–46.

limit our ability to use possible worlds to think otherwise than we thought before.[20]

I want to argue that by *emphasising* such logical features, most notably that notion of 'invariant across the worlds assertions', we can gain a deeper insight into the nature of Bunyan's narrative project (I will hyphenate the phrase 'invariant-across-the-worlds' from now on to bring out its adjectival role). Possible worlds theory helps us to understand the harshness of the logic of this project; what the author's beliefs will, and will not, allow him to do. Bannet feels that when 'we specify what is always or necessarily the case in all possible worlds, we in effect give ourselves a typology which not only excludes other possible constructions, but also tends, in practice, to make us blinder and more lazy readers'.[21] I think that Bunyan is dealing with just such a specification, but that, on the contrary, it invites his audience to be much more scrupulous and attentive readers in their decoding of the semiotics of salvation (and as Maxine Hancock, amongst others, has pointed out, we should never lose sight of 'the seriousness with which reading and interpreting were approached by both Bunyan and his readers).[22] It is certainly part of Bunyan's project to exclude other possible constructions of events than his own – latitudinarianism, for example.

---

20 Bannet, *Postcultural Theory*, p. 117. Pavel's work demonstrates something of a similar desire to break free from the more constraining aspects of philosophical logic.
21 Bannet, *Postcultural Theory*, p. 152.
22 Maxine Hancock, 'Bunyan as Reader: the Record of *Grace Abounding*', Bunyan Studies, 5 (1994), 68–84 (p. 68).

Necessity and Soteriology in Bunyan's Fiction

We turn now to Bunyan's fiction, in particular to consider the nature of the relationship between necessity and soteriology – a topic which raises some interesting questions regarding narrative shape and authorial freedom in *The Pilgrim's Progress, Mr. Badman* and *The Holy War*. Is it the case that soteriological necessity dictates certain narrative moves to the exclusion of others? Could there be counterfactual versions of Christian or Badman – worlds where Christian turned into Badman, or vice versa – or are they condemned to act the way they do, given a predestinarian schema? How much freedom does God or the author *have* when it comes to predestination? Behind such questions lies arguably the ultimate one in Bunyan's world: is the attainment of 'grace' always possible, or only *apparently* so?

Predestination, as interpreted by Calvin and his followers certainly, involves various paradoxes; such as the fact that the elect can take no credit for their salvation, but that, on the other hand, the reprobate are to blame for their own damnation. No credit can be taken because the state of the elect has been willed by God since before their birth; but as for the reprobate, 'the cause and occasion of it are found in themselves', in Calvin's typically unforgiving words.[23] The reasoning behind the paradox of reprobation is that all mankind is 'spotted and corrupted' by original sin and that no-one at all is *worth* saving: 'only as it so pleases him', as Calvin points out of God's practice in such matters, 'will he be merciful to one rather than to another'.[24] No individual has any grounds for complaint when he or she is passed over, since according to this doctrine none of us deserves the bestowal of divine grace on our person. The reprobate's case is as hopeless as that of the condemned criminal – an image used with considerable dramatic flair by Bunyan in his early work *The Doctrine of Law and Grace Unfolded* (1659):

---

23   Calvin, *Institutes*, 1: 957 (III.xxiii.8).
24   Calvin, *Institutes*, 1: 939 (III.xxii.6).

> Methinks the prisoners at the bar, having offended the Law (and the charge of a just Judge towards them) do much hold forth the Law, as it is a Covenant of Works, and how it deals with them that are under it. The prisoner having offended cries out for mercy; good my Lord mercy (saith he) pray my Lord pitty me; the Judge saith, What canst thou say for thy self, that sentence of Death should not be passed upon thee? Why nothing but this, I pray my Lord be merciful: But he answers again, Friend, the Law must take place, the Law must not be broken (*MW*, 2: 37–8).[25]

Such pleas fall on deaf ears, there being precious little leeway in a system where justice is so firmly in the ascendancy over mercy – as it generally is in Bunyan (Part II of *The Pilgrim's Progress* constituting the exception, with the figure of Mercy allotted a significant role).

The intense anxiety states that such a doctrine could induce in the sensitive individual are perhaps nowhere captured more memorably than in Bunyan's spiritual autobiography *Grace Abounding*, a major source of the fictional world of *The Pilgrim's Progress*:

> Thus, by the strange and unusual assaults of the tempter, was my Soul, like a broken Vessel, driven, as with the Winds, and tossed sometimes head-long into dispair; sometimes upon the Covenant of works, and sometimes to wish that the new Covenant, and the conditions thereof, might, so far forth as I thought myself concerned, be turned another way, and changed. But in all these, I was but as those that jostle against the Rocks; more broken, scattered, and rent. Oh, the unthought of imaginations, frights, fears, and terrors that are affected by a thorow application of guilt, yielding to desperation! (*GA*, §186).[26]

The new covenant referred to is the one favoured by Calvin: the covenant of faith, whereby it is one's faith and not one's actions (or 'works') that forms the ground of one's salvation. Already the individual's freedom to act is being called into question, as is the openness and availability of grace. On the face of it predestination, and the paradox of reprobation in particular, does not seem to offer many

---

25 For an analysis of the political implications of the covenant theology espoused in this treatise, see David Walker '"Heaven is prepared for whosoever will accept of it": Politics of the Will in Bunyan's *Doctrine of Law and Grace Unfolded*', *Prose Studies*, 21 (1998), 18–31.

26 For a reading of Bunyan emphasising the role of Calvinism in creating such anxiety states, see John Stachniewski, *The Persecutory Imagination: English Puritanism and the literature of religious despair* (Oxford, 1991).

loopholes for the individual to exploit: 'only as it so pleases him' hardly provides much encouragement for any such activity.

Spiritual autobiography in this period often has a Calvinist bias, and the author's use of that form in *The Pilgrim's Progress* demands that certain narrative moves be made; such as the recurrent sin-despair-repentance cycle that unfolds towards the soteriologically-defining conversion experience (the latter, critically, a consequence of the individual's faith rather than his works). In that sense, Christian is constrained as to what he can and cannot do over the course of his pilgrimage. He *must* perform certain actions, undergo certain experiences, more or less adhere to the route pointed out to him at the beginning of his journey by Evangelist ('Keep that light in your eye, and go up directly thereto, so shalt thou see the Gate; at which when thou knockest, it shall be told thee what thou shalt do' (*PP*, p. 10)), because of the predestinarian bias of his author's theology, and the narrative framework that has been developed to express this by several generations of Calvinist-influenced thinkers. By remaining within this narrative framework, with its highly distinctive semiotics, Bunyan positions himself within a cultural tradition with its own ideological certainties – or, we might say, 'invariant-across-the-worlds assertions' about belief and politics. *The Pilgrim's Progress* is a possible world that stands in a strict logical relationship to a range of other narrative worlds, stretching back through nonconformist and Puritan cultural history, with its catalogue of spiritual autobiographies, to such seminal works as Arthur Dent's *The Plaine Man's Pathway to Heaven* of 1601.[27]

So, too, with Ignorance, whose career can only unfold towards damnation and that final chilling dispatch to hell from the very gates of heaven, bound 'hand and foot' (*PP*, p. 163) like a criminal further to emphasise his guilt. It is hard to imagine that Ignorance could qualify for anything else *but* transworld depravity. To do so would be to cast doubt on the force of the author's predestinarian theology, where Ignorance is deemed to be damning *himself*, as he signals by

---

27 For more on this topic, see my *Negotiations with Paradox: narrative practice and narrative form in Bunyan and Defoe* (Hemel Hempstead, 1990), particularly chapter 1.

displaying a complacency about soteriological matters that amounts almost to spiritual pride. Bunyan certainly is not about to cast doubt on that theology from within the context of the Restoration settlement, where nonconformity has no reason to feel charitably inclined towards its perceived enemies – not even in another possible world.[28] Christian's response to the conduct of those two notable sceptics of the virtues of the 'straight and narrow' path (*PP*, p. 28), Formalist and Hypocrisy, tells us what to expect instead:

> I walk by the Rule of my Master, you walk by the rude working of your fancies. You are counted thieves already, by the Lord of the way; therefore I doubt you will not be found true men at the end of the way. You come in by your selves without his direction, and shall go out by your selves without his mercy (*PP*, p. 40).

Soteriological categories take on a considerable political resonance for the nonconformist cause in this period, and we have to assume their invariance across any possible world that God could create. Wherever the reprobate appear, they will be met with the same lack of mercy displayed towards Formalist and Hypocrisy in the instance above.

A predestinarian scheme demands that soteriological fate is decreed in advance and can never be altered – not even by God, it would seem, otherwise it would not *qualify* as predestinarian. Election will always be confirmed: 'But he that over-rules all things, having the power of their rage in his own hand, so wrought it about, that *Christian* for that time escaped them, and went his way' (*PP*, p. 97). Equally, so will damnation: 'You are counted thieves already'. To believe otherwise is to raise the spectre of works rather than faith being the determining factor in salvation; a possibility utterly rejected by Calvin, for whom, 'the salvation of believers [...] is not earned by works but comes from free calling'.[29] The sheer remorselessness of the predestinarian division of humanity into two forever opposed

---

28   For a counter-reading of Bunyan, de-emphasising the political side, see Michael A. Mullett, *John Bunyan in Context* (Keele, 1996). Mullett's Bunyan is 'not deeply interested in political questions' (p. 235), but the assumption that the spiritual can be so easily detached from the political in Bunyan's time is not one shared by many recent commentators.

29   Calvin, *Institutes*, 1: 937 (III.xxii.5).

categories, should bring home to us the enormity of original sin, the 'dregs' of which we can never expel from our actions. The only narrative suspense left once we accept the predestinarian schema lies in the way the semiotics of election and reprobation are revealed to us – as well as to the characters themselves, and whether they are endowed with the skill to read them correctly. Bunyan certainly expects some close reading skills on the part of his *audience* when it comes to these critical signs, and the way in which they irreparably divide an Ignorance from a Christian, recipients of grace from non-recipients.

Predestinarian soteriology is not designed to be a flexible theory with loopholes for good behaviour or change of heart on the part of the believer, therefore, but a judgement for all time; right up to, and including, the possible world of the Last Judgement. The covenant of works – in effect, a promise to amend one's conduct in a future possible world – simply fails to make any impression in this context. Predestination is to be considered, in Plantinga's terms of reference, a world-indexed condition that is not open to interpretation; a doctrine of unquestionable authority rather than a point of debate. (We can consider a predestinarian God as world-indexed too, rather than one who can choose to be other than he is, since that would suggest something less than perfection on his part in any one state of being.) Ignorance's semiotic blindness, as well as Talkative and Worldly Wiseman's cultural pragmatism, are to be regarded not as accidental, but as essential properties, world-indexed over time in such a manner that the characters can *never* manage to shed them – they would have no psychological impact on the audience otherwise. Neither can the Restoration regime escape the spiritual bad end that Bunyan's theology tells him must be its due. Although he would not conceive of it in these terms, Bunyan's God is not free to revise the facts of predestination, otherwise, as pointed out above, it would not really *be* predestination. Neither is Bunyan the author free to allow any scope for redemption on the part of his transworld depraved characters. Proposition $p - p$ for predestination, we might say – holds over all possible worlds or it ceases to have any capacity to compel fearful respect; not to mention induce the personally-harrowing anxiety states so frequently experienced by both Christian and his creator (the *Grace*

Abounding example above being but one of a host of such to be found throughout the text).

The respective progresses of Christian and Ignorance clearly reveal the harshness of the logic of Bunyan's narrative project. They are locked into the same fate across all possible worlds: the one to entry into, the other to expulsion from, the elusive Celestial City. For a figure from Bunyan's society, heaven and hell *must* operate across all possible worlds, and there is no necessity more inexorable than that attending predestinarian election or reprobation. As one of the shepherds remarks to Christian during his journey through the Delectable Mountains, the way to the Celestial City is 'Safe for those for whom it is to be safe', but for no others: *'transgressors shall fall therein'* (*PP*, p. 119).[30] It is hard to posit a counterfactual electee or reprobate, therefore; even to hint at the possibility of other spiritual outcomes would be to undercut one's theological position – to the ultimate detriment of one's ideological objectives also.

When we come to *Mr. Badman* we have yet another 'progress' – this time towards damnation:

> As I was considering with my self what I had written concerning the Progress of the Pilgrim from this World to Glory, and how it had been acceptable to many in this Nation: It came again into my mind to write, as then, of him that was going to Heaven, so now, of the Life and Death of the ungodly, and of their travel from this world to Hell (*MB*, p. 1).

We are also faced with the paradox of reprobation – 'the cause and occasion of it are found in themselves' – in its starkest form; the author encouraging us to believe, simultaneously, that grace is always available to Badman at any point on his progress, and that his descent

---

30 Bunyan is particularly adept at such sleights of hand, remarking in *The Heavenly Footman*, for example, that 'Heaven is prepared for whosoever will accept of it' (*MW*, 5: 167). The corollary of this is that if heaven is *not* prepared for you, then, clearly, it must be the case that you could not have 'accepted of it'; blame is invariably shifted onto the individual when it comes to all such judgements. For more on the importance of such sentiments in Bunyan's ideological outlook, see Walker, 'Politics of the Will'.

into reprobation is nevertheless absolutely inevitable.[31] That descent is also presented as past history right from the narrative's opening exchanges, just in case we are in any danger, as readers, of lapsing into inappropriate sympathy for his fate: 'He died that he might die, he went from Life to Death, and then from Death to Death, from Death Natural to Death Eternal' (*MB*, p. 14). Another way of describing this paradox would be to say that grace is both available and not available to Badman, or that counterfactualisation of his fate is both possible and impossible; leading to the problematical conclusion that contingency and necessity co-exist in the same narrative space (thus raising the spectre of the 'impossible world' so disliked by theorists such as Umberto Eco perhaps).[32] Predestinarian theology would seem to allow just that possibility, but with the sting in the tail that Badman is pre-programmed to refuse the ostensible offer of grace every time around, without fail – his '*Indwelling sin*' (*MB*, p. 17), as Mr. Attentive puts it, seeing to that.

Again, it is hard to see how this state of affairs could alter in any possible world; how the possibility of grace could ever be anything other than apparent only; how an indwelling sin, proceeding from that ineradicable original sin with which the entire human race is tainted for eternity, could ever be expelled. In order to be predestinarian, it has to be an *essentially* irreversible condition – and in order to be original sin it has to be an act that could never, ever, be retracted. Badman is not free to amend his conduct; nor God to change his mind regarding his subject's ultimate spiritual status (that would be to have performed a less than perfect act in the first instance); nor Bunyan to allow us as readers to think that either eventuality could ever be a real possibility. We are in the presence of the transworld depraved yet again, world-indexed over time repeatedly to commit the same election-excluding sins, with all the predictability in Badman's case of the return of '*the Dog to his vomit*' (*MB*, p. 17). The logic of predes-

---

31 For a fuller discussion of the impact of this figure on the fictional output of both Bunyan and Defoe, see again my *Negotiations with Paradox*.
32 For Eco, such a world, where contradictory states of affairs apply (and propositions can be true and false at the same time), produces 'a sense of logical uneasiness and of narrative discomfort' (Eco, *The Role of the Reader*, p. 234).

tinarian soteriology must be considered to be based on the principles of 'across-the-worlds' invariance, which is to say that there is a strict logical necessity encoded within soteriological necessity. There is no more room for manoeuvre with regard to one's fate in Badman's case than there is in Christian's or Ignorance's. The only difference between Christian and his reprobate counterparts Ignorance and Badman, is that the latter are also held to be world-indexing *themselves*: the reprobate are to blame for hardening their hearts against God, rather than God himself.

Similarly, in *The Holy War*, Mansoul is assured that Emanuel, having returned '*once and twice, and thrice to save thee from the poyson of those arrows that would have wrought thy death*' (*HW*, p. 249), will return yet again, no matter what new 'poysons' Diabolus and his minions might contrive to conjure up in the interim:

> And dost thou know why I at first, and do still suffer Diabolonians to dwell in thy walls, O Mansoul? it is to keep thee wakening, to try thy love, to make thee watchful, and to cause thee yet to prize my noble Captains, their Souldiers, and my mercy [...] I command thee to believe that my love is constant to thee. O my Mansoul, how have I set my heart, my love upon thee (*HW*, pp. 249, 250).

Even if there are unspecified dangers yet to be faced in the future, transworld election beckons, and it becomes impossible to envisage a world in which the saved and the damned could ever exchange places – or where grace could become a merely contingent property.

Conclusion: the Ideology of Bunyan's Possible Worlds

One is forced to conclude that soteriological necessity drives narrative necessity in Bunyan, and that counterfactualisation can only take place within the strictly-defined parameters of soteriological necessity. Which is to say that soteriological necessity, arguably the harshest form of necessity conceivable, applies across all possible worlds. It is invariant – even *God* could not change it, even if he wanted to – an unlikely scenario in itself. As Bunyan had assured the 'blessed saints' in *The Doctrine of Law and Grace Unfolded*, with appropriate rhetorical emphasis, 'you have received a kingdom which cannot, which cannot be moved' (*MW*, 2: 163). Answering the question I posed at the beginning, yes, there are worlds that neither God nor Bunyan could create: from a predestinarian perspective there is no possible world in which Badman can become Christian, or Christian Badman, or Mansoul fail to be rescued at the last minute by Emanuel. In *any* possible world Christian will receive the seal of election, Ignorance and Badman will be debarred forever from doing so on the grounds of their transworld depravity (their fault, not God's, it must always be emphasised, since the guilt for original sin can never be evaded by mankind), and Mansoul will survive to fight yet another day. Once saved, always saved; once reprobated, always reprobated; once the Law, always the Law.

In each case soteriological essence circumscribes God's range of creative options, giving us a synthesis of logical and theological necessity – a potent combination for an author like Bunyan to have at his ideological disposal. 'God could not have created any world *W* such that Curleyhood contains the properties *is significantly free in W* and *always does what is right in W*. Progresses may differ in incidental detail (as Christian's does from Christiana's or Mansoul's), but soteriological categories function invariantly across the entire progress spectrum. And that is the harsh, but to the embattled nonconformist individual suffering under the Restoration regime, singularly encouraging message to emerge from Bunyan's possible fictional worlds.

Bibliography of Secondary Sources

Achinstein, Sharon, *Milton and the Revolutionary Reader* (Princeton, 1994).
Appleby, Joyce Oldham, *Economic Thought and Ideology in Seventeenth-Century England* (Princeton, 1978).
Backscheider, Paula R., *A Being More Intense* (New York, 1984).
Baird, Charles W., *John Bunyan: a study in narrative technique* (Port Washington NY, 1977).
Bannet, Eve Tavor, *Postcultural Theory: critical theory after the Marxist paradigm* (Basingstoke, 1993).
Barnard, John, 'Bibliographical Context and the Critic', in *Text 3*, ed. D. C. Greetham and W. Speed Hill (New York, 1987), pp. 27–46.
Batson, E. Beatrice, *John Bunyan: allegory and imagination* (London, 1984).
Benjamin, Walter, *The Origin of German Tragic Drama*, trans. John Osborne (London, 1977).
Berry, Boyd, *Process of Speech: Puritan religious writings and 'Paradise Lost'* (Baltimore, 1976).
Bland, Mark, 'The Appearance of the Text in Early Modern England', *Text 11*, ed. W. Speed Hill and Edward M. Burns (Ann Arbor, 1998), pp. 91–127.
Bouwsma, William, *John Calvin: a sixteenth-century portrait* (New York and Oxford, 1988).
Brown, John, *John Bunyan (1628–1688): his life, times and work*, rev. edn. ed. Frank Mott Harrison (London, 1928).
Caarov, Ellen, 'A Wilderness of Opinions Confounded: Allegory and Ideology', *College English*, 34 (1972), 215–55.
Campbell, Gordon, *A Milton Chronology* (Basingstoke, 1997).
Campbell, Gordon *et al.*, 'The Provenance of *De Doctrina Christiana*', *Milton Quarterly*, 17 (1997), 67–121.

Camden, Vera J., 'Blasphemy and the Problem of the Self in *Grace Abounding*', *Bunyan Studies*, 2 (1989), 5–22.

—,'"Most Fit for a Wounded Conscience": the Place of Luther's "Commentary on Galatians" in *Grace Abounding*', *Renaissance Quarterly*, 50 (1997), 819–49.

Capp, B. S., *The Fifth Monarchy Men: a study in seventeenth-century English millenarianism* (London, 1972).

Carey, John, *Milton* (London, 1969).

Carlton, Peter J., 'Bunyan: Language, Convention, Authority', *English Literary History*, 51 (1984), 17–32.

Chartier, Roger, *The Order of Books*, trans. Lydia G. Cochrane (Cambridge, 1994).

Christianson, Paul, *Reformers of Babylon: English apocalyptic visions from the Reformation to the end of the Civil War* (Toronto, 1978).

Clapp, Sarah L. C., 'Subscription Publishers Prior to Jacob Tonson', *The Library*, 4th. ser., 13 (1932), 158–83.

Corns, Thomas N., 'Bunyan's *Grace Abounding* and the Dynamics of Restoration Nonconformity', in Neil Rhodes (ed.), *English Renaissance Prose: history, language, and politics* (Tempe, 1997), pp. 259–70.

Damrosch, Leopold, *God's Plot and Man's Stories: studies in the fictional Imagination from Milton to Fielding* (Chicago and London, 1985).

De Krey, Gary S., 'Rethinking the Restoration: Dissenting Cases for Conscience, 1667–1672', *Historical Journal*, 38 (1995), 53–83.

Dunn, Kevin, *Pretexts of Authority: the rhetoric of authorship in the Renaissance preface* (Stanford, 1994).

Eagleton, Terry, *Walter Benjamin, or Towards a Revolutionary Criticism* (London, 1981).

Eco, Umberto, *The Role of the Reader: explorations in the semiotics of texts* (Bloomington and London, 1979).

—, *The Limits of Interpretation* (Bloomington and London, 1990).

Evans, G. E., *Come Wind, Come Weather: chronicles of Tilehouse Street Baptist Church, 1669–1969* (London and Tonbridge, 1969).

Eyre, G. E. B., and C. R. Rivington (ed.), *A Transcript of the Registers of the Worshipful Company of Stationers, 1640–1708*, 3 vols (London, 1913–14).

Fellows, Jennifer, 'St. George as Romance Hero', *Reading Medieval Studies*, 19 (1993), 27–54.

Ferenczi, Sandor, *Sex in Psychoanalysis* (New York: 1960).

Fish, Stanley E., *Self-Consuming Artifacts: the experience of seventeenth-century literature* (Berkeley, Los Angeles CA and London, 1972).

Fletcher, Angus, *Allegory: the theory of a symbolic mode* (Ithaca, 1964).

Foucault, Michel, *Madness and Civilization: a history of insanity in the age of reason* (New York, 1965).

—, 'What Is an Author?', in Donald F. Bouchard (ed.), *Language, Counter Memory, Practice* (Oxford, 1977).

Freud, Sigmund, *Collected Papers*, 5 vols., trans. Alix and James Strachey (New York, 1959).

—, *The Standard Edition of the Complete Psychological Works*, ed. James Strachey, 24 vols. (London, 1953–66).

Frye, Northrop, *Anatomy of Criticism: four essays* (Princeton, 1957).

—, *The Secular Scripture: a study of the structure of romance* (Cambridge MA and London, 1976).

Furdell, Elizabeth, '"At the King's Arms in the Poultrey": The Bookshop Emporium of Dorman Newman 1670–1694', *London Journal*, 23 (1998), 1–20.

Furlong, Monica, *Puritan's Progress* (New York, 1975).

Gay, David, James G. Randall and Arlette Zinck (ed.), *Awakening Words: John Bunyan and the language of community* (Newark DE and London, 2000).

Golder, Harold,'John Bunyan's Hypocrisy', *North American Review*, 223 (1926), 323–32.

—, 'Bunyan's Valley of the Shadow', *Modern Philology*, 27 (1929), 55–72.

—, 'Bunyan's Giant Despair', *Journal of English and Germanic Philology*, 30 (1931), 361–78.

Goldie, Mark, 'The Theory of Religious Intolerance in Restoration England', in Ole Peter Grell (ed.), *From Persecution to Toler-*

ation: the Glorious revolution and Religion in England (Oxford, 1991), pp. 331–68.

Greaves, Richard L., *John Bunyan and English Nonconformity* (London and Rio Grande OH, 1992).

—, '"Let Truth Be Free": John Bunyan and the Restoration Crisis of 1667–73', *Albion*, 28 (1996), 587–605.

—, 'John Bunyan and the Fifth Monarchists', *Albion*, 13 (1981), 83–95.

Greaves, Richard L. and Robert Zaller, *Biographical Dictionary of British Radicals in the Seventeenth Century*, 3 vols. (Brighton, 1983).

Greetham, D. C., *Textual Scholarship: an introduction* (New York and London, 1994).

Gribben, Crawford, *The Puritan Millennium: literature and theology, 1550–1682* (Dublin, 2000).

Guibbory, Achsah, *The Map of Time: seventeenth-century English literature and ideas of pattern in history* (Urbana, 1986).

Hale, J. R., 'Incitement to Violence? English Divines on the Theme of War 1578–1631', in J. G. Rowe and W. H. Stockdale (ed.), *Florilegium Historiale* (Toronto, 1971), pp. 368–399.

Hancock, Maxine, 'Bunyan as Reader: The Record of *Grace Abounding*', *Bunyan Studies*, 5 (1994), 68–84.

Harrison, Frank Mott, 'Nathaniel Ponder: The Publisher of *The Pilgrim's Progress*', *The Library*, 4th ser. 15 (1934), 257–94.

Harrison, G. B., *John Bunyan: a study in personality* (North Haven CT, 1967).

Hawkins, Anne, 'The Double-Conversion in Bunyan's *Grace Abounding*', *Philological Quarterly*, 61 (1982), 259–76.

Hill, Christopher, *The World Turned Upside Down: radical ideas during the English revolution* (London, 1972).

—, *Milton and the English Revolution* (London, 1977).

—, *A Turbulent, Seditious, and Factious People: John Bunyan and his church 1628–88* (Oxford, 1988).

—, *The Experience of Defeat: Milton and some contemporaries* (London, 1984).

—, *The English Bible and the Seventeenth-Century Revolution* (London, 1993).

Hillyard, S., 'Memoir of the Late Rev. Ebenezer Chandler', *Evangelical Magazine*, 24 (1816), 497–500.
Hirschmann, Albert O., *The Passions and the Interests: political arguments for capitalism before its triumph* (Princeton, 1977).
James, William, *The Varieties of Religious Experience* (New York, 1919).
Jameson, Frederic, *Marxism and Form: twentieth-century dialectical theories of literature* (Princeton, 1971).
Johnson, Barbara A., *Reading 'Piers Plowmam' and 'The Pilgrim's Progress': reception and the Protestant reader* (Carbondale and Edwardsville, 1992).
Johnston, Arthur, *Enchanted Ground: the study of Medieval romance in the eighteenth century* (London, 1964).
Jones, Norman, *God and the Money-lenders: usury and law in early modern England* (Oxford, 1989).
Kaufmann, U. Milo, *The Pilgrim's Progress and Traditions in Puritan Meditation* (New Haven and London, 1966).
Keeble, N. H., *The Literary Culture of Nonconformity in later Seventeenth-Century England* (Leicester, 1987).
—, (ed.), *John Bunyan: Conventicle and Parnassus – tercentenary essays* (Oxford, 1988).
Knoppers, Laura Lunger, *Historicizing Milton: spectacle, power and poetry in Restoration England* (Athens GA, 1994).
Knott, John R., *The Sword of the Spirit: Puritan responses to the Bible* (Chicago and London, 1980).
Kripke, Saul, *Naming and Necessity* (Oxford, 1980).
Langholm, Odd, *The Aristotelian Analysis of Usury* (Oslo, 1984).
Laurence, Anne, W. R. Owens and Stuart Sim (ed.), *John Bunyan and His England, 1628–1688* (London and Ronceverte WV, 1990).
Lewis, C. S., *A Preface to Paradise Lost* (London, 1963).
—, 'The Vision of John Bunyan', in C. S. Lewis, *Selected Literary Essays*, ed. Walter Hooper (Cambridge, 1969), pp. 146–53.
Lewis, David, 'Truth in Fiction', *American Philosophical Review*, 15 (1978), 37–46.
—, *On the Plurality of Worlds* (Oxford, 1986).
Lindsay, Jack, *John Bunyan: maker of myths* (New York, 1969).

Luxon, Thomas, *Literal Figures: Puritan allegory and the Reformation crisis in representation* (Chicago, 1995).
McClelland, John, 'Text, Rhetoric, Meaning', in *Text 3*, ed. D.C. Greetham and W. Speed Hill (New York, 1987), pp. 11–26.
McGann, Jerome J., *The Textual Condition* (Princeton, 1991).
McHale, Brian, *Postmodernist Fiction* (New York and London, 1987).
McKenzie, D. F., *Bibliography and the Sociology of Texts* (1986; rpt. Cambridge, 1999).
—, 'Typography and Meaning: the Case of William Congreve', in Giles Barber and Bernhard Fabian (ed.), *Buch und Buchhandel im Europa im achtzehnten Jahrhundert* (Hamburg, 1981), pp. 81–125.
Mackenzie, Donald, 'Rhetoric versus Apocalypse: the Oratory of *The Holy War*', *Bunyan Studies*, 2 (1990), 33–45.
McKeon, Michael, *The Origins of the English Novel, 1600–1740* (Baltimore, 1987).
Maitre, Doreen, *Literature and Possible Worlds* (London, 1983).
Marcault, Emile, 'Le "Cas Bunyan" et le Temperament psychologique', *Melanges litteraires et philosophies* (Clermont-Ferrand, 1910).
Marx, Karl, *Capital: a critique of political economy*, trans. Ben Fowkes (London, 1976).
Merrell, Floyd, *Pararealities: the nature of our fictions and how we know them* (Amsterdam, 1988).
Mullett, Michael A., *John Bunyan in Context* (Keele, 1996).
Murrin, Michael, *The Veil of Allegory: some notes towards a theory of allegorical rhetoric in the English Renaissance* (Chicago, 1969).
—, *The Allegorical Epic: essays in its rise and decline* (Chicago, 1980).
Nelson, Benjamin, *The Idea of Usury: from tribal brotherhood to universal otherhood* (Princeton, 1949).
Newey, Vincent (ed.), *The Pilgrim's Progress: critical and historical Views* (Liverpool, 1980).
Noonan, John T., *The Scholastic Analysis of Usury* (Cambridge MA, 1957).
Olson, Richard, *The Emergence of the Social Sciences, 1642–1792* (New York, 1993).

Nussbaum, Felicity A., '"By these words I was sustained": Bunyan's *Grace Abounding*', *English Literary History*, 49 (1982), 18–34.
Patrides, C. A., *Milton and the Christian Tradition* (Hamden CT, 1979).
Pavel, Thomas, *Fictional Worlds* (Cambridge MA, 1986).
Plantinga, Alvin, *The Nature of Necessity* (Oxford, 1974).
—, 'God, Possible Worlds and the Problem of Evil', in Ted Honderich and Myles Burnyeat (ed.), *Philosophy As It Is* (Harmondsworth, 1979), pp. 417–46.
Plomer, Henry R., *A Dictionary of the Printers and Booksellers who Were at Work in England, Scotland and Ireland from 1668 to 1725* (London, 1922).
Pooley, Roger, 'The Structure of *The Pilgrim's Progress*', *Essays in Poetics*, 4 (1979), 59–70.
Quilligan, Maureen, *The Language of Allegory* (Ithaca, 1979).
Rescher, Nicholas, *A Theory of Possibility* (Oxford, 1975).
Rinson, Phillip, *Classical Theories of Allegory and Christian Culture* (Pittsburgh, 1981).
Roncaglia, Alessandro, *Petty: the origins of political economy*, trans. Isabella Cherubini (Armonck, 1985).
Ross, Trevor, *The Making of the English Literary Canon* (Montreal and London, 1998).
Rumrich, John P., *Milton Unbound: controversy and reinterpretation* (Cambridge, 1996).
Rusche, H., 'Astrology and Propaganda from 1644 to 1651', *English Historical Review*, 80 (1965), 322–333.
Salzman, Paul, *English Prose Fiction: a critical history* (Oxford, 1985).
Sasek, Lawrence A., *The Literary temper of the English Puritans* (Baton Rouge, 1961).
Scarry, Elaine, *The Body in Pain: the making and unmaking of the world* (New York, 1985).
Schwartz, Hillel, *The Culture of the Copy: striking likenesses, unreasonable facsmiles* (New York, 1996).
Schwartz, Regina M., *The Curse of Cain: the violent legacy of monotheism* (Chicago, 1997).
Sharrock, Roger, *John Bunyan* (London, 1954).

—, 'Spiritual Autobiography in *The Pilgrim's Progress*', *Review of English Studies*, 24 (1948), 102–20.
—, '*The Life and Death of Mr. Badman*: Facts and Problems', *Modern Language Review*, 82 1987), 15–29.
Shawcross, John T., *John Milton: the self and the world* (Lexington, 1993).
Sherman, Sandra, *Finance and Fictionality in the Early Eighteenth Century* (Cambridge, 1996).
Sim, Stuart, *Negotiations with Paradox: narrative practice and narrative form in Bunyan and Defoe* (Hemel Hempstead, 1990).
Sim, Stuart, and David Walker, *Bunyan and Authority: the rhetoric of dissent and the legitimation crisis in seventeenth-century England* (Bern, 2000).
Sizemore, Christine, 'The Literary Artistry of John Bunyan's *The Holy War*', University of Pennsylvania Ph.D. thesis (Ann Arbor, Michigan: University Microfilms, 1975).
Smith, Nigel, *Perfection Proclaimed: language and literature in English radical religion 1640–1660* (Oxford, 1989).
—, *Literature and Revolution in England, 1640–1660* (New Haven, 1994).
Spargo, Tamsin, *The Writing of John Bunyan* (Aldershot, 1997).
Spufford, Margaret, *Small Books and Pleasant Histories: popular fiction and its readership in seventeenth-century England* (London, 1981).
Stachniewski, John, *The Persecutory Imagination: English Puritanism and the literature of despair* (Oxford, 1991).
Stearns, Raymond Phineas, *The Strenuous Puritan: Hugh Peter 1598–1660* (Urbana, 1954).
Stein, Arnold, *Answerable Style: essays on 'Paradise Lost'* (Minneapolis, 1953).
Stranahan, Brainerd P., 'Bunyan and the Epistle to the Hebrews: his Source for the Idea of Pilgrimage in *The Pilgrim's Progress*', *Studies in Philology*, 79 (1982), 279–96.
Swaim, Kathleen, *Pilgrim's Progress, Puritan Progress* (Urbana, 1993).
Swiss, Margo, 'Satan's Obduracy in *Paradise Lost*', *Milton Quarterly*, 28 (1994), 56–61.

Talon, Henri, *John Bunyan: the man and his works*, trans. by Barbara Wall (London, 1951).
Tawney, R. H., *Religion and the Rise of Capitalism* (Gloucester MA, 1962).
Taylor, Gary, *Reinventing Shakespeare: a cultural history from the Restoration to the present* (London, 1990).
Thompson, E. P., *The Making of the English Working Class* (Harmondsworth, 1963).
Thompson, James, *Models of Value: eighteenth-century political economy and the novel* (Durham, 1996).
Tindall, William York, *John Bunyan, Mechanick Preacher* (New York, 1934).
Titlesla, P. J. H., 'The "pretty young man Civility": Bunyan, Milton and Blake and patterns of Puritan thought', *Bunyan Studies*, 6 (1995/6), 34–43.
Tuve, Rosamund, *Allegorical Imagery: some Medieval books and their posterity* (Princeton 1966).
van Os, M., and G. J. Schutte (ed.), *Bunyan in England and Abroad* (Amsterdam, 1990).
Walker, David, '"Heaven is prepared for whosoever will accept of it": Politics of the Will in Bunyan's *Doctrine of the Law and Grace Unfolded*', *Prose Studies*, 21 (1998), 18–31.
Watkins, Owen, *The Puritan Experience* (London, 1972).
Watt, Ian P., *The Rise of the Novel: studies in Defoe, Richardson and Fielding* (London, 1957).
Webber, Joan, *The Eloquent 'I': style and self in seventeenth-century prose* (Madison, 1968).
Werblowsky, R. J. Z., *Lucifer and Prometheus: a study of Milton's Satan* (London, 1952).
Ziff, Larzar, *Puritanism in America* (New York: 1973).
Zinck, Arlette M., '"Doctrine by Ensample": Sanctification through Literature in Milton and Bunyan', *Bunyan Studies*, 6 (1995/6), 44–55.

Index

Achinstein, Sharon 172
Addison, Joseph 23
Allegory 212, 213, 214
Allen, Don Cameron 202
Allen, Hannah 239
Alsop, Benjamin 63, 89
Ames, William 141
Anaximander 205
Antichrist, the 45–6, 48–9, 51, 53, 184
Antinomianism 44
Appleby, Joyce Oldham 215
Aristotle 205, 220–1, 230
Arminianism 43–4
Ascham, Roger 202
Asgill, John 219
Ashley, Mrs. Edward 24
Atheism 199–210

Backscheider, Paula 22
Bacon, Francis, Lord Verulam 91, 209
Barbon, Nicholas 217, 226
Barrow, Isaac 69,
Barry, Johnathan 58
Bates, William 69
Bauckham, Richard 192
Bauthumley, Jacob 23
Baxter, Richard 17, 21, 39–58, 62, 69, 77, 91, 108n, 130, 131n, 143, 205
Beaumont, Francis 69
Behn, Aphra 203
Berry, Boyd 136, 137
Besse, Joseph 56
Beverley, Thomas 47, 48
Bevis of Southampton 107, 108n, 111n, 115, 121n
Blake, William 199

Bland, Mark 68
Booth, Sir George 51
Boyle, Robert 203
Bouwsma, William J. 249
Brightman, Thomas 48
Brown, John 141
Buckley, Michael 203
Bunyan, Elizabeth 62, 63
Bunyan, John:
  Acceptable Sacrifice 88
  Advocateship of Jesus Christ 63, 89
  Antichrist and his Ruine, Of 45, 56, 125n, 187–8, 189, 196
  Book for Boys and Girls 100
  Christian Behaviour 82, 83
  Come & Welcome 88,
  Confession of My Faith 88
  Discourse of the ... House of God 88
  Discourse upon the Pharisee 89
  Exposition on ... Genesis 73
  Doctrine of the Law and Grace 30–1, 82, 112, 253, 261
  Few Sighs from Hell 42, 66, 82, 107
  Gospel-Truths Opened, Some 33–4, 66, 81
  Grace Abounding 18, 23, 28, 29, 38, 84, 85, 86, 88, 92, 116, 119, 121, 130n, 133–63,165–81, 207, 236, 239, 240, 241, 254
  Greatness of the Soul 189, 197
  Heavenly Foot-Man 74
  Holy City 52, 66, 83, 103, 105–6, 125n, 126
  Holy Life 189, 190, 197
  Holy War 18, 45, 55, 63, 75, 89, 93, 95, 99, 100,107, 127, 131, 183–98, 227, 229, 234, 253, 260

Instruction for the Ignorant 87, 97
Jerusalem Sinner Saved 88
Life and Death of Mr. Badman 18, 40–1, 45, 75, 89, 131, 138, 199–243, 253, 258–60
Light for Them that Sit in Darkness 87, 98
Mapp Shewing the Order of Salvation and Damnation 30, 206–7
Pilgrim's Progress 18, 22, 23, 24, 27, 31, 38, 45, 63, 65, 75, 76, 80, 88, 89, 91, 94, 95, 96, 98, 99, 103–32, 192, 193, 195, 198, 207, 209, 228, 232, 253, 254–6, 258
Prison Meditations 83
Profitable Meditations 82
Relation of the Imprisonment 27, 74, 124
Resurrection of the Dead 83
Seasonable Counsel 125n, 189, 190, 197
Treatise of the Fear of God 187, 189, 196
Vindication of Some Gospel-Truths Opened 33, 81
Works (1692) 17, 59–77, 86, 87, 206
Burnet Gilbert, bishop of Salisbury 25
Burton, John 66
Calvin, John 104, 106
Calvinism 43, 206, 247–50, 253
Camden, Vera 18
Campbell, Gordon 42–3, 45, 47
Carey, John 169
Caryl, John 70
Chandler, Ebenezer 71–3
Charles I, king 26, 57, 58, 184
Charles II, king 23, 24, 46, 54–5, 57, 58, 125n, 167
Charleton, Walter 204
Charnock, Stephen 69
Clapp, Sarah 64

Clarke, Samuel 206, 234
Cohn, Norman 39, 47,
Coleridge, Samuel Taylor 79, 228
Collinson, Patrick 40
Congreve, William 59
Constantine, emperor 46, 53, 54, 57
Corns, Thomas N. 17
Cox, Thomas 77
Crisp, Tobias 45, 70
Cromwell, Oliver, lord protector 51–2, 55, 57
Cromwell, Richard, lord protector 51–2, 55
Cudworth, Ralph 204, 205

Daniel, Samuel 68
Davies, Michael 18
Defoe, Daniel 22, 75
Delaune, Thomas 64
Dent, Arthur 185, 222–3, 234, 255
Descartes, Rene 91
Doe, Charles 17, 45, 63, 65–7, 70, 71–6, 86, 87
Dover, Joan 83
Dryden, John 22, 65
Dunan, Ann 200
Dunn, Kevin 89–92, 97

Ellwood, Thomas 32
Epicurus 204, 205

Febvre, Lucien 202
Ferenczi, Sandor 141
Fifth Monarchists 50, 57, 185
Fish, Stanley 16
Fisher, Edward 43
Flavel, John 69
Fletcher, John 69
Fowler, Alastair 168
Fowler, Edward, bishop of Gloucester 44, 45
Foucault, Michel 90, 147
Foxe, John 49, 50, 53, 54, 56, 57

Index 275

Franco, Odilon De Mello 154, 161
Freud, Sigmund 143, 144, 148, 150, 152–3, 154, 156
Furlong, Monica 200, 232
Frye, Northrop 108

Gay, David 16
Gibbs, John 66
Glanvill, Joseph 48, 205
Golder, Harold 108, 109
Goldie, Mark 122
Good, Thomas 208
Goodwin, John 29
Goodwin, Thomas 69
Greaves, Richard L. 15, 55, 124, 127, 129, 185

Hammond, Henry 69
Hancock, Maxine 252
Harrington, James 26
Harris, Jo 89
Harrison, G. B. 133, 135, 141
Hawkes, David 18, 19
Hawkes, Terence 139
Heaton, E. W. 193
Hill, Christopher 15, 21, 26, 36, 122, 165, 177, 200, 227, 233
Hobbes, Thomas 19, 201, 204, 214–15, 225
Homer 22, 23
Hooker, Richard 67
Hopkins, Ezekiel, bishop of Raphoe 69
How, Samuel 64
Howe, John 69
Hume, Patrick 23
Humfrey, John 48
Hunter, Michael 202
Hutchinson, colonel John 26

Iser, Wolfgang 16

James I, king 67
James II, king 47, 55, 58

James, William 134
Jews 52
Joan, pope 49
Johnson, Richard 111n, 115, 120, 121n
Jonson, Ben 68

Kaufmann, U. Milo 109, 112
Keach, Benjamin 64
Keeble, N. H. 21, 27, 37, 65, 85, 91, 161, 174, 177, 181
Kierkegaard, Søren 153, 154
Knollys, Hanserd 64
Knoppers, Laura Lunger 176
Knott, John R. 56

Larkin, George 88
Lamont, William 17
Lapthorne, Anthony 41
Lawrence, D. H. 39
Lawrence, Henry 35
Lewis, C. S. 113, 168
Lightfoot, John 69
Lilburne, John 37
Lilly, William 184
Louis XIV, king of France 56
Lucretius 203, 204
Ludlow, Edmund 62
Luther, Martin 91, 92, 97, 104, 106
Luxon, Thomas 16
Lyly, John 202

Machiavelli, Niccolo 204
MacKenzie, Donald 192, 195
McGann, Jerome J. 59, 60–1
McHale, Brian 250
McKenzie, D. F. 59, 60–1
Malory, Sir Thomas 104
Mandeville, Bernard 19, 218–19, 226
Marbais, Peter 19
Marcault, Emile 139, 140
Marlowe, Christopher 209
Marshall, John 76

Marshall, William 63, 64, 65, 70, 71, 74–6
Marvell, Andrew 21, 25, 53
Marx, Karl 211, 230
Maule, Jeremy 35
Mead, Matthew 70
Mede, Joseph 49
Millenarianism 39–58, 165, 183–98
Milton, John 17, 21–38, 62, 91, 108n
   De Doctrina Christiana 25, 31, 34
   Paradise Lost 22, 23, 29, 31, 64, 108n, 165–81
   Paradise Regained 38
   Samson Agonistes 26, 38
Modell, Arnold 151
Montaigne, Michel de 68
More, Henry 47, 48–9, 205
Morton, Charles 77
Mullett, Michael 199

Newman, Dorman 63, 89
Newton, Thomas 23
North, Sir Dudley 217
Nussbaum, Felicity A. 171

Orwell, George 54
Owen, John 64, 69, 70
Owens, W. R. 16, 17, 46, 55

Patrides, C. A. 166
Patterson, James 23
Paul, St. 73, 92, 97, 106
Pavel, Thomas 245, 250
Penington, Isaac 69
Penn, William 55, 69
Perkins, William 107n, 207
Peter, Hugh 28
Petty, William 216
Picard, Jeremy 25
Plantinga, Alvin 246–50, 257
Ponder, Nathaniel 61, 76, 89
Pooley, Roger 18, 108
Pope, Alexander 22, 65

Pythagoras 205

Quakers 27, 32–3, 37, 55–6, 69, 82, 186

Ranters 23, 149, 186
Rivers, Isabel 15
Romance 18, 103–32
Rosenfeld, Nancy 18
Ross, Aileen 129
Ross, Trevor 68
Rumrich, John P. 167

Salzman, Paul 108, 199
Sasek, Lawrence 85, 86
Scarry, Elaine 231–2, 235, 238, 242
Schwartz, Hillel 150, 157
Schwarts, Regina 145, 146
Scott, John 69
Shadwell, Thomas 203
Shakespeare, William 68, 104
Sharrock, Roger 15, 42, 135, 139, 161, 199, 234, 237
Shawcross, John T. 32
Sherman, Thomas 106–7, 131
Sidney, Sir Philip 68, 169
Sim, Stuart 16, 19, 103, 200
Sizemore, Christine 194, 195
Skinner, Cyriack 25
Smith, Nigel 36–7
Socrates 205
Spargo, Tamsin 16, 17, 174
Spenser, Edmund 53, 194
Stachniewski, John 16
Stein, Arnold 164
Stillingfleet, Edward, bishop of Worcester 69
Stranahan, Brainerd P. 137, 174, 175
Strato 205
Sturt, John 70
Swaim, Kathleen M. 15, 174
Swift, Jonathan 22
Sylvester, Matthew 45

Index

Talon, Henri 137
Tawney, R. H. 229
Taylor, Gary 68
Thomas, Roger 47
Tillotson, John, archbishop of Canterbury 69
Tindall, William York 122
Tonson, Jacob 64
Turner, James 203

Venner, Thomas 50, 124, 185
Vergil, Polydore 202
Virgil 22, 23
Voltaire 247
Von Rad, Gerhard 190

Waldock, A. J. A. 168
Walker, David 103, 200

Walzer, Michael 39, 40
Warton, Thomas 23
Wesley, Samuel 76
White, Robert 93
Whitefield, George 76
Wight, Sarah 239
William III, king 47, 50, 52, 55, 57
Williams, Daniel 45
Williamson, Sir Joseph 23
Wilson, John 71–3, 76
Wilson, Samuel 76
Winstanley, Gerrard 23, 34
Wootton, David 202

Young, Samuel 45

Zinck, Arlette 18

Religions and Discourse

Edited by James Francis

Religions and Discourse explores religious language in the major world faiths from various viewpoints, including semiotics, pragmatics and cognitive linguistics, and reflects on how it is situated within wider intellectual and cultural contexts. In particular a key issue is the role of figurative speech. Many fascinating metaphors originate in religion e.g. revelation as a 'garment', apostasy as 'adultery', loving kindness as the 'circumcision of the heart'. Every religion rests its specific orientations upon symbols such as these, to name but a few. The series strives after the interdisciplinary approach that brings together such diverse disciplines as religious studies, theology, sociology, philosophy, linguistics and literature, guided by an international editorial board of scholars representative of the aforementioned disciplines. Though scholarly in its scope, the series also seeks to facilitate discussions pertaining to central religious issues in contemporary contexts.
The series will publish monographs and collected essays of a high scholarly standard.

Volume 1 Ralph Bisschops and James Francis (eds):
Metaphor, Canon and Community
307 pages. 1999.
ISBN 3-906762-40-8 / US-ISBN 0-8204-4234-8

Volume 2 Lieven Boeve and Kurt Feyaerts (eds):
Metaphor and God Talk
291 pages. 1999.
ISBN 3-906762-51-3 / US-ISBN 0-8204-4235-6

Volume 3 Jean-Pierre van Noppen:
Transforming Words
248 pages. 1999.
ISBN 3-906762-52-1 / US-ISBN 0-8204-4236-4

Volume 4   Robert Innes:
           Discourses of the Self
           236 pages. 1999.
           ISBN 3-906762-53-X / US-ISBN 0-8204-4237-2

Volume 5   Noel Heather:
           Religious Language and Critical Discourse Analysis
           319 pages. 2000.
           ISBN 3-906762-54-8 / US-ISBN 0-8204-4238-0

Volume 6   Stuart Sim and David Walker:
           Bunyan and Authority
           239 pages. 2000.
           ISBN 3-906764-44-3 / US-ISBN 0-8204-4634-3

Volume 7   Simon Harrison:
           Conceptions of Unity in Recent Ecumenical Discussion
           282 pages. 2000.
           ISBN 3-906758-51-6 / US-ISBN 0-8204-5073-1

Volume 8   Gill Goulding:
           On the Edge of Mystery
           256 pages. 2000.
           ISBN 3-906758-80-X / US-ISBN 0-8204-5087-1

Volume 9   Kune Biezeveld and Anne-Claire Mulder (eds.):
           Towards a Different Transcendence
           358 pages. 2001.
           ISBN 3-906765-66-0 / US-ISBN 0-8204-5303-X

Volume 10 George Newlands:
           John and Donald Baillie: Transatlantic Theology
           451 pages. 2002.
           ISBN 3-906768-41-4 / US-ISBN 0-8204-5853-8

Volume 11 Kenneth Fleming:
           Asian Christian Theologians in Dialogue with Buddhism
           388 pages. 2002.
           ISBN 3-906768-42-2 / US-ISBN 0-8204-5854-6

Volume 12 N. H. Keeble (ed.):
    John Bunyan: Reading Dissenting Writing
    277 pages. 2002.
    ISBN 3-906768-52-X / US-ISBN 0-8204-5864-3

Volume 13 Robert L. Platzner (ed.):
    Gender, Tradition and Renewal
    Forthcoming
    ISBN 3-906769-64-X / US-ISBN 0-8204-5901-1